# Neither Liberty

*Fear, Ideology, and t*
*of Government*

Robert Higgs

The **INDEPENDENT INSTITUTE**

Oakland, California

The Independent Institute
100 Swan Way, Oakland, CA 94621-1428
Telephone: 510-632-1366 · Fax: 510-568-6040
Email: info@independent.org
Website: www.independent.org

Library of Congress Cataloging-in-Publication Data

Higgs, Robert.
    Neither Liberty Nor Safety: Fear, Ideology, and the Growth of Government
/ Robert Higgs
        p. cm.
    Includes index.
    ISBN 978-1-59813-012-6 (softcover)
    1. Political science. 2. Ideology. 3. Fear. I. Title.
JA71.H497 2007
320.5--dc22

                                                                    2007001637u

Printed in the United States of America

11 10 09 08 07                                                      1 2 3 4 5

# Neither Liberty Nor Safety

*Fear, Ideology, and the Growth of Government*

THE INDEPENDENT INSTITUTE is a non-profit, non-partisan, scholarly research and educational organization that sponsors comprehensive studies of the political economy of critical social and economic issues.

The politicization of decision-making in society has too often confined public debate to the narrow reconsideration of existing policies. Given the prevailing influence of partisan interests, little social innovation has occurred. In order to understand both the nature of and possible solutions to major public issues, The Independent Institute's program adheres to the highest standards of independent inquiry and is pursued regardless of political or social biases and conventions. The resulting studies are widely distributed as books and other publications, and are publicly debated through numerous conference and media programs. Through this uncommon independence, depth, and clarity, The Independent Institute expands the frontiers of our knowledge, redefines the debate over public issues, and fosters new and effective directions for government reform.

THE INDEPENDENT INSTITUTE
100 Swan Way, Oakland, California 94621-1428, U.S.A.
Telephone: 510-632-1366 • Facsimile: 510-568-6040
Email: info@independent.org • Website: www.independent.org

For Bill,
always my big brother

and

Henry,
dear friend since 1954

Those who would give up essential Liberty,
to purchase a little temporary Safety,
deserve neither Liberty nor Safety.

—Benjamin Franklin

# Contents

# Introduction

Twenty years have passed since the publication of my book *Crisis and Leviathan: Critical Episodes in the Growth of American Government* (New York: Oxford University Press, 1987). In that book, I presented a general framework for the analysis of government growth, followed by an analytical narrative of the growth of the federal government in the United States from the late nineteenth century to the late twentieth century. To complement the existing literature, which emphasized long-run trends, I focused my analysis on a succession of crisis episodes during which the government grew abruptly and left enduring legacies that affected the character and rate of its expansion during the "normal" periods that followed. Although the book reflected two decades of general study and several years of more focused research, I never supposed that it constituted the last word with regard to any aspect of the growth of government, and I expected to continue my research along similar lines to deepen and widen the analysis I had presented.

I am pleased that *Crisis and Leviathan* has been seen, at least in certain quarters, as a substantial contribution to political economy in general and to the study of the growth of government in particular. As expected, however, I did not rest content with what I had written, but continued to work on several of the subjects considered in the book, especially the nature and legacies of the political economy of war and defense (preparation for war) since 1939. This research was reported episodically in journal articles and chapters contributed to anthologies. The most substantial of these contributions have recently appeared (all in revised form) in my book *Depression, War, and Cold War: Studies in Political Economy* (New York: Oxford University Press, 2006). This material, however, composes only a portion of my writings that may be seen as research sequels to *Crisis and Leviathan*.

Other parts of my follow-up research appear in the present volume. Although two of the chapters (2 and 4) were originally written soon after the publication of *Crisis and Leviathan*, all of the others have been written in the past four years. Except for chapter 4, which has not been changed in a substantive way, everything published previously has been revised and updated for publication in the present book. Three of the chapters (3, 5, and 7) have not been published previously in any form, although, like everything in this volume, they draw on my earlier work. Therefore, the contents of this book represent the views I have come to hold after a long period of reading, research, discussion, debate, and publication stretching back more than forty-five years. (I do not exaggerate when I say that my serious education in the political economy of government in general and of the military in particular began in the summer of 1961, when as a seventeen-year-old boy I joined the United States Coast Guard.) So, for better or worse, the material that appears here represents my mature views.

It is said that as people mature, they become more conservative. In my case, however, at least as far as my understanding of government is concerned, the common wisdom requires reversal because as I have continued my studies, I have become more radical. If the tone of my exposition sometimes seems shrill, it nonetheless reflects the tenor of my mature judgment. In matters of ideology, the young are actually more easily bamboozled by the powers that be, more easily intimidated by parents, teachers, and governmental authorities—not for nothing does the army prefer to draft eighteen-year-olds. My lifelong learning has been, among other things, a process of sloughing off orthodoxy and "respectable" views. Thus, after a thorough postgraduate training in mainstream, neoclassical economics at Johns Hopkins, I moved toward the Austrian school of economics, and after exchanging my collegiate leftism for classical liberalism in my early twenties, I moved toward private-property anarchism.

H. L. Mencken famously said that "every decent man is ashamed of the government he lives under." By now, however, I am no longer ashamed, because I do not identify with the government under which I live. Rather, I view it as a criminal organization that without provocation has chosen to make war on my just rights—not only mine, of course, but everyone's. Although this vile enterprise is my problem, because it robs and bullies me relentlessly and without mercy, it is not my responsibility: the nail is not the hammer. I did not ask for it, and I do not want it. I fervently desire that it would simply disappear without a trace, leaving individuals free to conduct their affairs by means of voluntary cooperation, free of its incessant, gratuitous threats of force and violence against unoffending people, and free of the ceaseless, insulting drumbeat of its moronic propaganda.

Of course, the government is not about to disappear; indeed, it grows stronger daily. Social scientists therefore must understand how it operates and what consequences its operations have for the public. The foremost difficulty of understanding the threat of modern government is its nearly complete infiltration of society. Not only does it permeate virtually every part of social and economic life, but people constantly pass back and forth across the line that separates the predators and the prey—so commonly, in fact, that the masses easily fall for the myth that in our blessed democracy "we are the government."

In reality, however, most play no role in running the government except in wholly symbolic and inconsequential ways, such as casting a meaningless ballot from time to time or expressing their views to government officials in one of the many forums set up to allow the victims to vent their anger, frustration, and distress. Having had our "day in court," we are expected to go forth convinced that the whole rapacious setup is manifestly fair, desirable, and even indispensable. Our government usually allows people the freedom of speech, if no other freedom, almost as if the rulers had the wit to follow the advice Vilfredo Pareto once gave to Mussolini: "Let the crows caw, but be indefatigable in repressing [rebellious] deeds! Experience demonstrates that leaders who embark upon this path of censorship find headaches, rather than benefits." So we Americans may talk or even yell as much as we like—it's a free country, ain't it?—but our rulers' ears are deaf to our cries. Besides, they have more important things to do, for themselves.

In *Crisis and Leviathan*, I emphasized the importance of ideology in politicoeconomic affairs, and I devoted an entire chapter to a consideration of its nature and operation. Here, in chapter 3, I extend that analysis in an attempt to understand better how ideological change occurs. Moreover, striving to go deeper than social scientists and philosophers have generally gone in their study of "public opinion," I consider in chapter 1 how fear grounds nearly everything that governments do, including their manipulation of public opinion. Shortly before this book went to press, I thought it might be interesting to ask the Google search engine to find the terms *George W. Bush* and *politics of fear* jointly. Google reported about 128,000 instances of this pair of terms on the World Wide Web. Thus, I am scarcely the only observer to notice that the government routinely employs fear to cement its domination and to attain its objectives. I hope, however, that my analysis here helps to clarify the precise ways in which the government plays the fear card and the effects it produces by doing so.

The first three chapters and the final chapter are more conceptual than historical, although they contain plenty of empirical examples. Chapters 4–7 deal more fully and carefully with the historical details of how government has grown in the United States since the late nineteenth century. In chapter 4, I take up briefly the question of what accounts for the rise of Progressivism, the most momentous ideological change in United States history. Although I do not claim to have presented a full analysis—nothing less than a book-length treatment could do so—I do offer a more complete statement on this issue than I have made elsewhere in my writings, in the hope that it will prove suggestive. (More than one critic has faulted me for failure to give such an explanation in *Crisis and Leviathan*.) Chapter 5 pertains to the interwar period; chapter 6 deals with the world wars; and chapter 7 brings the historical analysis of the growth of government in the United States up to date by considering the period from 1945 to the present. The final chapter, besides presenting substantial conceptual material, relates not simply to the United States, but to all of the economically advanced countries. So, all in all, despite being fairly short, the present book covers a great deal of ground.

It can take this form because it builds on so much that has already been done, not only by me but by a host of other writers. I am not ashamed to stand on the shoulders of giants, and readers will readily see which scholars serve as my giants. None of them, however, escapes my criticism. I am not given to hero worship. As admirable and as impressive as my giants were (and, in some cases, are now), none was privy to unimpeachable Truth. All of them, in my view, have made at least a few mistakes, ill-founded interpretations, or other scholarly missteps; all of them, in short, were human. I like to think that if they could see how I have taken issue with their analysis, they might be inclined to nod and say, "Well, you may have a point."

If I myself am wrong on various points, my mistakes too may be corrected. I have learned much about history and political economy since putting on that uniform in 1961, but I am not finished yet. This book, like each of its predecessors, constitutes a progress report on one man's scholarly journey. If readers find it helpful, I will be gratified that they may not have to plow through all of the rocks and briars that impeded me as I made my way, often by a tortuous path, to the views expressed here.

A brief comment on the title may be in order. Benjamin Franklin's 1755 statement, from which the title is taken, is well known, and it appears here as the book's epigraph. For Franklin, those who would sacrifice essential liberty to purchase a little temporary safety deserve neither liberty nor safety. I agree, but my point in this book is not simply that they *deserve* neither; instead, it is that they will *get* neither. Destroying the village to save it is never a smart move. Indeed, it is an absurdity. The most fundamental tragedy of modern U.S. politics is that so many people have embraced this absurdity. By doing so, they have sacrificed not only their liberty and their safety, but in the end their very souls. Impelled by their fears and by a desire to evade self-responsibility, questing in vain for a secular savior, they have surrendered themselves to the government so fully that, in effect, it has become their god. The Christians and Jews among them might well have given greater weight to the First Commandment.

*Robert Higgs*
Covington, Louisiana
January 2007

# 1

## Fear: The Foundation of Every Government's Power

Neither a man nor a crowd nor a nation can be trusted to act humanely or to think sanely under the influence of a great fear.
> —Bertrand Russell, "An Outline of Intellectual Rubbish" (1943)

[F]ear can debilitate us, making us susceptible to the importunities of those who promise to alleviate our fears if only we will give the direction of our lives over to them. In this manner are institutions born, with the state demanding the greatest authority over us, and promising release from our uncertainties.
> —Butler Shaffer, "A World Too Complex to Be Managed" (2006)

All animals experience fear—human beings, perhaps, most of all. Any animal incapable of fear would have been hard pressed to survive, regardless of its size, speed, or other attributes. Fear alerts us to dangers that threaten our well-being and sometimes our very lives. Sensing fear, we respond by running away, by hiding, or by preparing to ward off the danger. To disregard fear is to place ourselves in possibly mortal jeopardy. Telling people not to be afraid is giving them advice they cannot take (Bloom 2004, 82–84). Even the man who acts heroically on the battlefield, if he is honest, admits he is scared. "He would be a sort of madman or insensible person," Aristotle wrote, "if he feared nothing, neither earthquakes nor the waves" (1938, 249). Our evolved psychological and physiological makeup predisposes us to fear actual and potential threats, even those that exist only in our imagination.

And thy life shall hang in doubt before thee; and thou shalt fear day and night, and shalt have none assurance of thy life. (Deuteronomy 28:66)

The people who have the effrontery to rule us, who dare call themselves our government, understand this basic fact of human nature. They exploit it, and they cultivate it. Whether they compose a warfare state or a welfare state, they depend on fear to secure popular submission, compliance with official dictates, and, on some occasions, affirmative cooperation with the state's enterprises and adventures (Bloom 2004, 85–93). Without popular fear, no government would endure more than twenty-four hours.[1]

David Hume argued that all government rests on public opinion, and many others have endorsed his argument (e.g., Mises [1927] 1985, 41, 45, 50–51, 180; Rothbard [1965] 2000, 61–62), but public opinion is not the bedrock of government. Public opinion itself rests on something deeper and more primordial: fear. Hume recognized that the opinions that support government receive their force from "other principles," among which he included fear, but he considered these other principles to be "the secondary, not the original principles of government." He argued: "No man would have any reason to *fear* the fury of a tyrant, if he [the tyrant] had no authority over any but from fear" ([1777] 1987, 34, emphasis in original). We may grant Hume's statement yet still maintain that, regardless of the nature of the bonds between the ruler and his palace guard, the government's authority over the *great mass* of its subjects rests fundamentally on fear.

Murray Rothbard considers fear briefly in his analysis of the anatomy of the state, classifying its instillment as "another successful device" by which the rulers secure from their subjects acceptance of or at least acquiescence in being dominated—"[t]he present rulers, it was maintained, supply to the citizens an essential service for which they should be most grateful: protection against sporadic criminals and marauders" ([1965] 2000, 65)—but Rothbard does not view fear as the *fundamental basis* on which the rulers rest their domination, as I do here. Of course, as many scholars have recognized, ideology is critical in the long-term maintenance of governmental power. Yet every ideology that endows government with legitimacy requires and is infused by some kind(s) of fear. Unlike Rothbard, who views the instillment of fear in the subjects as one "device" among several by which the government maintains its grip on the masses, I contend that public fear is a necessary (though perhaps not a sufficient) condition for the viability of government as we know it.[2]

Jack Douglas comes closer to my own view when he observes that *myths* (a term he uses in roughly the same way that I use the term *ideologies*) "are predominantly the voice of our emotions, the images of our passionate hopes and *fears,* or our passionate longings and hatreds" (1989, 220, emphasis added; see also 313 on "the very powerful fear of death that reinforces all of the others" [that is, all of the other natural passions]). In his extended argument about the longstanding, overarching "myth of the welfare state," however, Douglas places more emphasis on the element of hopes *(millennialism)* than on the element of fears. Yet even ideological hopes, I maintain, often center on people's hopes for governmental deliverance from their fears. As David Altheide remarks, "People do want to be 'saved' and 'freed,' but they want to be saved and freed from fear, and this is what makes the [mass media's] messages of fear so compelling and important for public policy and the fabric of our social life" (2002, 15–16).

The fear need not be of the government itself and indeed may be of the danger from which the government purports to protect the people. Of course, some of the threats that induce subjects to submit to government in the hope of gaining its protection and thereby calming their fears may be real. I am not arguing that people who look to government for their salvation act entirely under the sway of illusory threats, although I do insist that nowadays, if not always, many public fears arise in large part if not entirely from stimulation by the government itself. If the people's fears may be (1) of the government itself, (2) of real threats from which the people look to the government for protection, and (3) of spurious threats from which the people look to the government for protection, we must admit that the relative importance of each type of fear varies with time and place. In every case, however, the government seeks to turn public fear to its own advantage.[3] "Directing fear in a society is tantamount to controlling that society. Every age has its fears, every ruler has his/her enemies, every sovereign places blame, and every citizen learns about these as propaganda" (Altheide 2002, 17, see also 56, 91, 126–33, 196, and passim).

## THE NATURAL HISTORY OF FEAR

> And my heart owns a doubt
> Whether 'tis in us to arise with day
> And save ourselves unaided.
> —Robert Frost, "Storm Fear" (1913, reprinted in 1979, 10)

Thousands of years ago, when the first organized groups recognizable as governments were fastening themselves on people, they relied primarily on warfare and conquest.[4] As Henry Hazlitt observes, "There may have been somewhere, as a few eighteenth-century philosophers dreamed, a group of peaceful men who got together one evening after work and drew up a Social Contract to form the state. But nobody has been able to find an actual record of it. Practically all the governments whose origins are historically established were the result of conquest—of one tribe by another, one city by another, one people by another. Of course there have been constitutional conventions, but they merely changed the working rules of governments already in being" ([1976] 1994, 471).[5]

This view of the origin of the state has great antiquity. As long ago as the late eleventh century, Pope Gregory VII (1073–85), the leader of the momentous Papal Revolution that began during his papacy and ran its course over a span of nearly fifty years (even longer in England), wrote: "Who does not know that kings and princes derive their origin from men ignorant of God who raised themselves above their fellows by pride, plunder, treachery, murder—in short by every kind of crime—at the instigation of the Devil, the prince of this world, men blind with greed and intolerable in their audacity?" (qtd. in Berman 1983, 110).

Although certain analytical purposes may be served at times by likening government to a form of exchange between the ruler and the ruled, à la public-choice theory, or by supposing that government might "conceptually" reflect a unanimously accepted "social contract," à la constitutional economics, these characterizations fail to acknowledge government's "essentially coercive character" and bear little resemblance to the actual historical establishment of governments—or to their functioning today (Yeager 1985, 269–72 , 283–85, 291; see also Olson 2000, 2, 11). The subjugation theory, in stark contrast, rests upon a mountain of historical evidence. As Ludwig von Mises remarks, "For thousands of years the world had to submit to the yoke of military conquerors and feudal lords who simply took for granted that the products of the industry of other men existed for them to consume." Moreover, "[t]he supplanting of the militaristic ideal, which esteems only the warrior and despises honest labor, has not, by any means, even yet been completely achieved" ([1927] 1985, 151).

## Fear For Your Life and Pay Tribute to the Rulers

Losers who were not slain in the conquest itself had to endure the subsequent rape and pillage and in the longer term had to acquiesce in the continuing payment of tribute to the insistent rulers—the *stationary bandits,* as Mancur Olson (2000, 6–9) aptly calls them. Subjugated people, for good reason, feared for their lives. Offered the choice of losing their wealth or losing their lives, they tended to choose the sacrifice of their wealth. Hence arose taxation, variously rendered in goods, services, or money (Nock [1935] 1973, 19–22).[6] For example, in thirteenth-century Bavaria, perhaps the most advanced of all the German principalities at the time, "the entire population of the duchy was taxed, free and unfree, secular and ecclesiastical; and the taxes were administered by a corps of ducal officials" (Berman 1983, 510). Max Spindler remarks that this "tax obligation ... made the existence and the sovereignty of the state palpable to every single person" (from a 1937 work in German, qtd. in translation in Berman 1983, 510).

Subjugated people, however, naturally resent the imposed government and the taxation and other insults it foists on them. Such bitter people easily become restive; should a promising opportunity to throw off the oppressor's dominion present itself, they may seize it. A historical example demonstrates this point clearly. "In the early thirteenth century King Canute II [of Denmark] tried to issue taxes, collect fines, and, in general, assert royal authority, but he was overthrown and assassinated" (Berman 1983, 515). Even if the people mount no rebellion or overt resistance, however, they quietly strive to avoid their rulers' exactions and to undermine their rulers' apparatus of government. As Machiavelli observed, the conqueror "who does not manage this matter well, will soon lose whatever he has gained, and while he retains it will find in it endless troubles and annoyances" ([1513] 1992, 5). For the stationary bandits, therefore, force alone proves a very costly means of keeping people in the mood to disburse a steady, substantial stream of tribute. If the rulers are to sustain their predation at tolerable cost, they must gain legitimacy (Mises [1927] 1985, 41, 45, 50–51, 180).

## Fear For Your Soul and Pay Tribute to the Rulers

Sooner or later every government augments the power of its sword with the power of its priesthood, forging an iron union of throne and altar. The priests were "the ones who fabricated the holy texts purporting to tell how the world was created, how God decreed the ruler's power, how the king was necessary for everyone's welfare, and on and on" (Douglas 1989, 129, see also 153, 325, and passim). In ancient times, it was not uncommon for rulers to be declared gods—the Pharaohs of ancient Egypt made that claim for centuries—or the descendants of the gods or the earthly representatives of the gods (63, 107, 129). When Charlemagne was crowned emperor in 800, he took the title "Charles, most serene Augustus, crowned by God, great and pacific emperor, governing the Roman empire" (Berman 1983, 603). Doctrines of the divine right of kings have deep historical roots in many parts of the world. In Western civilization, they received powerful support in the early fifth century from St. Augustine's *City of God,* reached their zenith in the seventeenth century in the writings of Jacques-Benigne Bossuet on behalf of Louis XIV in particular, and did not go down—with a thud, as it were—until the French Revolution (Hooker 1996). As late as World War I, Kaiser Wilhelm found it expedient to exhort his troops: "Remember that the German people are the chosen of God. On me, on me as German emperor, the Spirit of God has descended. I am His weapon, His sword and His visor" (qtd. in Skidelsky 2005). To the extent that the subjects can be brought to fear not only the ruler's superior force, but also his supernatural powers or authority—brought, in Harold Berman's words, to a "belief in his sacred character and thaumaturgic powers" (1983, 406), the ruler gains an enormous edge in overawing the people.

Moreover, if people believe in an afterlife, where the pains and sorrows of this life may be sloughed off, the priests hold a privileged position in prescribing the sort of behavior in the here and now that best serves one's interest in securing a blessed condition in the life to come. Referring to the Roman Catholic Church of his own day, Machiavelli noted "the spiritual power which of itself confers so mighty an authority" ([1513] 1992, 7), and he heaped praise on Ferdinand of Aragon, who, "always covering himself with the cloak of religion ... had recourse to what may be called *pious cruelty*" (59, emphasis in original).[7] For Roman Catholics, "the church, and more specifically the pope, is considered to have jurisdiction over purgatory ... [and] the time to be spent in purgatory can be reduced by clerical decision" (Berman 1983, 171). This clerical power may be—and often has been—used to induce people to fall into line with projects that serve definite secular as well as spiritual interests. For example, "With the emergence of papal monarchy at the end of the eleventh century, the Council of Clermont under Pope Urban II granted the first 'plenary indulgence,' absolving all who would go on the First Crusade from liability for punishment in purgatory for sins committed prior to their joining the holy army of crusaders" (171). In our own time and place, a similar example pertains to the support that Protestant evangelicals have given to militarism in general and to the recent U.S. wars against Iraq in particular (Bacevich 2005a, 122–46), support that George W. Bush's administration has actively cultivated and exploited, counting the religious right a key part of the Republican Party's electoral and lobbying "base."

Naturally, the warriors and the priests, if not one and the same, almost invariably come to be cooperating parties in the apparatus of rule. In medieval western Europe, from the sixth through the eleventh centuries, secular rulers dominated the church and appointed the highest ecclesiastical officials. Even after the Papal Revolution, in which the church established its corporate independence and gained the power to choose the pope and appoint the bishops, however, churchmen and secular rulers continued to be intertwined in countless ways, not least by the often close kinship of their leading authorities. Although the clergy sometimes clashed with secular authorities, their relationship normally entailed cooperation and mutual support.[8] This close relationship between throne and altar did not end with the Protestant Reformation. Indeed, in many ways it persists even in today's more secular societies.

Thus, the martial element of government puts people in fear for their lives, and the priestly element puts them in fear for their eternal souls. These two fears compose a powerful compound—sufficient to prop up governments everywhere on earth for several millennia.

## Look to the Rulers For Protection and Pay Them Tribute

Over the ages, governments refined their appeals to popular fears, fostering an ideology that emphasizes the people's vulnerability to a variety of internal and external dangers from which their governors—of all people!—are represented to be their protectors (Higgs 2002). Government, it is claimed, protects the populace from external attackers and from internal disorder, both of which are portrayed as ever-present threats (Rothbard [1965] 2000, 65). Sometimes the government, as if seeking to nourish this mythology with grains of truth, *does* protect people in this fashion—even the shepherd protects his sheep, but he does so to serve his own interest, not theirs, and when the time comes, he will shear or slaughter them as his interest dictates.

Olson describes in simple terms why the stationary bandit may find it in his interest to invest in public goods (the best examples of which are domestic "law and order" and defense of the realm) that enhance his subjects' productivity. In brief, the ruler does so when the present value of the expected additional tax revenue he will be able to collect from a more productive population exceeds the current cost of the investment that renders the people more productive (2000, 9–10). Sometimes, in addition, the ruler charges directly for the use of his "public good." For example, "the introduction of a system of royal law into England [by the Anglo-Norman ruler Henry II] was in part a means of enriching royal coffers as well as royal power at the expense not only of barons and ecclesiastics but also of the general population" (Berman 1983, 439).[9]

Robert Bates argues that in western Europe the kings struck deals with the merchants and burghers, trading mercantilist privileges and "liberties" for a steady stream of tax revenue, in order to dominate the chronically warring rural dynasties and thereby to pacify the countryside (2001, 56–69, 102).[10] Unfortunately, kings who undertook these measures had foremost in their minds the same thought that the Meiji reformers had in nineteenth-century Japan when they gave their country the slogan "rich nation, strong army" (Kuroda 1997). As Bates recognizes, the kings sought to enlarge their revenue for the purpose of conducting ever more costly wars against other kings as well as against domestic opponents. Thus, their "pacification" schemes actually entailed amplified fighting on some front, leaving the net effect on overall societal well-being very much in question, especially when we consider that no single king undertook these measures in isolation: a better-funded king might have pacified his own realm internally, but other kings, also better funded, now presented greater external threats to this realm. Each king's foreign war entailed some other society's domestic devastation. Joseph Schumpeter remarks of the rising nation-states of Europe: "None of them had all it wanted; each of them had what others wanted. And they were soon surrounded by new worlds inviting competitive conquest.... [A]ggression ... became the pivot of policy.... [M]aximum public revenue—for the court and the army to consume—was the purpose of economic policy, conquest the purpose of foreign policy" (1954, 146–47).[11] Obviously, no one can demonstrate that the displacement of the feudal order by the rising kings and nation-states of Europe gave rise to a continent consistently at peace. Indeed, as traditionally told, the history of the early modern age unfolds in a succession of wars, often several at the same time, among the great European powers. Lesser powers, compelled to line up on one side or the other of these armed struggles, suffered a full measure of the destruction.

When the government fails to protect the people as promised, it always has a good excuse, often blaming some element of the population—scapegoats such as traders, money lenders, unpopular ethnic or religious minorities, or "economic royalists" (Franklin D. Roosevelt's choice). "[N]o prince," Machiavelli assures us, "was ever at a loss for plausible reasons to cloak a breach of faith" ([1513] 1992, 46). Just consider how many big heads have rolled in order to hold government officials accountable for the security lapses that permitted the attacks on the World Trade Center and the Pentagon on September 11, 2001. By my count, the total comes to exactly zero—not to mention that the commander in chief on whose watch these devastating attacks took place subsequently engineered his reelection to office, carrying his entire entourage onward to seize further opportunities for "greatness."

In the crunch, governments always attend first to their own protection, even if the people's protection must be sacrificed in the process (Lind 2005).

Vice President Dick Cheney has become notorious for periodically scurrying into an impenetrable bunker when frightened by specters of terrorism, but we ordinary citizens are strictly on our own when the dreaded weapons of mass destruction come our way.[12] Government penal codes routinely make offenses against government officials, agents, or property graver offenses than identical offenses against other persons or property (Rothbard [1965] 2000, 80–82). Nor is this kind of "class" inequity in the application of the law a modern development. In the *Liber Augustalis,* an advanced legal code promulgated by Frederick II, tyrant of the Norman Kingdom of Sicily, in 1231, "higher penalties were imposed for offenses against nobles by non-nobles, and greater weight was given to the oath of a noble in suits for debt" (Berman 1983, 428). In our own time and place the official reaction to the murder or attempted murder of a government official or even of a low-ranking police officer bears no comparison with the official reaction to the murder of an ordinary citizen: the former offense calls forth legions of SWAT teams ardent to dispatch any suspect on sight, whereas the latter may, all in good time, set in motion a lethargic investigation.

## Embrace a Collectivist Ideology and Pay Tribute to the Rulers

The religious grounds for submission to the ruler gods gradually transmogrified into secular notions of nationalism and popular duty to the state, culminating eventually in the curious ideology that in a democratic system the people themselves *are* the government, and hence whatever it requires them to do, they are really doing for themselves; as Woodrow Wilson had the impudence to declare when he proclaimed military conscription backed by severe criminal sanctions in 1917: "it is in no sense a conscription of the unwilling; it is, rather, selection from a nation which has volunteered in mass" (qtd. in Palmer 1931, 216–17).

Not long after the democratic dogma had gained a firm foothold, organized coalitions emerged from the mass electorate and joined the elites in looting the public treasury, and as a consequence, in the late nineteenth century the so-called welfare state began to take shape. From that time forward, people were told that the government can and should protect them from all sorts of workaday threats to their lives, livelihoods, and overall well-being—threats of destitution, hunger, disability, unemployment, illness, lack of income in old age, germs in the water, toxins in the food, and insults to their race, sex, ancestry, creed, and so forth. Nearly everything people feared and much that they found merely annoying, the government stood poised to ward off. Thus did the welfare state anchor its rationale in the solid rock of fear. Governments, having exploited popular fears of violence so successfully from time immemorial (promising "national security"), had no difficulty in cementing these new stones (promising "social security") into their foundations of rule.

In this quest, governments have enjoyed the support of a growing secular priesthood of intellectuals and far more numerous pseudointellectuals—F. A. Hayek called them "secondhand dealers in ideas"—who for various reasons have tended overwhelmingly to espouse collectivist doctrines (Hayek 1949; Mises [1956] 1972; Nozick [1986] 1998; Rothbard [1965] 2000, 61–70; Feser 2004). These idea peddlers, many of whom live at taxpayer expense these days, have advanced a succession of interpretations of the world's troubles and of its potential salvation in which they portray various private actions, especially those bundled in the concept of "capitalism," as the source of a plethora of threats to life, limb, and happiness. They depict the government as the savior that will descend from its heaven—located in Berlin, Paris, Brussels, Washington, or other such places—to remedy all the people's woes and to drive the evil doers, especially the private "money changers," out of the temple. Karl Marx famously declared that religion is the opiate of the people. Not so famously but equally correctly, Raymond Aron (1957) called collectivism, especially in its Marxist variant, "the opium of the intellectuals."

This ideology seeped out from the intellectuals to the masses. Once it gained sufficient acceptance among them, by the beginning of the twentieth century in Europe and slightly later in North America, it allowed government officials to exploit each great socioeconomic and political emergency to add new weapons to their arsenal of social control (Higgs 1987, 2004; Porter 1994). The upshot of each such crisis included not only a ratcheting up of the government's size, scope, and power, but also a further weakening of the ideological resistance that had for millennia reflected the people's instinctive appreciation that the government is at best an unavoidable nuisance and at worst an unbearable oppressor. Under the sway of the new dominant ideology—recently analyzed by Daniel Klein (2005) under the rubric of *The People's Romance*—many people affirmatively support governmental enterprises and adventures under the illusion that "we are all doing this together"—as if millions or even hundreds of millions of extremely heterogeneous individuals were nothing more than one big happy family. Although this bizarre phenomenon may well justify calling for the men in white coats to bring out the straitjackets, one cannot deny that it seems to motivate the political speech and actions of many opinion leaders as well as a substantial number of ordinary citizens. Thus has fear led people from a well-founded aversion to the government itself to a form of mass lunacy in which, like Winston Smith in George Orwell's *Nineteen Eighty-Four,* they finally love Big Brother—a Stockholm Syndrome writ large (Clark 2002).

## THE POLITICAL ECONOMY OF FEAR

> The whole aim of practical politics is to keep the popu-
> lace alarmed (and hence clamorous to be led to safety) by
> menacing it with an endless series of hobgoblins, all of them
> imaginary.
> —H. L. Mencken, "Women as Outlaws" ([1921] 1949, 29)

Fear, like every other "productive" resource, is subject to the laws of production. Thus, it cannot escape the law of diminishing marginal productivity: beyond a certain point, as successive doses of fear mongering are added to the government's "production" process, the incremental public clamor for governmental protection declines. The first time the government cries wolf, the public is frightened; the second time, less so; the third time, still less so. If the government plays the fear card too much, it overloads the people's sensibilities, and eventually they discount almost entirely the government's attempts to frighten them further. Having been warned in the 1970s about catastrophic global cooling (see, for example, "The Cooling World" 1975; Holcombe 2006), then, soon afterward, about catastrophic global warming, the populace may grow weary of heeding the government's warnings about the dire consequences of alleged global climate changes—dire unless, of course, the government takes stringent measures to bludgeon the people into doing what "must" be done to avert the foretold disaster.

Former homeland-security czar Tom Ridge revealed recently that other government officials had overruled him when he wanted to refrain from raising the color-coded threat level to orange, or "high" risk of terrorist attack, in response to unlikely threats. "You have to use that tool of communication very sparingly," Ridge remarked astutely (qtd. in Hall 2005). Other Bush administration figures persisted, however, in drawing from the well of fear. When the president gave still another of his "same old same old" speeches midway through 2005, justifying the war in Iraq by tying it to the emotionally evocative attacks of September 11, the speech fell flat, even with the troops who composed his audience at Fort Bragg. "The president has no one to blame but himself," commented Frank Rich. "The color-coded terror alerts, the repeated John Ashcroft press conferences announcing imminent Armageddon during election season, the endless exploitation of 9/11 have all taken their numbing toll. Fear itself is the emotional card Mr. Bush chose to overplay, and when he plays it now, he is the boy who cried wolf" (2005).

Fear is a depreciating asset. As Machiavelli observed, "the temper of the multitude is fickle, and ... while it is easy to persuade them of a thing, it is hard to fix them in that persuasion" ([1513] 1992, 14). Unless the foretold threat eventuates, the people come to doubt its substance or its predicted magnitude. The government must make up for the depreciation by investing in the maintenance, modernization, and replacement of its stock of fear capital. For example, during the Cold War, the general sense of fear of the Soviets tended to dissipate unless refreshed by periodic crises, many of which took the form of officially announced or leaked "gaps" between U.S. and Soviet military capabilities: troop-strength gap, bomber gap, missile gap, antimissile gap, first-strike-missile gap, defense spending gap, thermonuclear-throw-weight gap, and so forth (Higgs 1994, 301–2).[13]

Lately, a succession of official warnings about possible forms of terrorist attack on the homeland has served the same purpose: keeping the people "vigilant," which is to say, willing to pour enormous amounts of their money into the government's bottomless budgetary pits dubbed "defense" and "homeland security" (Higgs 2003a; Bender 2006; Bennett 2006). Investigative journalist James Bamford notes that the Bush administration has made effective use of "the politics of fear" by exploiting "the threat of terrorism to push for harsh assaults on constitutional liberties." Moreover, Bamford declares, government officials "are succeeding to a remarkable degree, largely because of the nonstop drumbeat of fear and paranoia generated over the issue and the steady, numbing regularity of their attacks on civil liberties" (interviewed in Zeese 2005).

This same factor helps to explain the synchronous drumbeat of fears pounded out by the mass media: besides serving their own interests in capturing an audience, the news media buy insurance against government retribution by playing along with whatever program of fear mongering the government is conducting currently. Anyone who watches, say, CNN's *Headline News* programs can attest that a day seldom passes without some new announcement of a previously unsuspected Terrible Threat—I call it the danger du jour.[14] *New York Times* columnist John Tierney refers to "what is known in the [journalism] business as the 'Fear Stalks' story, as in, 'We need a Fear Stalks suburban bus riders'" (2005). By keeping the population in a state of artificially heightened apprehension, the government-cum-media prepares the ground for planting specific measures of taxation, regulation, surveillance, reporting, and other invasions of the people's wealth, privacy, and freedoms.[15] As Altheide observes, "The mass media, and especially the news media, are the main source and tool used to 'soften up' the audience, to prepare them to accept the justificatory account of the coming action" in an alleged crisis (2002, 12). Left alone for a while, relieved of this ceaseless bombardment of warnings, people would soon come to understand that hardly any of the announced threats have any substance—that they are "mostly fertilizer," as Charley Reese (2005) has described them—and that they can manage their own affairs quite well without the security-related regimentation and tax extortion the government seeks to justify.

Large parts of the government and the "private" sector participate in the production and distribution of fear. (Beware: many of the people in the ostensibly private sector are in reality mercenaries living ultimately at taxpayer expense. True government employment is much greater than officially reported [Light 1999; Higgs 2005a].) Bamford describes the activities of "a shadowy American company, The Rendon Group, that had been paid close to $200 million by the CIA and Pentagon to spread anti-Saddam propaganda worldwide.... Its specialty is manipulating thought and spreading propaganda" (2004, 295). Among many other achievements, Rendon created the Iraqi National Congress, a group whose paid informants and assorted con men profited handsomely by serving as critical sources of the disinformation the U.S. government employed to gain support for its 2003 attack on Iraq (296, see also 297–98). Defense contractors, of course, have long devoted themselves to stoking fears of enemies big and small around the globe who allegedly seek to crush our way of life at the earliest opportunity. Boeing's TV spots, for example, assure us that the company is contributing mightily to protecting "our freedom." If you believe that claim, I have a shiny hunk of useless Cold War hardware that I will sell you at an astronomical price. The news and entertainment media enthusiastically jump on the bandwagon of foreign-menace alarmism—anything to get the public's attention and to keep up its already elevated pulse rate.

Consultants of every size and shape clamber onboard, too, facilitating the distribution of billions of dollars to politically favored suppliers of phony-baloney "studies" that give rise to thick reports, the bulk of which amounts to nothing but worthless filler restating the problem and speculating about how one might conceivably go about discovering workable solutions. All such reports agree, however, that a crisis looms and that more such studies must be made in preparation for dealing with it. Hence, a kind of Say's Law of the political economy of crisis applies: supply (of government-funded studies) creates its own demand (for government-funded studies). Truth be known, government officials commission studies when they are content with the status quo but desire to write hefty checks to political favorites, cronies, and old associates who now purport to be "consultants." At the same time, the government demonstrates to the public in this way that it is "doing something" to avert impending crisis X.

At every point, opportunists latch onto existing fears and strive to invent new ones to feather their own nests. Thus, public-school teachers and administrators agree that the nation faces an "education crisis." Police departments and temperance crusaders insist that the nation faces a generalized "drug crisis" or at times a specific drug crisis, such as "an epidemic of crack cocaine use." Public-health interests foster fears of "epidemics" that in reality consist not of the spread of contagious pathogens, but of the lack of personal control and self-responsibility, such as the "epidemic of obesity" or the "epidemic of juvenile homicides." By means of this tactic, a host of personal peccadilloes are medicalized and consigned to the "therapeutic state" (Szasz 1965, 2001; Nolan 1998; Higgs 1999). In this way, people's fears that their children may become drug addicts or gun down a classmate become grist for the government's mill—a mill that may grind slowly, but at least it does so at immense expense, with each dollar falling into some fortunate recipient's pocket (a psychiatrist's, a social worker's, a public-health nurse's, a drug-court judge's; the list is almost endless). In this manner and in countless others, private parties become complicit in sustaining a vast government apparatus fueled by fear.

## FEAR WORKS BEST IN WARTIME

> It is not bad. Let them play.
> Let the guns bark and the bombing-plane
> Speak his prodigious blasphemies.
> —Robinson Jeffers, "The Bloody Sire" (1941,
> reprinted in 1965, 76)

Even tyrants can get bored. The exercise of great power may become tedious and burdensome—underlings are always disturbing one's serenity with questions about details; victims are always appealing for clemency, pardons, or exemptions from one's rules. Charlemagne traveled from place to place in his empire, living off the local nobleman's fief and the local serfs' labor as he went, but at each new venue, before he could settle down to sustained feasting, he had to attend to those with a gripe. "When he arrived in a place he would hear complaints and do justice" (Berman 1983, 89, see also 483–4). Likewise, Henry

II, the Norman monarch of England and parts of the Continent, "circuited his kingdom at a wearing pace to hear cases in the provinces" (439). What a grind.

Besides being a tiresome bore, the efficient and just administration of the laws brings the rulers little credit. Hardly anybody puts Martin Van Buren or Grover Cleveland at the top of a list of "great U.S. presidents."[16] Condemned to spend their time in high office during peacetime, rulers are necessarily destined to go down in history as mediocrities at best. In wartime, however, they come alive. Nothing equals war as an opportunity for greatness and public acclaim, as all leaders understand (Higgs 1997).[17]

Moreover, upon the outbreak of war, the exhilaration of the hour spreads through the entire governing apparatus. Army officers who had languished for years at the rank of captain may now anticipate becoming colonels. Bureau heads who had supervised a hundred subordinates with a budget of $10 million may look forward to overseeing a thousand with a budget of $400 million. Powerful new control agencies must be created and staffed. New facilities must be built, furnished, and operated. Politicians who had found themselves frozen in partisan gridlock can now expect that the torrent of money gushing from the public treasury will grease the wheels for putting together humongous legislative deals undreamed of in the past. Apparatchiks who had long harbored grand ideological visions—such as Paul Wolfowitz, perhaps the most important architect of the second U.S. war against Iraq—may find the doors finally opened for the attempted realization of their fantasies. As Andrew Bacevich has observed, "[F]or Wolfowitz, therefore, the unspeakable tragedy of 9/11 also signified a unique opportunity, which he quickly seized" (2005b).[18] Everywhere the government turns its gaze, the scene is flush with energy, power, and money. For those whose hands control the machinery of a government at war, life has never been better.

Small wonder that John T. Flynn, writing about the teeming bureaucrats during World War II, titled his chapter "The Happiest Years of Their Lives": "Even before the war, the country had become a bureaucrat's paradise. But with the launching of the war effort the bureaus proliferated and the bureaucrats swarmed over the land like a plague of locusts.... The place [Washington, D.C.] swarmed with little professors fresh from their $2,500-a-year jobs now stimulated by five, six and seven-thousand-dollar salaries and whole big chunks of the American economy resting in their laps" (1948, 310, 315).

Sudden bureaucratic dilation on such a scale can happen only when the nation goes to war and the public relaxes its usual resistance to the government's exactions. As Adam Smith wrote in *The Wealth of Nations*, "When a nation is already overburdened with taxes, nothing but the necessities of a new war, nothing but either the animosity of national vengeance, or the anxiety for nation security, can induce the people to submit, with tolerable patience, to a new tax" ([1776] 1937, 873). Legislators know that they can now get away with taxing people at hugely elevated rates; rationing goods; allocating raw materials, transportation services, and credit; authorizing gargantuan borrowing; drafting men into the armed forces; and generally exercising vastly more power than they exercised before the war. Although people may groan and complain about the specific actions the bureaucrats take in implementing the wartime mobilization, few dare to resist overtly or even to criticize publicly the overall mobilization for the war or the government's entry into the war. By resisting or criticizing, they would expose themselves not only to legal and extralegal government retribution, but also to rebuke and ostracism by their friends, neighbors, and business associates. As the conversation stopper went during World War II, "Don't you know there's a war on?" (Lingeman 1970).

Because during wartime people fear for the nation's welfare, perhaps even for its very survival, they surrender wealth, privacy, and liberties to the government far more readily than they would during peacetime. As Murray Rothbard observed, "In war, State power is pushed to its ultimate, and, under the slogans of "defense" and "emergency," it can impose a tyranny upon the public such as might be openly resisted in time of peace" ([1965] 2000, 80). Government and its private contractors therefore have a field day. Opportunists galore join the party, each claiming to be performing some "essential war service," no matter how remote the business may be from contributing directly to the military program. Using popular fear to justify its predations, the government lays claim to great expanses of the economy and the society. As the government's taxation, borrowing, expenditure, and direct controls dilate, individual rights shrivel into insignificance. "Frightful enemies coalesce the fear-ridden into obedient and manageable herds" (Shaffer 2005), and few people protest. Of what importance are the rights of a few grouchy individuals when the entire nation is in peril? After the September 11 attacks, pollster John Zogby reported: "I've never seen anything like it before. The willingness to give up personal liberties is stunning, because the level of fear is so high" (qtd. in Polman 2001).[19]

Finally, of course, every war ends, but it leaves legacies that persist, sometimes permanently. In the United States, the War Between the States (see Hummel 1996) and both world wars (see Higgs 1987, 2004) in particular left a multitude of such legacies. Likewise, as Corey Robin writes, "one day, the war on terrorism will come to an end. All wars do. And when it does, we will find ourselves still living in fear: not of terrorism or radical Islam, but of the domestic rulers that fear has left behind." Among other things, we will find that "various security agencies operating in the interest of national security have leveraged their coercive power in ways that target dissenters posing no conceivable threat of terrorism."[20] Not by accident, "the FBI has targeted the antiwar movement in the United States for especially close scrutiny" (2004, 25, 189).

Such targeting is scarcely a surprise because war is, in Randolph Bourne's classic phrase, "the health of the state," and the FBI is a core agency in protecting and enhancing the U.S. government's health. Over the years, the FBI has also done much to promote fear among the American populace, most notoriously perhaps in its COINTELPRO operations during the 1960s, but in plenty of others ways, too (Linfield 1990, 59–60, 71, 99–102, 123–28, 134–39). Of course, it has scarcely worked alone in these endeavors.[21] From top to bottom, the government wants us to be afraid, needs us to be afraid, and invests greatly in making us afraid.

## CONCLUSION

The Lord is my light and my salvation; whom shall I fear?
the Lord is the strength of my life; of whom shall I be afraid?
—Psalms 27:1

Were we ever to stop being afraid of the government itself and of the bogus threats it fosters, the government would shrivel and die, and the host would disappear for the tens of millions of parasites in the United States—not to speak of the vast number of others in the rest of the world—who now sap the public's wealth and energies directly and indirectly by means of government power. On that glorious day, everyone who has been living at public expense will have to get an honest job, and the rest of us, recognizing government as the false god it has always been, can set about assuaging our remaining fears in more productive and morally defensible ways.

## NOTES

1. In this chapter, I make no distinction between the *government* and the *state*. I also include every part of the governing apparatus within this designation, including the legislative, executive, and judicial branches.
2. What David Campbell claims about foreign policy we may claim with equal validity about a much wider range of government policies: "The constant articulation of danger through foreign policy is thus not a threat to a state's identity or existence: it is its condition of possibility" (qtd. in Altheide 2002, 178).
3. In this book, I am concerned only with "public" fears, not with personal apprehensions

such as Pedro's fear that Maria will decline his marriage proposal or Stephen's fear that people will laugh at him when he plays the role of Abraham Lincoln in the school play.

4. No doubt the primitive clans and bands in which human beings lived from time immemorial had various forms of authoritative social control, yet the authorities in these societies differed qualitatively from the coercive, predatory organizations that have been recognized as governments in the more economically advanced parts of the world during the past several millennia. As Jack Douglas observes, "There is leadership within these [primitive] groups, but it tends strongly to be a very subtle, complex, situated (task-oriented) form of consensus leadership closely related to parental authority" (1989, 107).

5. One might view the autonomous cities founded in Europe in the High Middle Ages as counterexamples. According to Harold Berman, "Many cities and towns were founded by a solemn collective oath, or series of oaths, made by the entire citizenry to adhere to a charter that had been publicly read aloud to them. The charter was, in one sense, a social contract; it must, indeed, have been one of the principal historical sources from which the modern contract theory of government emerged" (1983, 393). It is not clear, however, whether the unanimous approval given in these cases has a clear meaning, because people who would not accept the terms of the town's "contract" may have been required to leave the town, threatened, or harmed in other ways. Moreover, the town's law was but one of several to which its denizens might also be subject; the others included royal law, ecclesiastical law, and merchant law.

6. Nock relies on and credits the pioneering historical research of Ludwig Gumplowicz and Franz Oppenheimer.

7. One naturally wonders whether President George W. Bush has taken a page from Ferdinand's book; see, in particular, Higgs 2003b and, for additional aspects, Higgs 2005b.

8. For many fascinating details of this complex matter, see the magnificent account given in Berman 1983.

9. Exclusion of nonpayers demonstrates, of course, that enforcement of the royal law was not a true public good, but only a service that later commentators chose to dignify or justify by placing it in this category.

10. Both Olson and Bates argue along lines similar to those Douglass C. North developed in a series of articles and books published over the past four decades; see especially North and Thomas 1973, and North 1981 and 1990.

11. Mises characterizes the policies of the national monarchs in essentially the same way ([1927] 1985, 121).

12. For a description of the various bunkers and other high-security hideaways to which leading officials of the U.S. government fled on September 11, 2001, see Bamford 2004, 89.

13. One of the most memorable and telling lines in the classic Cold War film *Dr. Strangelove* occurs as the president and his military bigwigs, facing unavoidable nuclear devastation of the earth, devise a plan to shelter a remnant of Americans for thousands of years in deep mine shafts, and General "Buck" Turgidson, still obsessed with a possible Russian advantage, declares: "Mr. President, we must not allow a mine-shaft gap!"

14. CNN is hardly unique in this regard, of course; the mass media in general work relentlessly to foster an atmosphere of fear. For a book-length analysis of this phenomenon, see Altheide 2002.

15. Anyone who imagines that the government's massive surveillance in particular might actually serve its ostensible purpose would be well advised to ponder the analysis of Rudmin 2006. See also Moore 2005 for an example (one of many) of how the surveillance state serves as a pretext for dispensing political pork.

16. Among libertarians, however, each man has his partisans: on Van Buren, see Hummel 1999; on Cleveland, see Higgs 1997, 2.

17. According to investigative reporter James Bamford, one of the leading neoconservative instigators of the Iraq War, David Wurmser (currently Vice President Dick Cheney's Middle East adviser), released a paper in January 2001 urging a massive U.S.–Israeli attack on the Middle East and North Africa to bring that area under U.S.–Israeli domination. Declared Wurmser, "crises are opportunities" (quoted by Bamford in an interview by Zeese 2005). In his 2004 book *A Pretext for War*, Bamford says Wurmser wrote that "crises can be opportunities" (269).

18. Another leading figure who viewed the September 11 attacks as an opportunity was the president's national-security adviser (currently secretary of state) Condoleezza Rice. Shortly after the attacks, she asked the senior staff members of the National Security Council to think seriously about "How do you capitalize on these opportunities?" (qtd. in Ball 2004).

19. In a careful, systematic study of a large number of public-opinion surveys, Eric Larson and Bogdan Savych conclude that the extremely high levels of public support for the global war on terrorism after September 11, 2001, reflected "the view that nearly existential stakes were involved," or, in other words, "a widespread belief that the United States faced a critical threat" (2005, 103, 127).

20. Utterly typical is the FBI's recent surveillance of the American Civil Liberties Union and the environmentalist group Greenpeace under the guise of antiterrorism (see Sherman 2005).

21. For a revealing recent analysis of how "[f]ederal law enforcement agencies have also been expanding their power in the name of combating terrorism, whether or not such expansion has anything to do with enhancing security," and how they have been misusing and abusing their new powers in the process, see Scarborough 2005 (quotation from executive summary on p. 1).

## REFERENCES

Altheide, David L. 2002. *Creating Fear: News and the Construction of Crisis*. New York: Aldine de Gruyter.

Aristotle. 1938. *Aristotle: Selections*. Edited by W. D. Ross. New York: Charles Scribner's Sons.

Aron, Raymond. 1957. *The Opium of the Intellectuals*. Garden City, N.Y.: Doubleday.

Bacevich, Andrew J. 2005a. *The New American Militarism: How Americans Are Seduced by War*. New York: Oxford University Press.

———. 2005b. Trigger Man: In Paul Wolfowitz, Messianic Vision Meets Faith in the Efficacy of Force. *The American Conservative*, June 6. Available at: http://www.amconmag.com/2005_06_06/article1.html.

Ball, Tom. 2004. Top 27 Pieces of Evidence That Show Rice Perjured Herself in Front of the 9/11 Commission: A Reference for Seekers of Truth. *Daily News Online*, April 9. Available at: http://www.dailynewsonline.com/founder_ball_tom/2004_04_09_archive_article.php.

Bamford, James. 2004. *A Pretext for War: 9/11, Iraq, and the Abuse of America's Intelligence Agencies*. New York: Doubleday.

Bates, Robert H. 2001. *Prosperity and Violence: The Political Economy of Development*. New

York: Norton.

Bender, Bryan. 2006. Major Arms Soar to Twice Pre-9/11 Cost: Systems to Have Little Direct Role in Terror Fight. *Boston Globe,* August 19. Available at: http://www.boston. com/news/nation/articles/2006/08/19/major_arms_soar_to_twice_pre_911_cost/.

Bennett, James T. 2006. *Homeland Security Scams.* New Brunswick, N.J.: Transaction.

Berman, Harold J. 1983. *Law and Revolution: The Formation of the Western Legal Tradition.* Cambridge, Mass.: Harvard University Press.

Bloom, Sandra L. 2004. Neither Liberty nor Safety: The Impact of Fear on Individuals, Institutions, and Societies. Part I. *Psychotherapy and Politics International* 2, no. 2: 78–98.

Clark, Paul. 2002. Government and the Stockholm Syndrome. November 22. Available at: http://www.lewrockwell.com/orig2/clark6.html.

The Cooling World. 1975. *Newsweek,* April 28. Available from the Global Climate Coalition at: http://www.globalclimate.org/Newsweek.htm.

Douglas, Jack D. 1989. *The Myth of the Welfare State.* New Brunswick, N.J.: Transaction.

Feser, Edward. 2004. Why Are Universities Dominated by the Left? *Tech Central Station,* February 13. Available at: http://www2.techcentralstation.com/1051/ printer.jsp?CID=1051-021304A.

Flynn, John T. 1948. *The Roosevelt Myth.* Garden City, N.Y.: Garden City Books.

Frost, Robert. 1979. *The Poetry of Robert Frost: The Collected Poems, Complete and Unabridged.* Edited by Edward Connery Lathem. New York: Holt, Rinehart and Winston.

Hall, Mimi. 2005. Ridge Reveals Clashes on Alerts: Former Homeland Security Chief Debunks "Myth." *USAToday.com,* May 11. Available at: http://aolsvc.news.aol.com/news/ article.adp?id=20050511071809990020.

Hayek, F. A. 1949. The Intellectuals and Socialism. *University of Chicago Law Review* 16 (spring): 417–33.

Hazlitt, Henry. [1976] 1994. Is Politics Insoluble? *The Freeman* 44 (September): 468–73.

Higgs, Robert. 1987. *Crisis and Leviathan: Critical Episodes in the Growth of American Government.* New York: Oxford University Press.

———. 1994. The Cold War Economy: Opportunity Costs, Ideology, and the Politics of Crisis. *Explorations in Economic History* 31 (July): 283–312.

———. 1997. No More "Great Presidents." *The Free Market* 15 (March): 1–3.

———. 1999. We're All Sick, and Government Must Heal Us. *The Independent Review* 3, no. 4 (spring): 623–27.

———. 2002. Government Protects Us? *The Independent Review* 7, no. 2 (fall): 309–13.

———. 2003a. All War All the Time: The Battle on Terrorism Is an Excuse to Make Fighting Permanent. *San Francisco Chronicle,* July 6. Available at: http://www.independent. org/newsroom/article.asp?id=1178.

———. 2003b. Impending War in Iraq: George Bush's Faith-Based Foreign Policy. *San Francisco Chronicle,* February 13. Available at: http://www.independent.org/newsroom/ article.asp?id=443.

———. 2004. *Against Leviathan: Government Power and a Free Society.* Oakland, Calif.: The Independent Institute.

———. 2005a. The Ongoing Growth of Government in the Economically Advanced Countries. *Advances in Austrian Economics* 8: 279–300.

———. 2005b. *Resurgence of the Warfare State: The Crisis since 9/11.* Oakland, Calif.: The Independent Institute.

Holcombe, Randall G. 2006. Should We Have Acted Thirty Years Ago to Prevent Global Climate Change? *The Independent Review* 11, no. 2 (fall): 283–88.

Hooker, Richard. 1996. Divine Right of Kings. In *The European Enlightenment Glossary.*

Available at: http://www.wsu.edu/~dee/GLOSSARY/DIVRIGHT.HTM.

Hume, David. [1777] 1987. Of the First Principles of Government. In *Essays Moral, Political, and Literary,* rev. ed., edited with a foreword, notes, and glossary by Eugene F. Miller, 32–36. Indianapolis: Liberty Fund.

Hummel, Jeffrey Rogers. 1996. *Emancipating Slaves, Enslaving Free Men: A History of the American Civil War.* La Salle, Ill.: Open Court.

———. 1999. Martin Van Buren: The Greatest American President. *The Independent Review* 4, no. 2 (fall): 255–81.

Jeffers, Robinson. 1965. *Selected Poems.* New York: Vintage Books.

Klein, Daniel B. 2005. The People's Romance: Why People Love Government (as Much as They Do). *The Independent Review* 10, no. 1 (summer): 5–37.

Kuroda, Akira. 1997. Origins of Japanese Production: From Fukoku Kyohei to Zero Defects. *SOAS Economic Digest* 1 (January). Available at: http://www.soas.ac.uk/SED/Issue-1/akira.html.

Larson, Eric V., and Bogdan Savych. 2005. *American Public Support for U.S. Military Operations from Mogadishu to Baghdad.* Santa Monica, Calif.: RAND Corporation.

Light, Paul Charles. 1999. *The True Size of Government.* Washington, D.C.: Brookings Institution Press.

Lind, William S. 2005. Of Cabbages and Kings. May 26. Available at: http://www.lewrockwell.com/lind/lind66.html.

Linfield, Michael. 1990. *Freedom under Fire: U.S. Civil Liberties in Times of War.* Boston: South End Press.

Lingeman, Richard R. 1970. *Don't You Know There's a War on?* New York: G. P. Putnam's Sons.

Machiavelli, Niccolò. [1513] 1992. *The Prince.* New York: Dover.

Mencken, H. L. [1921] 1949. Women as Outlaws. In *A Mencken Chrestomathy,* 28–30. New York: Knopf.

Mises, Ludwig von. [1956] 1972. *The Anti-capitalistic Mentality.* South Holland, Ill.: Libertarian Press.

———. [1927] 1985. *Liberalism: In the Classical Tradition,* 3rd ed. Translated by Ralph Raico. San Francisco: Cobden Press and the Foundation for Economic Education.

Moore, Martha T. 2005. Cities Opening More Video Surveillance Eyes. *USA Today,* July 18. Available at: http://www.usatoday.com/news/nation/2005-07-17-cameras-cities_x.htm.

Nock, Albert J. [1935] 1973. *Our Enemy, the State.* New York: Free Life Editions.

Nolan, James L. 1998. *The Therapeutic State: Justifying Government at Century's End.* New York: New York University Press.

North, Douglass C. 1981. *Structure and Change in Economic History.* New York: Norton.

———. 1990. *Institutions, Institutional Change, and Economic Performance.* Cambridge, U.K.: Cambridge University Press.

North, Douglass C., and Robert Paul Thomas. 1973. *The Rise of the Western World: A New Economic History.* Cambridge, U.K.: Cambridge University Press.

Nozick, Robert. [1986] 1998. Why Do Intellectuals Oppose Capitalism? *Cato Policy Report,* January–February. Available at: http://www.cato.org/pubs/policy_report/cpr-20n1-1.html.

Olson, Mancur. 2000. *Power and Prosperity: Outgrowing Communist and Capitalist Dictatorships.* New York: Basic.

Palmer, Frederick. 1931. *Newton D. Baker: America at War.* New York: Dodd, Mead.

Polman, Dick. 2001. Fearful Americans Shun Liberties Lobby: Citizens Are Making Sacri-

fices, Some Experts Say. *Philadelphia Inquirer,* December 10. Available at: http://www.
zogby.com/soundbites/ReadClips.dbm?ID=4138.

Porter, Bruce D. 1994. *War and the Rise of the State: The Military Foundations of Modern Politics.* New York: Free Press.

Reese, Charley. 2005. Mostly Fertilizer. July 18. Available at: http://www.lewrockwell.com/reese/reese208.html.

Rich, Frank. 2005. The Two Wars of the Worlds. *New York Times,* July 3. Available at: http://www.nytimes.com/2005/07/03/opinion/03rich.html?ex=1121054400&en=61c0ffce6b638317&ei=5070&emc=eta1.

Robin, Corey. 2004. *Fear: The History of a Political Idea.* New York: Oxford University Press.

Rothbard, Murray N. [1965] 2000. The Anatomy of the State. In *Egalitarianism as a Revolt Against Nature and Other Essays,* 2d ed., 55–88. Auburn, Ala.: Ludwig von Mises Institute.

Rudmin, Floyd. 2006. The Politics of Paranoia and Intimidation: Why Does the NSA Engage in Mass Surveillance of Americans When It's Statistically Impossible for Such Spying to Detect Terrorists? *CounterPunch,* May 24. Available at: http://www.counterpunch.org/rudmin05242006.html.

Russell, Bertrand. 1943. An Outline of Intellectual Rubbish. Available at: http://www.solstice.us/russell/intellectual_rubbish.html.

Scarborough, Melanie. 2005. *The Security Pretext: An Examination of the Growth of Federal Police Agencies.* Cato Institute Briefing Paper no. 94. Washington, D.C.: Cato Institute, June 29.

Schumpeter, Joseph A. 1954. *History of Economic Analysis.* Edited from manuscript by Elizabeth Boody Schumpeter. New York: Oxford University Press.

Shaffer, Butler. 2005. Meeting a Suicide Bomber. July 21. Available at: http://www.lewrockwell.com/shaffer/shaffer113.html.

———. 2006. A World Too Complex to Be Managed. May 11. Available at: http://www.lewrockwell.com/shaffer/shaffer137.html.

Sherman, Mark. 2005. FBI Says It Has Files on Greenpeace, ACLU. *New Orleans Times-Picayune,* July 18.

Skidelsky, Edward. 2005. Review of *Earthly Powers: Religion and Politics in Europe from the French Revolution to the Great War,* by Michael Burleigh. *New Statesman* (October 10). Available at: http://www.newstatesman.com/Bookshop/300000105041.

Smith, Adam. [1776] 1937. *An Inquiry into the Nature and Causes of the Wealth of Nations.* New York: Modern Library.

Szasz, Thomas S. 1965. Toward the Therapeutic State. *The New Republic* (December 11): 26–29.

———. 2001. The Therapeutic State: The Tyranny of Pharmacracy. *The Independent Review* 5, no. 4 (spring): 485–521.

Tierney, John. 2005. Tune Out the Fear. *New Orleans Times-Picayune,* July 12 (reprinted from the *New York Times*).

Yeager, Leland B. 1985. Rights, Contract, and Utility in Policy Espousal. *Cato Journal* 5 (spring–summer): 259–94.

Zeese, Kevin B. 2005. A Pretext for War: An Interview with James Bamford. May 26. Available at: http://www.lewrockwell.com/orig6/zeese1.html.

Acknowledgments: For useful comments on an earlier version of this chapter, I thank Donald Boudreaux, Laurie Calhoun, Paul Clark, Jack Douglas, Randall Holcombe, Daniel Klein, and Pierre Lemieux. Beth Hoffman kindly helped me track down a reference. Others, too numerous to name, responded with sometimes thought-provoking comments on a briefer, preliminary version circulated extensively on the World Wide Web in May 2005.

# 2

# Eighteen Problematic Propositions in the Analysis of the Growth of Government

When you cannot express it in numbers, your knowledge is of a meagre and unsatisfactory kind.

—Lord Kelvin

Yes, and when you can express it in numbers, your knowledge is of a meagre and unsatisfactory kind.

—Jacob Viner

Economists, public-choice analysts, political scientists, and other scholars have made many studies of the growth of government, especially since the late 1970s. As the literature grew, a number of conventions became established with respect to concepts, measures, assumptions, and modes of analysis. Certain contributions came to be viewed as paradigmatic and hence served as models for subsequent contributors. However, no analytical consensus emerged. One can perceive the outlines of several competing "schools": a Chicago school, a Washington school (see Proposition 16), a mainstream economics school, a libertarian school, several distinct positions within the public-choice community of scholars, and others.

Despite the diversity of approaches and conclusions, much of this work has been premised, implicitly if not explicitly, on the acceptance of propositions that are questionable at best. In what follows, I state these propositions and criticize them. Although I provide citations and examples of scholars who have advanced or accepted the flawed propositions, my aim is not to compile a catalog of sinners. The examples are intended only to provide concrete illustrations of how various analysts have proceeded and to demonstrate that I am not quarreling with phantoms.

The discussion that follows pertains mainly to the growth of government as it has occurred in the countries of western Europe and their overseas off-shoots during the past two centuries, especially during the twentieth century. I have specific expertise with regard to only one case, the United States, so much of my discussion relates especially to that case. This restriction of the frame of reference does little harm, however, because the ideas I criticize have themselves been employed, for the most part, in the same empirical domain. Further, I believe that attempts to achieve universally applicable explanations of the growth of government are doomed to fail in any event. I disavow at the start any pretension of contributing to the construction of a single all-encompassing theory.

## PROPOSITION I

*Government activities can be reduced to a single variable, the "size" of government, which can be measured accurately.*

Modern governments undertake many distinct activities. They take money away from people by taxation and fines; they deliver mail; they operate law courts where citizens resolve various disputes and tennis courts where people work on their backhands; they conduct medical research; and so forth in nearly endless variety. To sum up the various activities, one must measure each of them in a common unit—persons on the government payroll, for example, or dollars spent by the government. These methods of achieving commensurability seem to make sense until one inquires a bit deeper.

Suppose that, ceteris paribus, the government has added a billion dollars to its spending for the operation of law courts and cut a billion dollars from its spending for farm subsidies. Has the government grown? If the changes had been reversed, would the government have grown? The answers are far from obvious. Government (as a set of activities) is what government (as a group of people) does, but because governments do so many diverse things, no common unit of account can scale the underlying reality satisfactorily.

Government employees or dollars often work at cross purpose in their effect on the economy. Many analysts have noted the prodigious "cross hauling" or "churning" associated with modern government activities (Becker 1983, 389, 1985, 341; Musgrave 1985, 305). On the one hand, government wheat researchers develop higher-yielding varieties of the crop, thereby increasing the supply and decreasing the price. On the other hand, government acreage restrictions or conservation set-asides decrease the supply and increase the price. Such examples can be multiplied indefinitely. I do not mean to suggest that the churning is accidental or politically irrational in its inception, because interested parties set each part of the process in motion with their eyes open and their hands grasping. The implication for muddled measurement remains, however, regardless of the motives involved.

In view of the heterogeneity, incommensurability, and offsetting effects of many government activities, the information content of any one-dimensional measure of "the" size of government verges on nil (Peters and Heisler 1983, 178–81, 186; Rose 1983, 7). Much more informative would be an answer to the question: What in particular is the government doing more frequently or less frequently? Most analysts of government growth simply ignore this problem.

## PROPOSITION 2

*The best measure of the size of government is relative government spending—the ratio of government spending to the gross national or domestic product (GNP, GDP). Good alternative measures include relative tax revenues (the ratio of tax revenues to GDP) and relative government employment (the ratio of government employees to labor force).*

Many analysts forgo entirely an attempt to justify measurement of the size of government as the ratio of government spending to GNP or GDP. (Net national product or national income occasionally serves as the denominator.) They just plunge ahead (Lowery and Berry 1983, 666–67; Mueller 1987, 115), noting, if anything, that "everybody does it." But choices still must be made. Should the analyst include all government spending, including transfer payments, or only the government's "exhaustive" spending for newly produced final goods and services, which is a component of GDP as conventionally defined? Both measures are used. Frequently, however, as in the United States during the past fifty years, the two measures behave quite differently—in this case the all-spending ratio tends to rise more or less steadily, whereas the "exhaustive" measure remains more or less level (U.S. Council of Economic Advisers 2006, 280–81, 379). Regardless of the exact measure selected, using relative government spending to measure the size of government raises many curiosities.

Consider some cases. (1) Suppose the breakfast-cereal manufacturers produce and sell more corn flakes, but nothing else changes. Implication: government has shrunk. (2) Suppose people from the Defense Department sit down with people from Lockheed Martin and agree to pay more per unit for this year's purchase of (the same number of) F-16s, but nothing else changes. Implication: government has grown. (3) Suppose the government switches, as it did in 1973, from military conscription to an all-volunteer military force, which entails payment of higher salaries to military personnel, but nothing else changes. Very strange implication: government has grown. (4) Suppose local governments across the country stop operating and spending money for sewage treatment plants, mandating instead that every home or business releasing sewage into the system ensure that the effluent meets strict treatment standards, with all costs to be borne by the private sewage generators, but nothing else happens. Implication: government has shrunk. Such examples can be produced virtually without limit. And the examples are not merely contrived. Arbitrary and counterintuitive determinants of change in the government's relative spending are part and parcel of this measure of the government's size.

Similar observations and others might be made with respect to using relative tax revenues as an index of the size of government. Whenever an index is a ratio with GNP as its denominator, all sorts of oddities may arise. In the workaday world of government fiscal reports, the repeated shuffling of various taxes, especially some or all of the Social Security tax, between on-budget and off-budget status further confuses the historical record (U.S. Office of Management and Budget 1989, 6).

Michael Boskin has concluded that for various reasons "the accounting problems are so fundamental and pervasive that federal budget figures cannot be used to compile an accurate representative of our fiscal history" (1987, 60, emphasis added). (See also Stiglitz's [1989, 68] strictures on the misleading way the national accounts treat government enterprises.) A fortiori, these figures cannot serve as a reliable basis for measuring the overall size of government in all of its significant economic dimensions.

How, for instance, should one take into account the government's various activities in the credit markets? Governments now make many types of loans, insure private loans, subsidize or grant tax breaks on the extension of certain private loans, and insure—sometimes far beyond the explicit promise—deposits in banks and savings institutions. Joseph Stiglitz notes that "in the U.S. today, approximately a quarter of all lending (to the private sector) is either through a government agency or with government guarantees.... The magnitudes of the implicit subsidies and costs—both the total value, and who receives how much—are hidden" (1989, 63).

Government employment also is a fragile index of the size of government, in part because governments obtain the labor services of millions of "contractors" and grant recipients who are not officially classified as government employees (Blumenthal 1979; Hanrahan 1983; Light 1999, 2003). These workers are classified as members of the private labor force, even though they work exclusively on projects set in motion by governments and receive compensation entirely, if often indirectly, from government outlays. They are considered "private" employees, rather than regular government employees, only because of legal technicalities and accounting conventions. Thus, as the composition of the total effective government workforce (regular government employees plus "private" government contractors and grant recipients) changes, as it often does, the standard index of relative government employment becomes a spurious indicator of whether government has grown or shrunk.


## PROPOSITION 3

*Even if relative government spending (or one of the commonly employed "good alternative measures") does not properly measure the true size of government, the two magnitudes are highly correlated over time, so relative government spending is an adequate—indeed an indispensable—proxy variable for empirical analysis.*

Many analysts know that acceptance of this proposition is risky (Borcherding 1985, 376–77; Lindbeck 1985, 314, 325). Yet most proceed, often into extremely intricate modeling and highly sensitive econometric analysis, without further ado. Sam Peltzman, in a widely read and cited study, should be commended for his candor: "I am going to equate government's role in economic life with the size of its budget. This is obviously wrong since many government activities (for example, statutes and administrative rules) redirect resources just as surely as taxation and spending, but the available data leave no other choice. My operating assumption has to be that large and growing budgets imply a large and growing substitution of collective for private decision in allocating resources" (1980, 209).

This rationale, accepted by many others besides Peltzman, has several defects. Most important, it simply is not true that one has no choice. There are mountains of evidence not only about the details of spending and taxing, but about the multifarious commands expressed in statutes, regulations, and judicial rulings, all of which sit in the archives and libraries awaiting researchers. Perhaps the study of such nitty-gritty evidence is beneath the dignity of modern, "high-powered" economists. To preserve their self-esteem, they need only make an "operating assumption" that a single data series, which can be retrieved from a standard statistical source, provides all the information required for an adequate analysis of the complex phenomena that constitute the actual behavior in question. One is reminded of the old joke about the people marooned on an island with cans of food but no can opener. After a chemist and a physicist propose esoteric technical solutions, the economist in the group proposes: "Let us assume we have a can opener."

As for the assumed high correlation between the observed data series and the unobserved reality, how does one know? Unless one makes an effort to establish at least the likelihood of a close correlation, one is simply making a raw assertion, a leap into the void. (Borcherding frankly recognizes the problem but does nothing about it [1985, 377].)

## PROPOSITION 4

*Point-to-point or trend-rate measures are adequate explicanda for the analysis of the growth of government.*

Analysts of the growth of government often rely on only a portion of their data (forget for the moment all that is wrong with the data anyhow). They may simply compare the size of government at one time with its size at a later time. Noting that government grew X-fold between the two dates, they proceed to explain the One Big Change by relating it to Other Big Changes in explanatory variables during the interim (Borcherding 1985, 362–69). Others fill in more blanks, examining measures for "selected years" (North and Wallis 1982, 337; Bernholz 1986, 662–63; Mueller 1987, 116–17). Still others compute from annual or semiannual data a series of decade averages or a trend rate of change, making the result of their calculation the explicandum (Bernholz 1986, 664, 676, 678). In each case, valuable information is ignored at great risk to the validity of the analysis.

For example, Gerald Scully makes much of a shift from local government spending to state and federal government spending in the United States between the average for 1902–27 and the average for 1960–88 (1989, 6.93). Had he examined all the available data, however, he would have discovered that almost the entire shift occurred between 1932 and 1936 (Wallis 1985, 5). The change obviously had more to do with the Great Depression and New Deal politics than with the long-term changes in the focus of rent seeking that Scully emphasizes.

Aside from the inadvisability of throwing away information in an empirical analysis, one has a more fundamental reason for examining the full sequence of data: the growth of government has been a path-dependent process. Because understandings gained from experience shape social beliefs and constrain social actions, where the relation of government to the economy can go depends on exactly where it has already been—that is, it depends on what precisely people's experiences have been. One needs to examine the entire profile of the growth of government to discover the dynamic interrelations between ideas and events over time. (Analysts who emphasize path dependency include Hughes [1977]; Higgs [1987a]; and North [1990, 92–104 and 2005, 48–64].)

Some analysts believe that it is better to smooth the data or even to omit certain deviant years from consideration (Meltzer and Richard 1983). These analysts view the unruly observations as unlikely stochastic deviations from a smoothly changing central tendency; they prefer that their statistical analysis not be contaminated by "outliers" (and maybe that their coefficients of determination not be diminished). I criticize the theoretical foundation of these views when I discuss Proposition 7. For now it suffices to observe that the crises of history, when government expanded abruptly, were real. People did not forget them. Indeed, people were deeply affected by such experiences and later behaved differently as a result.

## PROPOSITION 5

*Government can be analyzed as something having an abstract "functional" relation to the economy; it is unnecessary to consider government officials as autonomous decision makers having genuine discretion and making real choices.*

The approach implied by this proposition appears frequently as what I call the Modernization Hypothesis, which maintains that a modern, urban-industrial, technologically advanced economy simply must have a big, active government. Modern socioeconomic affairs are very complex. How can they possibly take place successfully without the guiding, regulating, coordinating hand of government? "The increased complexities and interrelationships of modern life," wrote Calvin Hoover, "necessitate this extension of power of the state" (1959, 373). Supreme Court justice William Brennan echoed this view in a 1985 speech. "The modern activist state," he declared, "is a concomitant of the complexity of modern society; it is inevitably with us" (quoted in Kozinski n.d., 6).

One doubt arises immediately. Why is government apparently so much bigger in some countries than in other, equally modernized countries (say, Sweden vis-à-vis Switzerland)? This issue, however, is not the most fundamental problem.

Anyone who has understood Adam Smith's message, not to speak of Ludwig von Mises and Friedrich Hayek's more penetrating and pertinent contributions, immediately doubts the Modernization Hypothesis. Indeed, it seems completely backwards, for whereas government might conceivably coordinate a simple premodern economy, it certainly cannot coordinate successfully a complex modern economy. The now undeniable failure of all the centrally planned economies, confirming the early insights of Mises and Hayek, clearly supports the Austrian school position on this question.

My point is different, however; it relates to methodological individualism. Even if it were true that a modern economy "requires" bigger government for its effective coordination, the Modernization Hypothesis would be virtually worthless as an explanation of the growth of government. The fatal flaw is the absence of willing human actors. Just because a course of action is "necessary" in some systemic sense for the successful operation of an economy does not ensure that anyone has a personal incentive to work toward fulfilling the requirement. In the Modernization Hypothesis, the process is magical: the economy "needs" bigger government, and POOF! the government grows. But who did what to bring about that growth? And why did those actors find it in their interest to take such actions? To these questions, the Modernization Hypothesis, like every other "functional necessity" explanation, has no answer.

Functional necessity explanations implicitly view government officials as robots who lack genuine discretion and make no real choices, automatons programmed to accomplish whatever is necessary to serve the known, unambiguous "public interest" optimally. Besides being mystical and obscurantist, this view is patently, empirically wrong. (For more general observations on methodological individualism and "the false organismic analogies of scientism," see Rothbard [1979, 15–17, 57–61] and sources cited there.)

## PROPOSITION 6

*Government can be analyzed as if it were a single decision maker; it is unnecessary to consider conflicts of interest within government or migration back and forth between the ruling group and the ruled group.*

The difficulties of formal modeling and the analytical attractions of simplicity have enticed many analysts to embrace this proposition. (An outstanding example is Auster and Silver [1979].) In ordinary oral and written discourse, of course, we frequently encounter statements that "the government" did something or "the government" decided such and such, without any specification of which government officials in particular took the action. Sometimes this vague attribution is harmless, but more is at stake when analysts continually adopt such misleading language.

Even the Nobel laureate Douglass C. North built his "neoclassical theory of the state" on the assumption of "a state with a single ruler ... a wealth- or utility-maximizing ruler" who can act in a way that his subjects cannot because, as a single person, "he has no free rider problem" (1981, 20, 32). However useful this conception may be in understanding a medieval lord of the manor or the court of Louis XIV, it has virtually no applicability to governmental growth in the Western world during the past two centuries.

Modern governments consist of thousands of important decision makers, not to mention millions of minions who have at least a bit of discretion in carrying out delegated activities. Today, for example, the United States has more than eighty-seven thousand separate governments, more than sixty thousand with the power to tax (Higgs 1987a, 6; U.S. Bureau of the Census 2000, 299–300). Moreover, people are constantly passing back and forth between the ruling group and the ruled group. The "revolving door" is notorious at the Department of Defense, but a similar phenomenon occurs at many other places in the government. In many instances, one would be warranted to regard certain persons formally outside the government as more a part of it than most of those who are formally inside it—just think of the exogovernmental potency of such notable figures as Walter Lippmann, Felix Frankfurter, John J. McCloy, David Rockefeller, Henry Kissinger, and Richard Perle. (For more examples, see Dye 1990.) In any event, no one person, no small group, calls the shots for the whole hydra-headed creature that constitutes "the state." Although people within the ruling circles typically share at least one goal—retaining their own powers and privileges—they constantly engage in internecine struggles. The assumption that the government operates as if it were a single decision maker cannot take us far toward a realistic understanding of modern government or its growth.

## PROPOSITION 7

*There exists a structure of politicoeconomic behavioral relations—an "underlying model"—whose workings generate the growth of government as a dynamic equilibrium outcome; this structure does not change over time.*

Whether analysts think about it or not, those who test their theories of the growth of government by fitting a linear regression model to the time-series data for a certain period are accepting this proposition. Econometric theory admits of no exception if the estimated coefficients are to have the meaning they are supposed to have. Thus, if the theory contains the equation

$$(1) \quad G = \alpha + \beta X + u$$

and, using linear regression techniques, one estimates the parameters $\alpha$ and $\beta$ from time-series data for the years 1901–99 as $a$ and $b$, respectively, then one is assuming, inter alia, that the politicoeconomic world was working so that whenever $X$ took the value of $x'$, then $G$ as a result took the value $a + b(x')$, plus or minus a purely random amount $u'$, and this result was the case regardless of whether $X$ took the value $x'$ in 1901, in 1999, or in any other year during the time period to which the model is fitted. That is, the underlying model is assumed to be invariant as specified by equation (1). The econometric estimation is designed only to ascertain the numerical values of the parameters, not to test or otherwise call into question the functional specification of the model. The specification is presumed to be given to the investigator by his theory, independent of any empirical observation—in effect, by divine revelation, though the source may well be one of the lesser deities.

Suppose that $G$ denotes total government spending and $X$ denotes total personal income as defined in the standard national-income accounts. Suppose further that the estimated value of $\beta$ turns out to be $b = 0.3$. The interpretation would be that every additional dollar of personal income gave rise to an additional thirty cents of government spending, no matter when during the period that extra dollar came into people's possession: the identical quantitative linkage existed for income changes occurring between 1901 and 1902, between 1998 and 1999, and, indeed, between any two years in the test period, whether the pairs be 1933–34, 1945–46, or any other adjacent years. The dates simply do not matter—by assumption.

Is the assumption plausible? No. The world of 1901 differed in many pertinent ways from the world of 1999. Among other differences, people at the two dates had quite different ideas about what they wanted the government to do. In the United States in 1901, many people still thought in terms of a variant of classical liberal ideology. They wanted not much more than a night-watchman state, and they already had more than that (Higgs 1983, 1987a, 77–105, 1989b, 92–98). In 1999, in contrast, most Americans had relatively inflated ideas about the range of social and economic "problems" they wanted the government to solve (Smith 1987; Higgs 1989b, 101–3, 2004a, 271–95). Even if the ideology had not changed—and historians may reasonably differ about precisely how and when it did shift—socioeconomic and political conditions certainly had changed enormously in the interim. In 1901, a majority of the population still lived in rural areas, and 43 percent of the labor force worked in farming, fishing, and mining. In 1999, less than one-quarter of the population lived in rural areas (many of them with easy access to a city), and less than 4 percent of the labor force worked in farming, fishing, and mining. These differences in socioeconomic conditions are but two of the many that starkly distinguish the people of 1901 from those of 1999. Would it not be strange if people so differently situated, even without subscribing to different views concerning the desirable scope of government, should just happen to get thirty cents of additional government spending every time their personal incomes rose by a dollar? That circumstance would be very strange indeed. If such constancy were found to be the case, would the analyst not be on firmer ground to interpret it as a coincidence, a parametric peculiarity, rather than as the manifestation of a politicoeconomic law? After all, the meaning of thirty cents of additional government spending—the precise collection of goods and services associated with it—differed dramatically in 1901 and 1999.

Further, given that people's behavior depends on their ideas and that people learn from their experiences, it is extremely unlikely that an aggregative "behavioral" relation between a more or less inaccurate index of government activity and any of the usual "explanatory" variables would have remained invariant over a century of tumultuous experience—wars, depressions, deflations, labor upheavals, inflations, energy crises, environmental panics, and so forth (contra Becker [1985, 332], who postulates a similar sort of constancy, and Peltzman [1985], who claims to have confirmed a related political stability econometrically). Can we really believe that none of these great events budged the people's commitment to or acquiescence in the government's spending an additional thirty cents for every additional dollar of personal income? Even with regard to much shorter periods, similar doubts may be raised. Can anyone really believe, for example, that the structure of politicoeconomic behavioral relations did not change in the United States between 1929 and 1939?

We might well take seriously the conclusion reached by Assar Lindbeck: "there is no compelling reason to model a process of an expansion of public spending [or the growth of government in other dimensions] as a series of static equilibria positions at different values of a set of exogenous variable, or even as a dynamic sequence of equilibria." We are dealing with "a disequilibrium process, the speed of which is determined by characteristics of political competition" (1985, 325–26).

A final caveat, noted by Johan Myhrman, pertains to the example itself: "we have to avoid the temptation that many have fallen for and that is to conclude that rising income is the cause of the growth of government" (1985, 279). Temporal association, no matter how close, does not establish a causal relation in any event. (I raise additional questions about the correlation between income and the size of government in my discussion of Proposition 16.)

## PROPOSITION 8

*Which particular persons compose or influence the government does not matter. Only broad socioeconomic changes and the relative strengths of interest groups need be considered.*

In analyzing the operation of the market system, economists are accustomed to ignoring the personal identities of the actors; and usually they are justified in doing so. We can probably understand the demand for and supply of potatoes well enough without naming consumer Jones as a demander and farmer Smith as a supplier. In markets with many small demanders and suppliers, no one in particular has any perceptible influence over the prevailing price or the volume of sales. Therefore, nothing is gained by worrying about the particularities of specific people.

When economic methodology has been carried over to the analysis of political, governmental, and legal matters, the nameless quality of the analysis also has been carried over. Hence, public-choice scholars speak of voters, legislators, bureaucrats, and others only as anonymous members of categories of actors. The theory is supposed to apply regardless of which particular person occupies a theoretical category. The theory is supposed to be—indeed, one of its imagined glories is that it is—general in the sense of being abstract. (Like physics, you see: no one cares which uranium atom we work with because presumably they are all the same.) For some analytical purposes, this approach may be satisfactory, but it has limits well short of its pretensions.

One fact that should give pause to the analysts is that political actors themselves certainly seem to have acted as if particular personalities mattered to them. Legions of Roosevelt haters seethed with animosity toward "that man"; he is said to have agitated them so mightily that they could not stand even the sound of his name! Would they have hated any other Democratic president as much and acted the same—say, if Al Smith had been elected in 1932? Not likely. Smith himself served as an officer of the leading Roosevelt haters' group, the Liberty League (Leuchtenburg 1963, 92). Would nothing have changed had someone other than Woodrow Wilson been president during and immediately after World War I? Would the events of the 1980s have unfolded without essential difference if, say, Howard Baker had been president instead of Ronald Reagan? In the mid-1930s, when the Supreme Court was more or less evenly divided between those eager to affirm and those eager to deny the constitutionality of major New Deal programs, did nothing of substance turn on the personal character of Justice Owen J. Roberts, the famous "swing man"?

If merely raising these questions does not indicate obvious answers to them, then it must at least create serious doubts about political explanations devoid of personalities. To most historians, the significance of particular persons in determining the course of political history seems manifest. Politics is not, in this regard, like economics. (Maybe economics [in reality] is not always like economics [in the models], either.) In politics, one person can make a difference—not that very many can or do, but the potential exists when the right person and the right occasion conjoin. To understand the growth of government, which is obviously the outcome of a political process, we may need to attend to the roles that particular actors have played at critical junctures.

## PROPOSITION 9

*In studying the growth of government, econometric analysis is superior to historical analysis.*

The idea that econometrics trumps history seems warranted if one accepts Proposition 7 (invariant structural model) and Proposition 8 (personalities are irrelevant). I have already criticized those propositions, but additional objections may still be raised.

One problem has to do with the distinction between the creation of a new government power and its exercise, say, by means of government spending or employment. In the United States, authorization must precede the appropriation of public funds. After political events prompt the creation of new authority, a long time may pass before much money is spent under that authority.

Consider, for example, the Social Security system created in 1935. Clearly the program reflected the unique configuration of socioeconomic and political conditions in the mid-1930s (C. Weaver 1983). For the next twenty years, it remained a minor element in federal spending; as late as 1955, only $4.3 billion was spent for Social Security (Old Age and Survivors Insurance [OASI]) transfers to the aged and to eligible survivors (U.S. Office of Management and Budget 2006, 281). In 2005, these types of transfers exceeded $430 billion, exactly one hundred times more, thereby accounting for a large share of the increase in federal spending over the preceding fifty years—a period when OASI payments grew from about 6 percent to more than 17 percent of all federal spending (291) (note that these data do not include other Social Security transfers, authorized later, such as disability payments or Medicare).

Of course, the increase in OASI transfers from 1955 to 2005 reflects the unfolding of political events during those years, as members of Congress catered to a segment of the electorate by expanding the scope of eligibility and increasing the allowable amount of payment per eligible recipient. But someone who has tracked the yearly pulling and hauling of events that resulted in changing amounts of aggregate spending, as the econometrician does in an abstract way, is attending to only one aspect of the growth of government, and it is a consequential or derivative aspect, not a fundamental one. The increase in Social Security transfers during each year of the 1960s, for example, resulted not simply from the playing out of politics in the 1960s. It was also a lagged effect of the events and political actions of the 1930s. The increased OASI payments in the 1960s could not have occurred without a Social Security system in place, and that system owed its existence to much earlier events and actions. As Richard Rose has remarked, the growth of government taxing and spending "is not so much a function of new laws as it is a consequence of the continuance of old laws" (1984, 21).

An even more compelling example is the veterans' program. As described nearly twenty years ago by Julie Johnson:

> The VA [Department of Veterans Affairs] serves 27 million veterans and 53 million dependents and survivors, more than a third of the population. It is the largest independent agency in the Federal bureaucracy, with an annual budget of $27 billion and more than 240,000 employees. It operates one of the largest health care systems in the world, and the number of patients it treats is expected to skyrocket as more World War II veterans age; it administers one of the largest home loan guarantee programs in the Federal Government, having guaranteed some $263 billion in mortgage loans since 1944; and it has helped 18 million veterans go to college or get job training. (*New York Times*, December 13, 1987)

Here is a welfare state in itself. Again, one can ascertain that spending for the veterans' programs grew in connection with an ongoing political process during the past sixty years. Yet no one can really understand how this gargantuan complex of government activities emerged unless one understands how the GI Bill of 1944 gained enactment: 12 million people, most of them draftees, were serving in the armed forces, and an election was coming up (Ross 1969; Higgs 1987a, 229). Once the institutional apparatus of the VA had been established, its vast potential to serve as a single-agency welfare state had only to be exploited at the margin as events and political conditions permitted. To use an analogy from cosmology, none of this evolution could have occurred without the original Big Bang.

Econometric models of the growth of government typically relate the explicandum to contemporaneous events alone or to events a year or two earlier. Such models are ill suited to capture the distinction between what is essential or fundamental (creation of new powers expanding the scope of government action) and what is consequential or derivative (increased government spending within an unchanged scope of government powers). As a rule, the econometrician "falsely assumes that the causes of government growth represent current choice rather than the inertia force of established commitments" (Rose 1983, 6). In modern democratic political systems, it is much easier to start a program than to terminate one; just keeping programs from growing, far from killing them, requires political courage and commitment of a sort rarely evinced.

Other problems arise because, by admitting only one aspect of reality (the quantifiable), econometric models of the growth of government in effect throw away information. Because no number can measure a politician's personality and its political import, the econometrician has no way to appreciate the difference in the potential for the growth of government between, say, a government headed by Franklin Roosevelt and a government (that might have been) headed by Herbert Hoover in 1933. Except as the measured variables allow, the econometrician cannot appreciate any difference between, say, 1929 and 1933. A year is a year is a year; a variable is a variable is a variable; and real people with all their quirks and fickleness do not exist at all. This quantitative homogenization squeezes all the life, blots all the color, freezes all the feeling out of human history in general and out of political strife in particular.

By characterizing only abstract aggregative variables linked by rigid functional relations, an econometric model of the growth of government implicitly affirms that people had no real choice. They could not have done otherwise but to act in accordance with fixed formulas; the only deviations allowed are stochastic, as if those who deviate from the formulaic central tendency are lunatics acting randomly. This way of representing human history is not just a simplification; it is a basic distortion, a denial of the very thing the Austrian school economists call human action (Mises 1957, 1966, 1978; Rothbard 1979; Buchanan 1979, 39–63).


## PROPOSITION 10

*The process generating the growth of government is internal to each country; each one's relations with the rest of the world may safely be ignored.*

Virtually all existing economic models of the growth of government are models of a behaviorally closed economy—that is, an economy operating and developing independently vis-à-vis the rest of the world. Of course, external events may enter the explanatory framework indirectly. For example, the GNP may increase because net exports increase, and the rise in GNP may be assumed to increase the public's demand for government services. In this model, however, an identical effect would have resulted from an increase in GNP occasioned by a rise in domestic spending; there is nothing distinctive about external demand as such.

"Rigorous" analysts usually ignore genuinely external causes of the growth of government in part because their models exclude any role for changes in economic or political ideas, which are readily "imported" and "exported." So analysts of the twentieth-century growth of government in the United States suppose that the same politicoeconomic structure persisted throughout the past one hundred years even though, roughly speaking, (a) traditional, balanced-budget fiscal doctrines held sway during the first third of the period, but Keynesian (and derivative) macroeconomic theory and chronic-deficit politics prevailed during the following two-thirds; (b) traditional "isolationist" doctrines had great influence on foreign policy during the first third of the period but virtually no influence during the following two-thirds; and (c) peacetime military spending usually amounted to about 1 percent or less of GNP during the first third but more than 7 percent during the following two-thirds. (Higgs 1990b, xv–xviii, 2006, 126–31).

Increased military spending by itself accounts for a substantial part (roughly 45 percent) of the increase in federal spending relative to GDP between fiscal years 1940 and 2005 (U.S. Office of Management and Budget 2006, 25–26, 46, 54), if we make due allowance for budgetary items that are genuinely military-related but are not classified as such in the budget, such as veterans programs, homeland security, international arms assistance, current interest on past debt-financed military spending, and so forth (Higgs 2004b). Can anyone seriously contend that this increase had nothing to do with external military and political events and hence with the ideas Americans held about international communism and the threats they came to believe it posed for their well-being after World War II? Readily available facts refute such a supposition (Higgs 2006, 137–44).

Readily available facts also attest to the power of ideas imported from abroad in various other realms of thought. Information about social and economic developments in the European welfare states, for example, has heavily influenced the political thinking and practices of Americans ever since the late nineteenth century with regard to income taxation, central banking, nationalized retirement and health insurance, public housing, and countless other matters. Keynes's ideas alone had an immense influence on macroeconomic policy in the quarter century after World War II, an influence that is still alive today (Stein 1969, 1984; Buchanan and Wagner 1977), not to mention his influence and that of other British economists in establishing postwar institutions for reconstruction of the international financial system, including the International Monetary Fund and the World Bank. From the late nineteenth century to the present, western European thinking has exerted a magnetic attraction pulling American thinking toward collectivism. To ignore this powerful external influence on the course of events is to abstract from an essential aspect of the process whereby government has grown in the United States.

## PROPOSITION 11

*Putative "public demand," especially as expressed by voting, drives the political-governmental system. Elected officials and hence the bureaucracy subordinate to them may be viewed as perfect agents of the electorate.*

Adherence to this proposition characterizes the bulk of all analysis dealing with the growth of government in the West, regardless of analytical tradition or ideological leaning. (Specific citations seem unnecessary, but see virtually any issue of *Public Choice*, as well as the widely cited articles by Meltzer and Richard [1978, 1981, 1983], Peltzman [1980, 1984, 1985], Becker [1983, 1985], and Borcherding [1977, 1985]. The most recent and most extreme contribution along these lines is by Wittman [1989].) This approach displays a professional deformity related to the economist's basic tool of analysis—the theory of markets, with its component theories of demand and supply. Economists, applying their familiar tools to the analysis of politics, immediately look for analogues. What is the "good" being traded? Who is the "supplier," and who is the "demander"? What is the "price"? The answers seem obvious to economists. Public policy is the good; the elected legislators are the suppliers; the voters are the demanders; votes are the currency with which political business is being transacted. Thus, voters "buy" the desired policies by spending their votes; the legislators "sell" policies in exchange for the votes that elect them to office. (See Benson and Engen 1988 for a straightforward application of such analogues.) Economists view consumer demand in ordinary markets as ultimately decisive for the allocation of resources; hence, they speak of consumer "sovereignty," thus importing a political metaphor into economics. Applying their familiar apparatus of thought to politics, economists tend to think that the political system ultimately gives the voters what they want. In the words of the authors of a recent survey of economic theories of the growth of government, "Voters decide which goods the government will provide and which negative externalities the government will correct" (Garrett and Rhine 2006, 18, emphasis added). Therefore, if the government grows, it does so because that growth is what the people want (Musgrave 1985, 306; Stiglitz 1989, 69). Demand creates its own supply. Voting is ultimately all that matters for determining the growth of government. As Dennis Mueller has observed, "In the public choice literature the state often appears as simply a voting rule that transforms individual preferences into political outcomes" (1987, 142).

It is easy—and probably healthy—to mock this view of the political process. Joseph Schumpeter called it "the perfect example of a nursery tale" (1954, 429). There are, after all, many significant differences between ordinary markets and the "political market" (Higgs 1987a, 14–15; Boudreaux 1996, 115–19). Even Benson and Engen, adherents of this model, describe their output variable as "somewhat artificial and very restrictive" and their price variable as "clearly an incomplete proxy" (1988, 733, 741).

Not least of the problems is that voters rarely vote directly for or against policies. Rather, they vote for candidates who run for office. Winning candidates subsequently enact a multitude of policies, many of which neither the voters nor their representatives had considered at the time of the campaign. It is not enough that voters know something about office seekers' general ideological reputation (à la Dougan and Munger 1989); the devil is in the details. Besides, notwithstanding the elaborate theoretical and econometric attempts to show that politicians are perfect agents (Becker 1983, 1985; Peltzman 1984, 1985; Wittman 1989), we can easily demonstrate that political representatives frequently act in ways that must necessarily run counter to the dominant preference of their ostensible constituents. We see this in the U.S. Senate, for instance, every time the two senators who represent the same state split their votes—and such splitting occurs commonly (Higgs 1989c). Remarkably, and quite damningly for models that presume tight linkages between voters and their elected representatives, many of the vote-splitting senators are reelected time and again. So elections are reliable neither as an ex ante check nor as an ex post check on the substantial autonomy of officeholders.

Perhaps the most important case in which legislators and other officials (including many nonelected functionaries) act independently of control by the voters concerns political action during crises. How many voters could possibly have known in the election of 1940 what the elected federal officials would do during their upcoming terms in office, which were to include, depending on the office, some or all of the years of World War II? How many voters in the election of 1972 had any idea how they wished their representatives to deal with the "energy crisis" of 1973–74 or even that such a crisis would arise? Who anticipated that George H. W. Bush would send U.S. troops to the Persian Gulf to eject the Iraqis from Kuwait? How many anticipated the military invasion and endless, bloody occupation of Iraq when they cast their ballots for George W. Bush in 2000? During crises, government officials, lacking any reliable means of discovering dominant constituent preferences, necessarily exercise considerable discretion. Even if leaders cannot know what "the people" desire, however, they do act, often in dramatically important ways.

Once those actions have been taken, the course of events is changed irrevocably in a world of path-dependent historical processes (Brennan and Buchanan 1985, 16, 74; Higgs 1987a, 30–33, 57–74). (Rasler and Thompson [1985] confirm statistically, using Box-Tiao tests, the increasing growth of government spending associated with participation in global wars.) In the election of 1942, if U.S. voters actually had preferred that the nation not go to war, it was too late to rectify the legislators' mistake—the fat was already in the fire. If they preferred the removal of U.S. troops from Iraq in 2004, they were out of luck because neither candidate for the presidency espoused that alternative.

Further, political actions are usually accompanied by carefully crafted rationalizations, excuses, and propaganda emanating from the politicians and their friends who initiated or supported the actions. (How often do politicians admit policy mistakes?) From this vantage point, it is easy to see how political preferences, public opinion, even the dominant ideology may be altered, becoming more congruent with what has been done and thereby reversing the direction of causality usually assumed in political models. (On ideology and policy as interactive, see Higgs 1985, 1987a, 67–74, 1989b, 96–98, 2006, 202–5.)

## PROPOSITION 12

*A corollary of Proposition 11: the judicial branch of government may safely be ignored.*

If analytical political economists have greatly overstated the role of legislators (too often viewed as perfect agents of voters) in the growth of government, they have understated to an even greater degree the role of judges, at least in U.S. history, where legislation must withstand judicial review of its constitutionality to survive and have ongoing effect. The public-choice and related analytical literatures contain almost nothing empirically concrete about the judiciary's role in the growth of the U.S. government, although the literature of law and economics offers some useful insights (several chapters in the volume edited by Gwartney and Wagner [1988], as well as Hughes 1977, are pertinent), and the literature on constitutional political economy offers suggestive insights, albeit at a very abstract, quasi-philosophical level (e.g., Friedrich Hayek's *Law, Legislation, and Liberty* or various works by James Buchanan and his collaborators). The index of the admirably comprehensive survey of public choice by Dennis Mueller (1989) has no entry for judges or judiciary. Mueller mentions but does not dwell on an oft-cited paper by William Landes and Richard Posner, enticingly titled "The Independent Judiciary in an Interest-Group Perspective" (1975). Unfortunately, the thesis of this paper—legislators tolerate an independent judiciary only to augment the longevity and hence to enhance the value of the legislative products they sell—is difficult to take seriously, at least for anyone who has spent much time studying the constitutional history of the United States. (Cogent critics of the Landes-Posner paper include Buchanan [1975], Samuels [1975], and North [1981, 56–57].)

The U.S. Supreme Court—nine persons appointed for life, answerable to no electorate, legislature, or interest group—played a key role in the growth of the U.S. government over the past century. (The relevant legal and historical literature is enormous. For selected references, see the footnotes and bibliography of Higgs 1987a.) Evidently, no one wants to deny this fact, but many analysts seem content to ignore it. The reason, one suspects, is that it doesn't fit into the profession's standard set of puzzles or lend itself to solution by the usual methods of analysis. It requires that one pay attention to particular autonomous individuals with specific values and beliefs. As North has observed, the behavior of the independent judiciary presents us with "the clearest instance of the dominant role of ideology" (1981, 56–57). That fact makes most economists either run for cover or take up arms in visceral opposition.

## PROPOSITION 13

*Ideology does not matter.*

Indeed, the idea that people act on the basis of ideology strikes most mainstream economists, including many of those who have written about the growth of government (e.g., Becker and Stigler 1977; Peltzman 1984, 1985), as utterly anathematic. They flee from it as a vampire flees from holy water—perhaps for the same reason, too. Surprisingly, in view of his leading position in the Chicago school, Gary Becker once wrote that "undoubtedly, the decline in laissez faire ideology contributed to the growth of government." He immediately backed away, however, issuing the obiter dictum: "but most of the decline was probably induced by the arguments and propaganda of the many groups seeking public largess" (1985, 345).

More than twenty-five years ago, when a few neoclassical economists began to toy with the idea that ideologically motivated behavior might be the cause of certain apparent anomalies of public-choice theory (e.g., why people vote), the economic literature took an unfortunate turn. Economists, political scientists, and public-choice analysts began to produce an outpouring of problematic econometric studies of roll-call voting in the U.S. Congress. (Notable contributions, with many references to earlier literature, include Lott 1987, 1988; Nelson and Silberg 1987; McArthur and Marks 1988; Davis and Porter 1989; Dougan and Munger 1989; Lott and Reed 1989; Nollen and Iglarsh 1990; Richardson and Munger 1990; Zupan 1990; Grier 1993; and Levitt 1996.) Roll-call voting was a poor choice of observations for testing whether ideology matters—it was seized upon because it produces numbers that can be cranked through the econometric mill—though even in these studies it seems fairly clear that ideology does matter, insofar as the indexes used to measure it mean what they are supposed to mean.

Elsewhere, I have tried to clarify the concept of ideology, to show how ideology can be understood as consistent with, rather than as the antithesis of, rational action, and to document how ideology affected and in turn was affected by the growth of governments at all levels during the past 125 years (Higgs 1983, 1985, 1987a, 1989b). I am not going to repeat everything I have written on this subject, but one point requires restatement and emphasis.

The existing thrust of the economic literature—the quest to determine econometrically whether ideology mattered in determining a certain set of political actions—seeks to answer a nonquestion. Of course it mattered. It always matters because people cannot even think about political questions, much less undertake political actions, without an ideology (Siegenthaler 1989; Higgs

1989b, 98–100, 1989d).

How can I make such a claim? Economists are supposed to believe, or at least to postulate for analytical purposes, that people pursue their "economic interests." Open any mainstream text on economic theory and check the arguments of the utility function: sure enough, they consist of amounts of "goods" consumed by the individual; there's nothing about ideas here—just pounds of potatoes, bottles of beer, trips to the shore, hours of leisure, and so forth. In the words of Gary Becker, "the utility of each person . . . depends only on own commodities" (1983, 374, emphasis added). To consume more of these things, the mainstream economist supposes, is precisely what is meant when one speaks of people's acting in their self–interest. In this context, to speak of a person's economic or material interest would be redundant because the theory recognizes no other kind. Thus, Thomas Borcherding declares it "an open question whether after the obvious elements of self-interest are separated from political action, scope for ideology remains" (1985, 378, emphasis added).

The most charitable thing I can say about this view is that it is simply wrong. No one ever explained why it is wrong more clearly and succinctly than Mises: "In the world of reality, life, and human action there is no such thing as interests independent of ideas, preceding them temporally and logically. What a man considers his interest is the result of his ideas. . . . Free men do not act in accordance with their interests. They act in accordance with what they believe furthers their interests" (1957, 140, 142, emphasis added). Nor are the Austrian school economists alone in appreciating the dependence of interest on belief. Jon Elster, for example, has written: "What explains the action is the person's desires together with his beliefs about the opportunities. Because beliefs can be mistaken, the distinction is not trivial" (1989, 20).

Ideologies are belief systems about social relations. Chief among their dimensions is the cognitive: ideologies structure and give meaning to a person's perceptions of social life. They also place moral weight on those perceptions, designating some things good or right and other things bad or wrong. They also point toward a justifiable political program and open up the potential for solidarity with like-minded comrades. Such solidarity serves as an important means of establishing and maintaining a social identity; it helps to determine people's psychologically essential conceptions of what kind of persons they are.

In myriad ways, the growth of government has involved collective action, a transcendence of the free-rider problem that neoclassical theorists regard as paralyzing. This transcendence reflects ideologically motivated action. It poses no great puzzle for those who understand that real people act on the basis of two equally propulsive—but inextricably intertwined—motives: to get something and to be someone (Higgs 1987b). (See also the discussions of "artifactual man" by Buchanan [1979, 93–112]; of "preferences for preferences" and "the role of norms" by Brennan and Buchanan [1985, 68–73, 146–47]; and of self–interest and the free-rider problem by Hummel and Lavoie [1990].)

## PROPOSITION 14

*Government grows in order to correct the distortions stemming from externalities.*

This proposition, along with Proposition 5 and 15, lies at the heart of the theory of the growth of government that mainstream economists usually embrace, teach, and write about (e.g., Baumol 1965; Stiglitz 1989, 57). The theory asserts that governments have grown in a process of correcting emerging "market failures" associated with private monopoly power, externalities, and public goods. As a positive theory of the growth of government the idea suffers, as already indicated, from reliance on magic: a market failure emerges, and POOF! government undertakes a program to remedy the associated deviation from the "efficient" allocation of resources. In the words of Richard Musgrave, "the assumption was that government, once advised of proper action, will proceed to carry it out" (1985, 287). No account is given, however, of, first, why either the public or specific government officials know or care about systemic efficiency, and of, second, what personal incentives they have to take the implied corrective action, even if they do know about systemic efficiency. In short, a black box stands between the alleged cause and its presumed effect. What actually fills the black box are the Two Big Collectivist Assumptions (some might call them myths): government officials know what needs to be done to promote the public interest, and they act on the basis of that knowledge.

Apart from the implausibility of the theory because it has nothing to say about the personal incentives and constraints of actual decision makers, the theory does not stack up empirically. A reasonable survey of how the government has grown—that is, an accounting of what it has come to do more often and what it has undertaken episodically to do for the first time—must conclude that only a small proportion of all government activities has anything to do with externalities. One need only examine an organization chart for the government, leaf through the *Federal Register*, or scrutinize *U.S. Statutes at Large*, not to mention the detailed budget documents, to discover that evidence of the alleged connections rarely appears. Studies that have sought to find a relation between the growth of government and proxies for growing externality problems (e.g., population density, urbanization, ratio of manufacturing to agricultural activities) have found little or nothing (Borcherding 1977, 53; 1985, 368; Mueller 1987, 119).

The theory that represents government as the corrector of externalities is often completely backwards. Governments themselves compose "the prototypical sector in which decision makers do not take accurate account of all the costs as well as all the benefits of each activity" (Yeager 1983, 125). In reality, the government is more likely to cause a negative externality than to reduce one. In the wake of the revelations that came forth from eastern Europe and the Soviet Union after the fall of communism, everyone has become aware of the vast environmental destruction wreaked by government officials there, but one need not rely on these egregious cases to establish the point. According to studies of the United States cited by James Bennett and Manuel Johnson, "Federal government agencies emit huge quantities of pollutants into the water and atmosphere. The U.S. Department of Defense alone discharges over 335 million gallons of human waste per day, of which 30 percent received secondary treatment or less. The Tennessee Valley Authority (TVA) is the country's largest sulfur dioxide polluter, accounting for 38 percent of total sulfur emissions in the Southeast U.S., and its compliance record with pollution laws is only 16 percent as compared to 74 percent for all utilities nationally" (1980, 133–34).

Press reports tell us, and government spokesmen such as Energy secretary James Watkins admit (*Wall Street Journal*, November 27, 1989), that government plants for manufacturing nuclear materials have been poisoning the surrounding air, land, and water for decades while hiding behind their top-secret national-security classification. In the late 1980s, the Energy Department forecast that the future expense of cleaning up these messes would accumulate to more than $80 billion (*Wall Street Journal*, December 12, 1988). Nor are nuclear-weapons plants the only problem of this sort. By 1990, eighty-seven military installations were slated for the Superfund list of the nation's most dangerous toxic-waste sites, and more than one hundred other military facilities were candidates for addition to the list. A *Newsday* study concluded that "the armed forces have been slow to move, have resisted state regulators' efforts to force compliance with environmental laws, and continue to violate anti-pollution laws even as officials in Washington, D.C., insist their bases are trying to be better neighbors" (*Seattle Times*, February 5, 1990).

Still, one should not leap to the conclusion that the growth of government had nothing to do with programs in response to emerging externality problems, although one ought to refrain from immediately labeling those perceived problems as "market failures." Historically, for example, urbanization created severe externality problems in relation to the spread of contagious diseases, and the (mainly local) governments' public-health programs responded to these problems in a fashion that in retrospect seems remarkably successful (Higgs 1971, 67–72, 1979; Meeker 1974). Other examples also might be found, perhaps in other areas where public health and safety are at stake. The point, however, is that such examples cannot bear much weight as significant explanations of the growth of government. They do not add up empirically to a big part of the relevant record.

## PROPOSITION 15

*Government grows in order to supply public goods that the public demands but the free market will not supply.*

As already indicated, this proposition belongs to the class of "market-fail-ure" explanations of the growth of government. Like all such explanations, it suffers from the infirmities of the behavioral black box. Empirically, however, it seems to possess greater warrant than its cousin, the externality proposition. Although many examples of public goods are problematic—they do not actu-ally involve goods that are totally nonrival in consumption or nonpayers who cannot be excluded—at least one potentially important case remains, namely, national defense. Especially when one conceives of defense as the deterrence of nuclear or other widely devastating attacks against national territory, it seems to be a genuine public good for which the free market might make insufficient provision. Nor is the necessity of government provision affirmed only by main-stream economists. Mises himself concluded that "in a world full of unswerv-ing aggressors and enslavers ... isolated attempts on the part of each individual to resist are doomed to failure [and therefore] the only workable way is to orga-nize resistance by the government." Indeed, Mises went even further, support-ing conscription of people to serve in the armed forces (1966, 282).

As indicated earlier, increases in military spending over the past sixty-five years account for a substantial share, perhaps as much as 45 percent if a com-plete accounting were made, of the rise of federal government spending relative to GDP. The arms industries also have become the most heavily regulated sector of the U.S. economy (Kovacic 1990). It would seem, then, that Proposition 15 has a great deal to recommend it, both theoretically and empirically, to students of the growth of government. Of course, the empirical weight that this expla-nation will bear needs to be kept in perspective: all military-related spending (including items previously mentioned that are not classified as military in the official budget) now amounts to only about 40 percent of federal spending, less than one-fourth of all government spending, and only about 8 percent of GDP, and the defense spending shares are substantially below their levels during the 1950s and 1960s (U.S. Office of Management and Budget 2006, 206–7, 216–17; official amounts are doubled, as suggested by the findings in Higgs 2004b).

Before embracing Proposition 15 fully, however, one needs to consider a rather difficult question: how much of the observed increase in the government's military activity represents a response to the public-good dilemma (the free-rider problem) and how much represents self-serving exploitation of the public's insecurities by people who make little or no contribution to the maintenance of genuine national security (the free-loader problem)?

No simple answer can be given, but some things are fairly obvious. Much military activity has served the interests not of the general public, but of the government itself (Hummel and Lavoie 1990; Higgs 2006). The invasions of Grenada, Panama, and Iraq are good examples. Moreover, far from seeking a "revelation" of the public's true demand for defensive actions and the derived demand for arms production, the national-security establishment has engaged in a series of mendacious efforts to scare the public and stampede the taxpayers into supporting higher levels of military spending. Just recall all of the weapons "gaps" announced from time to time during the Cold War, most of which were eventually revealed to be overblown or completely bogus (Higgs 2006, 138–39). Much military spending has done nothing to promote national security—for example, lavish officers' clubs and golf courses, cushy military retirement systems, and maintenance of obsolete facilities such as Fort Monroe, the fort with a moat. Members of Congress have twisted the defense program again and again to aid their quest for reelection (Higgs 1988, 1989a, 1990b; many of the chapters in the volume *Arms, Politics, and the Economy*, edited by Higgs [1990a]; and Higgs 2006, 152–85). Anyone who reads the newspapers, not to mention the literature on military procurement, knows that the big defense contractors, in league with their friends at the Pentagon and in Congress, have siphoned hundreds of billions of dollars in rents out of the public treasury during the past sixty-five years, especially during the Cold War buildups (Stubbing 1985; Fitzgerald 1989) and during the buildup under George W. Bush since 2001 (Higgs 2004a, 260–63, 2005; U.S. Department of Defense 2006, 206–7, 216–17).

In sum, it is obvious that the growth of government via increased military activities represents far more than a straightforward effort to achieve a solution to the public-good problem. To a large extent, it represents a poorly disguised form of redistributive politics—if we are perfectly frank, an enormous racket.

## PROPOSITION 16

*Government grows in order to reduce the transaction costs inherent in a complex modern economy, thereby facilitating a high degree of division of labor and enhancing productivity.*

I call this proposition, which is a more sophisticated variant of the Modernization Hypothesis, the theory of the Washington school. Its prime proponent is Douglass C. North, long of the University of Washington (Seattle) and more recently of Washington University (St. Louis). North draws from theoretical work on measurement and transaction costs by Steven N. S. Cheung (formerly of the University of Washington) and Yoram Barzel (still there). Collaborating with North on empirical work connected with the theory was John Wallis, who earned his Ph.D. at the University of Washington. The thesis began to take shape more than twenty-five years ago and appeared in North's *Structure and Change in Economic History* (1981, especially 187–98 on the United States). Later articles (North and Wallis 1982; North 1985; Wallis and North 1986) and North's 1990 book *Institutions, Institutional Change and Economic Performance* clarified and extended the argument and presented empirical materials in support of it.

An early summary conveys the essence of the argument: "The wedding of science and technology in the late nineteenth century made possible a technology of production whose potential was only realizable with an enormous increase in the resources devoted to political and economic organization—the transactions sector of the economy. A substantial part of this increase has occurred in the market and through voluntary organization, and a substantial share has also been undertaken by government" (North and Wallis 1982, 336). The government's part evidently has outpaced the market's part; hence the growth of government.

North's argument traces virtually everything back to a single aspect of societal modernization: the increase in specialization. That increase caused the rise in productivity, hence economic growth; it necessitated more "contracts across time and space and with unknown second parties," hence a demand for bigger government to supply "effective third party enforcement" (North 1989, 113); it fostered ideological divisions, hence the proliferation of politicized interest groups (North 1981, 51, 196–98; 1985); it cheapened tax collection and hence shifted outward the supply curve of government activities. (Becker [1985, 345] tells a similar tale.)

Although Wallis and North's empirical exercises in creative national-income accounting are not compelling, in part because the empirical categories simply do not match the theoretical counterparts (for some details, see Davis

1986), the Washington thesis may have some merit. North continually emphasizes that government has grown throughout the Western world and elsewhere over the past century; and, by conventional measures, government is bigger in the more developed countries than it is in the less developed. A good theory, it seems, ought to account for the apparently pervasive association of economic progress and growth of government in the West. Because rising specialization marks every case, it would appear to resolve the issue. Perhaps to some extent it does, but questions remain.

One difficulty is that the theory is too general. Although it seems to match the long-term trend in every Western country—and many others as well—it cannot account for the marked irregularities that have appeared in most cases. The specific shape of the historical profile must be explained by auxiliary theories or in some ad hoc manner. The abrupt growth of government that occurred in the United States during the world wars and the Great Depression, for instance, would seem to have little to do, in any immediate way, with changes in the degree of societal specialization (Higgs 1987a, 123–236). Similar questions may be raised about the precise paths other countries have followed.

Another problem: the theory is rather vague, and the attempts that have been made to give it empirical substance only heighten one's misgivings in this regard. The concepts of "transaction cost" and "transaction sector" have been stretched to the breaking point. The distinction between "transaction" and "production transformation," though central to the thesis, is blurry at best and may be completely arbitrary. Nin Wang remarks in a recent survey that "[d]espite the voluminous literature in the new institutional economics, a theoretical consensus on what transaction costs are is still out of sight" (2003, 4). Of course, what cannot be defined theoretically cannot be measured empirically.

Further, the explanation of why remote transactions and other features of modern economic life cannot be accommodated in the market—an explanation that appeals to "moral hazard, adverse selection, and the demand for public goods" (North 1985, 392)—is offered almost in passing and needs a much more extensive argument before it can become persuasive. (See Lindbeck [1985, 315–16] for criticism about the alleged roles of adverse selection and moral hazard.) Myhrman argues that although North's thesis may explain why governments grew bigger during the early stages of economic development, it does not account for why the growth of government has continued to exceed the growth of the private sector (1985, 277). (Davis makes a similar point [1986, 158].)

Finally, stepping back from the theory and viewing it as a whole, one may get an eerie feeling of unreality. Many of us are convinced that modern governments hugely *increase* the costs of transacting mutually beneficial exchanges in comparison with what those costs would be in a minimal or night-watchman state. In view of all of the taxes, all of the direct, highly politicized government participation in markets, all of the regulations, all of the laws infringing economic liberties on every side, how can anyone suppose that on balance the growth of government has reduced transaction costs and promoted economic growth? Perhaps cause and effect have been reversed in the Washington Thesis; perhaps only economically progressive societies can afford the deadweight costs of ever bigger governments.

## PROPOSITION 17

*Government is nothing but an engine of redistribution.*

Many of the most cited contributions to the literature make this assumption their point of departure (Meltzer and Richard 1978, 1981, 1983; Peltzman 1980, 1985; Becker 1983, 1985; Benson and Engen 1988; and others cited by Mueller 1987, 122–28). Analysts evidently adopt the assumption because it facilitates the construction of tractable formal models. To simplify the analysis further, investigators usually assume that the redistribution runs from richer to poorer. There is something to be said for simple models, but in this case it is not much.

These models lack even the elementary saving grace of positivism: they do not generate predictions that fit the facts. (For criticism, see Higgs 1987a, 12–15, and Mueller 1987, 126–28.) Peltzman, in his influential 1980 article, claims to present empirical confirmation, but the claims are too ill founded to be acceptable. Indeed, the econometric methods employed in that article—presumptuous proxy variables, ad hoc substitutions for "missing" data, unwarranted specification switches, inter alia—fill a chamber of horrors sufficient to discredit the entire undertaking. The methods employed in Peltzman's 1985 article warrant a similar evaluation.

More fundamentally, the assumption that government only redistributes wealth simply is not true; it is not even close to the truth. Although hard-core anarchists do not easily swallow this fact, governments in the West probably do provide some widely desired services. Deterrence of foreign aggression, some local protection of life and property, a body of property law and a system of courts for resolving civil disputes, a public-health system, public water supplies and sewage disposal, the roads and the traffic rules—all seem to qualify as more or less public goods and as goods genuinely demanded by the overwhelming majority of the public. Of course, even these goods are supplied in ways that one might lodge many complaints against, and conceivably they might be supplied privately (and in some cases they already are, to some extent). Yet the point remains: they are not merely means of redistribution, even though their financing, production, and distribution have many undeniable redistributive aspects.

National defense, perhaps the most important example, surely receives much political impetus from those who privately appropriate benefits from its provision (Higgs 1990b; Lee 1990 and other chapters in the Higgs 1990a volume; Higgs 2004a, 235–68). Still, not many citizens favor unilateral disarmament. Most people want the government to maintain a military establishment adequate to deter foreign aggression. (The evidence of public-opinion polls and elections indicates that a substantial number also support military aggression against others, although one might apologize for at least some of those who maintain this position on the grounds that they have been duped to believe that the aggression is actually defensive [e.g., support for the U.S. invasion of Iraq in 2003].) In any event, they do not support simply handing money to the owners and employees of General Dynamics (GD) in the same way that they support Temporary Assistance for Needy Families. Most of them want the military potency produced by the nuclear submarines, and only a few of them care whether GD or another company supplies the vessels. For the general public, GD's rents are incidental, though of course they are far from incidental in the actual political process by which that company becomes the supplier (Goodwin 1985).

## PROPOSITION 18

*The modern welfare state merely "filled the vacuum" left by the deterioration of private institutions.*

This proposition is still another variant of the Modernization Hypothesis. Modern economic development, it is said, caused socioeconomic transformations (e.g., urbanization, greater personal mobility, increased survival of the aged) that sapped the vitality of private institutions. Families, churches, and voluntary associations became less and less able to accomplish their traditional tasks. Hence, government increasingly substituted for them "as the principal institution assisting individuals in time of economic or social misfortune" (Fuchs 1979, 13). Government had to hold the "safety net" when others no longer could or would.

Certainly government activities in immense profusion—countless programs ranging from sex education to mental-health care to the federal Foster Grandparents Program—may be viewed as illustrating this thesis. Perhaps the proposition contains more than a grain of truth. As an explanation of the growth of government, however, the proposition by itself does not carry us far, and even that little bit is partly illusory.

A serious defect of the proposition is that once the alleged process of "vacuum filling" had got under way, if not before, the direction of causality must have run in both directions. Perhaps certain socioeconomic changes did promote the breakdown of individual responsibility among family members, but the availability of governmentally provided substitute services lowered the cost of irresponsible private actions and hence increased their frequency. Government did not simply substitute for responsible private efforts; it also crowded them out. Without narrowing the focus to a specific activity, not much more can be said. The crowding-out theory, however, is logically unimpeachable, and those with normal eyesight and a little knowledge of history can see evidence of such crowding out on all sides (Higgs 2004a, 21–29). (See Wagner 1989 for an extended discussion and references.)

Of course, Proposition 18, as an explanation of the growth of government, presents us with yet another case of the black box. When we fill the box in a theoretically and empirically warranted manner, the nature of the explanation changes completely. Question: How do the kinds of people who need a government safety net—presumably those who are destitute, physically or mentally disabled, aged and infirm, or otherwise in dire straits—exert enough political pressure to elicit the creation of a safety net by those who control the political process? Short answer: They don't. Notice, however, the millions of middle-class administrators, school teachers, social workers, lawyers, urban planners, doctors, nurses, professional and technical specialists, and all the others who act as well-paid providers and facilitators of governmentally funded services for the helpless, and then the politics of the welfare state becomes a lot plainer. Also transparent is that the rise of the welfare state involved far more than unvarnished altruism (P. Weaver 1978; Higgs 1987a, 248–51, 2004a, 9–19).

Not surprisingly, it involved a great deal of redistributive politics: redistribution not so much from the fortunate to the unfortunate as from the taxpayers to the bureaucrats, providers, and hangers-on. As Lindbeck puts it, "the original 'welfare state,' designed mainly to provide basic economic security, has gradually developed into a free-for-all competition for favors from the state, with 'every politician trying to buy votes from everybody'" (1985, 327).

## CONCLUSION

In the literature on the growth of government, much that is misguided may be seen as unwarranted reduction. This in turn may be seen as arising almost inevitably from the positivist pretensions that underlie modern social science in general and modern mainstream economics in particular.

The drive toward reduction takes several forms. First, analysts strive to reduce empirical reality to one measure of the explicandum, or dependent variable. Second, they strive to reduce the theory to one independent variable that can carry the entire explanatory load. Third, they strive to reduce historical and geographical diversity so that one general explanation applies to all times and places. In the words of the authors of a recent survey of economic theories of the growth of government, "the challenge facing economists is to develop a single unifying theory of government growth" (Garrett and Rhine 2006, 13, emphasis added). In sum, the goal appears to be an equation of the form $G = f(X)$, where $G$ is one simple measure of the size of government, $X$ is one simple explanatory variable, and $f$ is a fixed-coefficient functional relation connecting the values of $X$ and $G$ by what amounts to a law of history.

This reductionist quest is nothing more than a species of scientism, the attempt to conduct the study of human action with the same methods employed to study nonhuman nature. Research in political economy is being carried out as if it were research in physics or chemistry. But people are not atoms; the political economy is not a molecule; and the growth of government is not analogous to the natural growth processes analyzed in biochemistry. The prevailing reductionism, which is both positivist and historicist, founders on the reality that people are purposive actors whose actions are shaped by their (changeable) beliefs and values and whose personal and societal histories are marked by contingencies with significant consequences, including path dependencies (Mises 1957, 1966, 1978; Rothbard 1979; Higgs 1987a).

Strange to say, one can describe a large part of the recent research on the growth of government as attempts by researchers who neither know nor care much about history to discover laws of history. It is scarcely surprising that black boxes litter the field. Here, however, as in other areas of serious empirical research, there is no good substitute for knowing, quite literally, what we are talking about. One must therefore study history; one must comprehend the great variety of acting and interacting individuals whose actions compose our subject and the diverse and changing beliefs and institutions that condition the actors' choices.

To this recommendation, a positivist might respond: If there are no laws of history to be discovered, what is the point of studying history? The answer is that much valuable knowledge exists in the gap between invariable law and utter chaos. Although no laws of history exist—indeed, as Mises explained, "the notion of a law of historical change is self-contradictory" (1957, 212)—the study of history can reveal patterns and probable relations and rule out certain correspondences (Hayek 1967, 3–21). Mises called the search for this kind of empirical understanding of human action "thymology" and contrasted it with the study of the pure logic of action, or "praxeology" (1957, 264–84). He maintained that "[w]hat thymology achieves is the elaboration of a catalogue of human traits. It can moreover establish the fact that certain traits appeared in the past as a rule in connection with certain other traits. But it can never predict in the way the natural sciences can. It can never know in advance with what weight the various factors will be operative in a definite future event" (274).

Therefore, even though one cannot rely on historical understanding to be apodictic, as one can rely on the pure logic of choice, which the Austrian school economists call economic theory, one must, both in everyday life and in empirical research, constantly place bets. Although one cannot be certain that the relations on which one places the bets will prevail (or did in the past), one confidently expects to come closer to the truth by taking thymological understanding into account than by closing one's eyes and throwing darts at the dartboard of all possibilities.

It is no accident that many of the leading lights of the Austrian school of economics—Mises, Hayek, Rothbard—have taken historical understanding seriously and devoted much effort to historical research. Mises went so far as to describe historical understanding as not only essential for practical action, but worthwhile in another sense as well. "It opens the mind toward an understanding of human nature and destiny. It increases wisdom. It is the very essence of that much misinterpreted concept, a liberal education" (1957, 293).

In view of the wide extent to which the problematic propositions criticized here have been accepted by contributors to the recent literature on the growth of government, a Misesian might well reach the following conclusion. Many of the analysts thought they were formulating and testing economic theory, but in the Austrian school sense they were not. Few of them thought they were writing economic history, but in the Austrian school sense they actually were. Unfortunately, much of this inadvertently written economic history has been deeply flawed.

## REFERENCES

Auster, Richard D., and Morris Silver. 1979. *The State as a Firm: Economic Forces in Political Development*. Boston: Martinus Nijhoff.

Baumol, William J. 1965. *Welfare Economics and the Theory of the State*, 2d ed. Cambridge, Mass.: Harvard University Press.

Becker, Gary S. 1983. A Theory of Competition among Pressure Groups for Political Influence. *Quarterly Journal of Economics* 98 (August): 371–400.

———. 1985. Public Policies, Pressure Groups, and Dead Weight Costs. *Journal of Public Economics* 28: 329–47.

Becker, Gary S., and George J. Stigler. 1977. De Gustibus Non Est Disputandum. *American Economic Review* 67 (March): 76–90.

Bennett, James T., and Manuel H. Johnston. 1980. *The Political Economy of Federal Government Growth: 1959–1978*. College Station, Texas: Center for Education and Research in Free Enterprise.

Benson, Bruce L., and Eric M. Engen. 1988. The Market for Laws: An Economic Analysis of Legislation. *Southern Economic Journal* 54 (January): 732–45.

Bernholz, Peter. 1986. Growth of Government, Economic Growth, and Individual Freedom. *Journal of Institutional and Theoretical Economics* 142: 661–83.

Blumenthal, Barbara. 1979. Uncle Sam's Army of Invisible Employees. *National Journal* (May 5): 730–33.

Borcherding, Thomas E. 1977. The Sources of Growth of Public Expenditures in the United States, 1902–1970. In *Budgets and Bureaucrats: The Sources of Government Growth*, edited by Thomas E. Borcherding, 45–70. Durham, N.C.: Duke University Press.

———. 1985. The Causes of Government Expenditure Growth: A Survey of the U.S. Evidence. *Journal of Public Economics* 28: 359–82.

Boskin, Michael J. 1987. Follow the Money. *Regulation* 11: 60–62.

Boudreaux, Donald J. 1996. Was Your High-School Civics Teacher Right After All? Donald Wittman's *The Myth of Democratic Failure*. *The Independent Review* 1 (spring): 111-28.

Brennan, Geoffrey, and James M. Buchanan. 1985. *The Reason of Rules: Constitutional Political Economy*. Cambridge, U.K.: Cambridge University Press.

Buchanan, James M. 1975. Comment on the Independent Judiciary in an Interest Group Perspective. *Journal of Law and Economics* 18 (December): 903–5.

———. 1979. *What Should Economists Do?* Indianapolis, Ind.: Liberty Fund.

Buchanan, James M., and Richard E. Wagner. 1977. *Democracy in Deficit: The Political Legacy of Lord Keynes*. New York: Academic Press.

Davis, Lance E. 1986. Comment. In *Long–Term Factors in American Economic Growth*, edited by Stanley L. Engerman and Robert E. Gallman, 149–61. Chicago: University of Chicago Press.

Davis, Michael L., and Philip K. Porter. 1989. A Test for Pure or Apparent Ideology in Congressional Voting. *Public Choice* 60 (February): 101–11.

Dougan, William R., and Michael C. Munger. 1989. The Rationality of Ideology. *Journal of Law and Economics* 32 (April): 119–42.

Dye, Thomas R. 1990. *Who's Running America? The Bush Years*. Englewood Cliffs, N.J.: Prentice Hall.

Elster, Jon. 1989. *Nuts and Bolts for the Social Sciences*. New York: Cambridge University Press.

Fitzgerald, A. Ernest. 1989. *The Pentagonists*. Boston: Houghton Mifflin.

Fuchs, Victor R. 1979. The Economics of Health in a Post-industrial Society. *Public Interest* (summer): 3–20.

Garrett, Thomas A., and Russell M. Rhine. 2006. On the Size and Growth of Government. *Federal Reserve Bank of St. Louis Review* 88 (January–February): 13–30.

Goodwin, Jacob. 1985. *Brotherhood of Arms: General Dynamics and the Business of Defending America*. New York: Times Books.

Grier, Kevin B., ed. 1993. Empirical Studies of Ideology and Representation in American Politics. Special issue of *Public Choice* 76, nos. 1–2.

Gwartney, James D., and Richard E. Wagner, eds. 1988. *Public Choice and Constitutional Economics*. Greenwich, Conn.: JAI

Hanrahan, John D. 1983. *Government by Contract*. New York: Norton.

Hayek, F. A. 1967. Degrees of Explanation. In *Studies in Philosophy, Politics, and Economics*, 3–21. Chicago: University of Chicago Press.

Higgs, Robert. 1971. *The Transformation of the American Economy, 1865–1914: An Essay in Interpretation*. New York: Wiley.

———.1979. Cycles and Trends of Mortality in 18 Large American Cities, 1871–1900. *Explorations in Economic History* 16 (October): 381–408.

———. 1983. When Ideological Worlds Collide: Reflections on Kraditor's *Radical Persuasion*. *Continuity: A Journal of History* (fall): 99–112.

———. 1985. Crisis, Bigger Government, and Ideological Change: Two Hypotheses on the Ratchet Phenomenon. *Explorations in Economic History* 22 (January): 1–28.

———. 1987a. *Crisis and Leviathan: Critical Episodes in the Growth of American Government*. New York: Oxford University Press.

———. 1987b. Identity and Cooperation: A Comment on Sen's Alternative Program. *Journal of Law, Economics, and Organization* 3 (spring): 140–42.

———. 1988. Hard Coals Make Bad Law: Congressional Parochialism versus National Defense. *Cato Journal* 8 (spring–summer): 79–106.

———. 1989a. Beware the Pork-Hawk: In Pursuit of Reelection, Congress Sells Out the Nation's Defense. *Reason* 21 (June): 28–34.

———. 1989b. *Crisis and Leviathan*: Higgs Response to Reviewers. *Continuity: A Journal of History* (spring–fall): 92–105.

———. 1989c. Do Legislators' Votes Reflect Constituency Preference? A Simple Way to Evaluate the Senate. *Public Choice* 63 (November): 175–81.

———. 1989d. Organization, Ideology, and the Free Rider Problem: Comment. *Journal of Institutional and Theoretical Economics* 145 (March): 232–37.

———. ed. 1990a. *Arms, Politics, and the Economy: Historical and Contemporary Perspectives*. New York: Holmes and Meier for The Independent Institute.

———. 1990b. Introduction: Fifty Years of Arms, Politics, and the Economy. In *Arms, Politics, and the Economy: Historical and Contemporary Perspectives*, edited by Robert Higgs, xv–xxxii. New York: Holmes and Meier for the Independent Institute.

———. 2004a. *Against Leviathan: Government Power and a Free Society*. Oakland, Calif.: The Independent Institute.

———. 2004b. The Defense Budget Is Bigger Than You Think. *San Francisco Chronicle*, January 18. Available at: http://www.independent.org/newsroom/article.asp?id=1253.

———. 2005. *Resurgence of the Warfare State: The Crisis since 9/11*. Oakland, Calif.: The Independent Institute.

———. 2006. *Depression, War, and Cold War: Studies in Political Economy*. New York: Oxford University Press for The Independent Institute.

Hoover, Calvin B. 1959. *The Economy, Liberty, and the State*. New York: Twentieth Century Fund.

Hughes, Jonathan R. T. 1977. *The Governmental Habit: Economic Controls from Colonial Times to the Present*. New York: Basic Books.

Hummel, Jeffrey Rogers, and Don Lavoie. 1990. National Defense and the Public-Goods Problem. In *Arms, Politics, and the Economy: Historical and Contemporary Perspectives*, edited by Robert Higgs, 37–60. New York: Holmes and Meier for The Independent Institute.

Kovacic, William E. 1990. The Sorcerer's Apprentice: Public Regulation of the Weapons Acquisition Process. In *Arms, Politics, and the Economy: Historical and Contemporary Perspectives*, edited by Robert Higgs, 104–31. New York: Holmes and Meier for the Independent Institute.

Kozinski, Alex. n.d. The Collision Between Government Activity and Individual Rights. *Econ Update* 1: 5–9.

Landes, William M., and Richard A. Posner. 1975. The Independent Judiciary in an Interest–Group Perspective. *Journal of Law and Economics* 18 (December): 875–901.

Lee, Dwight R. 1990. Public Goods, Politics, and Two Cheers for the Military-Industrial Complex. In *Arms, Politics, and the Economy: Historical and Contemporary Perspectives*, edited by Robert Higgs, 22–36. New York: Holmes and Meier for The Independent Institute.

Leuchtenburg, William E. 1963. *Franklin D. Roosevelt and the New Deal 1932–1940*. New York: Harper Colophon Books.

Levitt, Steven D. 1996. How Do Senators Vote? Disentangling the Role of Voter Preferences, Party Affiliation, and Senator Ideology. *American Economic Review* 86 (June): 425–41.

Light, Paul C. 1999. *The True Size of Government*. Washington, D.C.: Brookings Institution Press.

———. 2003. Fact Sheet on the New True Size of Government. September 5. Available at: http://www.brook.edu/gs/cps/light20030905.pdf.

Lindbeck, Assar. 1985. Redistribution Policy and the Expansion of the Public Sector. *Journal of Public Economics* 28: 309–28.

Lott, John R. 1987. Political Cheating. *Public Choice* 52: 169–86.

———. 1988. Ideological Shirking or Ideological Priors? Comments on Kalt-Zupan and Dougan-Munger. Unpublished typescript.

Lott, John R., and W. Robert Reed. 1989. Shirking and Sorting in a Political Market with Finite-Lived Politicians. *Public Choice* 61: 75–96.

Lowery, David, and William D. Berry. 1983. The Growth of Government in the United States: An Empirical Assessment of Competing Explanations. *American Journal of Political Science* 27 (November): 665–94.

McArthur, John, and Stephen V. Marks. 1988. Constituent Interest vs. Legislator Ideology: The Role of Political Opportunity Cost. *Economic Inquiry* 26 (July): 461–70.

Meeker, Edward. 1974. The Social Rate of Return on Investment in Public Health, 1880–1910. *Journal of Economic History* 34 (June): 392–431.

Meltzer, Allan H., and Scott F. Richard. 1978. Why Government Grows (and Grows) in a Democracy. *Public Choice* (summer): 111–18.

———. 1981. A Rational Theory of the Size of Government. *Journal of Political Economy* 89 (October): 914–27.

———. 1983. Tests of a Rational Theory of the Size of Government. *Public Choice* 41: 403–18.

Mises, Ludwig von. 1957. *Theory and History: An Interpretation of Social and Economic Evolution*. New Haven, Conn.: Yale University Press.

———. 1966. *Human Action: A Treatise on Economics*, 3rd rev. ed. Chicago: Henry Regnery.

———. 1978. *The Ultimate Foundation of Economic Science*. Kansas City: Sheed Andrews and McMeel.

Mueller, Dennis C. 1987. The Growth of Government: A Public Choice Perspective. *IMF Staff Papers* 34 (March): 115–49.

———. 1989. *Public Choice II*. New York: Cambridge University Press.

Musgrave, Richard A. 1985. Excess Bias and the Nature of Budget Growth. *Journal of Public Economics* 28: 287–308.

Myhrman, Johan. 1985. Introduction: Reflections on the Growth of Government. *Journal of Public Economics* 28: 275–85.

Nelson, Douglas, and Eugene Silberberg. 1987. Ideology and Legislator Shirking. *Economic Inquiry* 25 (January): 15–25.

Nollen, Stanley D., and Harvey J. Iglarsh. 1990. Explanations of Protectionism in International Trade Votes. *Public Choice* 66 (August): 137–53.

North, Douglass C. 1981. *Structure and Change in Economic History*. New York: Norton.

———. 1985. The Growth of Government in the United States: An Economic Historian's Perspective. *Journal of Public Economics* 28: 383–99.

———. 1989. Comments 2. In *The Economic Role of the State*, edited by Arnold Heertje, 107–15. Oxford: Basil Blackwell.

———. 1990. *Institutions, Institutional Change, and Economic Performance*. Cambridge, U.K.: Cambridge University Press.

———. 2005. *Understanding the Process of Economic Change*. Princeton, N.J.: Princeton University Press.

North, Douglass C., and John Joseph Wallis. 1982. American Government Expenditures: A Historical Perspective. *American Economic Review* 72 (May): 336–40.

Peltzman, Sam. 1980. The Growth of Government. *Journal of Law and Economics* 23 (October): 209–87.

———. 1984. Constituent Interest and Congressional Voting. *Journal of Law and Economics* 27 (April): 181–210.

———. 1985. An Economic Interpretation of the History of Congressional Voting in the Twentieth Century. *American Economic Review* 75 (September): 656–75.

Peters, Guy, and Martin O. Heisler. 1983. Thinking about Public Sector Growth: Conceptual, Operational, Theoretical, and Policy Considerations. In *Why Governments Grow: Measuring Public Sector Size*, edited by Charles Lewis Taylor, 177–97. Beverly Hills, Calif.: Sage.

Rasler, Karen A., and William R. Thompson. 1985. War Making and State Making: Governmental Expenditures, Tax Revenues, and Global Wars. *American Political Science Review* 79 (June): 491–507.

Richardson, Lilliard E., Jr., and Michael C. Munger. 1990. Shirking, Representation, and Congressional Behavior: Voting on the 1983 Amendments to the Social Security Act. *Public Choice* 67: 11–33.

Rose, Richard. 1983. The Programme Approach to the Growth of Government. *Studies in Public Policy* no. 120. Glasgow: Center for the Study of Public Policy, University of Strathclyde.

———. 1984. Are Laws a Cause, a Constraint, or Irrelevant to the Growth of Government? *Studies in Public Policy* no. 124. Glasgow: Center for the Study of Public Policy, University of Strathclyde.

Ross, Davis R. B. 1969. *Preparing for Ulysses: Politics and Veterans during World War II*. New York: Columbia University Press.

Rothbard, Murray N. 1979. *Individualism and the Philosophy of the Social Sciences*. San Francisco: Cato Institute.

Samuels, Warren J. 1975. Comment on the Independent Judiciary in an Interest Group Perspective. *Journal of Law and Economics* 18 (December): 907–11.

Schumpeter, Joseph A. 1954. *History of Economic Analysis*. New York: Oxford University Press.

Scully, Gerald W. 1989. Liberty and Human Progress. Typescript prepared for the Liberty Fund Conference "Liberty and Human Progress," Seattle, April 6–8, 1990.

Siegenthaler, Hansjörg. 1989. Organization, Ideology, and the Free Rider Problem. *Journal of Institutional and Theoretical Economics* 145 (March): 215–31.

Smith, Tom W. 1987. The Polls—A Report: The Welfare State in Cross–National Perspective. *Public Opinion Quarterly* 51 (fall): 413–20.

Stein, Herbert. 1969. *The Fiscal Revolution in America: Policy in Pursuit of Reality*. Chicago: University of Chicago Press.

———. 1984. *Presidential Economics: The Making of Economic Policy from Roosevelt to Reagan*. New York: Simon and Schuster.

Stiglitz, Joseph E. 1989. On the Economic Role of the State. In *The Economic Role of the State*, edited by Arnold Heertje, 9–85. Oxford: Basil Blackwell.

Stubbing, Richard. 1985. *The Defense Game: An Insider Explores the Astonishing Realities of America's Defense Establishment*. New York: Harper and Row.

U.S. Bureau of the Census. 2000. *Statistical Abstract of the United States: 2000*. Washington, D.C.: U.S. Government Printing Office.

U.S. Council of Economic Advisors. 2006. *Annual Report*. Washington, D.C.: U.S. Government Printing Office.

U.S. Department of Defense, Office of the Under Secretary of Defense (Comptroller). 2006. *National Defense Budget Estimates for FY2007 (March 2006)*. Washington, D.C.: U.S. Department of Defense.

U.S. Office of Management and Budget. 1989. *Budget of the United States Government, Fiscal Year 1990: Historical Tables*. Washington, D.C.: U.S. Government Printing Office.

Wagner, Richard E. 1989. *To Promote the General Welfare: Market Processes vs. Political Transfers*. San Francisco: Pacific Research Institute for Public Policy.

Wallis, John Joseph. 1985. Why 1933? The Origins and Timing of National Government Growth, 1933–1940. In *Emergence of the Modern Political Economy*, edited by Robert Higgs, 1–51. Greenwich, Conn.: JAI.

Wallis, John Joseph, and Douglass C. North. 1986. Measuring the Transaction Sector in the American Economy, 1870–1970. In *Long–Term Factors in American Economic Growth*, edited by Stanley L. Engerman and Robert E. Gallman, 95–148. Chicago: University of Chicago Press.

Wang, Nin. 2003. Measuring Transaction Costs: An Incomplete Survey. February. *Ronald Coase Institute Working Papers no. 2*. Available at: http://www.coase.org/workingpapers/wp–2.pdf.

Weaver, Carolyn L. 1983. On the Lack of a Political Market for Compulsory Old-Age Insurance Prior to the Great Depression: Insights from Economic Theories of Government. *Explorations in Economic History* 20 (July): 294–328.

Weaver, Paul H. 1978. Regulation, Social Policy, and Class Conflict. *Public Interest* (winter): 45–63.

Wittman, Donald. 1989. Why Democracies Produce Efficient Results. *Journal of Political Economy* 97 (December): 1395–1424.

Yeager, Leland B. 1983. Is There a Bias Toward Overregulation? In *Rights and Regulation: Ethical, Political, and Economic Issues*, edited by Tibor R. Machan and M. Bruce Johnson, 99–126. Cambridge, Mass.: Ballinger.

Zupan, Mark A. 1990. The Last Period Problem in Politics: Do Congressional Representatives Not Subject to a Reelection Constraint Alter Their Voting Behavior? *Public Choice* 65 (May): 167–180.

Acknowledgments: An earlier version of this chapter was prepared for the Liberty Fund Conference "Liberty and Human Progress," Seattle, April 6–8, 1990. For comments on that version, I am grateful to conference participants and to Murray Rothbard, Walter Block, Price Fishback, and two anonymous referees for the *Review of Austrian Economics*. A later version appeared in the *Review of Austrian Economics* 5 (1991): 3–40. It appears here (in substantially revised form) with the permission of the Ludwig von Mises Institute.

# 3

# The Complex Course of
# Ideological Change

We know all too little about the way such belief systems
evolve.
                    —Douglass C. North (2005, 167)

In the early 1980s, when I was composing my book *Crisis and Leviathan,* I devoted substantial effort to considering what scholars had written
about the nature of ideology, its role in the social system, its causes, and its
consequences. In studying the growth of government, I had become convinced
that ideological change had played a critical role in propelling that growth. In
the century analyzed in my book, from the 1880s to the 1980s, various forms of
large-group collective action had obviously helped to bring about increases in
the government's size, scope, and power. Yet most economists (and some other
analysts as well), convinced by Mancur Olson's (1965) pioneering analysis of
collective action, seemed to find such collective action paradoxical: in the light
of Olson's analysis, the historical actors appeared to have behaved irrationally,
and social scientists have little, if anything, to say about irrational action. Beyond mere descriptions of what has been called "extraordinary popular delu-
sions and the madness of crowds," what systematic account can anyone give of
actions that make no sense?

As I developed my ideas about ideology, I came to understand that ideologically motivated action is no less rational than the actions economists routinely explain by appealing to so-called material self interest. In the light of this
understanding, I advanced consistent explanations of various sorts of collective
action, including those that had played crucial roles in bringing about the modern growth of government. One might criticize or condemn those actions on
many grounds, but, as I had come to understand them, the cloud of irrational-
ity no longer hung over them.

Moreover, in this view, any shrinkage of the enormous governments that had come into existence by the middle of the twentieth century and had continued to grow relentlessly thereafter would require ideologically motivated action just as much as their creation had required such action in the first place. A reversal hinged only on changing the content of the reigning ideology by reversion to something like the classical liberal ideology that had dominated the thinking of many western Europeans in the mid-nineteenth century and most American opinion leaders as late as the 1880s or 1890s, with its emphasis on individualism, steadfast private-property rights, and limited government (Higgs and Close 2006).

With regard to the causes of ideological *change,* however, I had reached few satisfying conclusions. In my account of changes in politicoeconomic institutions, I resigned myself, for the most part, to treating ideological change as exogenous. The one notable exception was that in dealing with the great crises of the twentieth century, I had developed what I called *a (partial) hypothesis on ideological change* (1987a, 67–72) to help me account for the ratchet effect on the size, scope, and power of the U.S. government that characterized its growth most visibly during the world wars and the Great Depression. Although I continue to believe that my partial hypothesis has substantial validity, I have never supposed that it provides a complete theory of ideological change. Ultimately, we also need, at the very least, a compelling way to understand the long-term drift of ideology that seems to have been so decisive in determining secular changes in the fundamental character of the political economy throughout the Western world.

In this chapter, I review elements of my previous analysis of ideology, discuss further some important aspects of ideological change, indicate how certain notable thinkers have tried to account for such change, and suggest how we might think more productively about some open questions that invite further research.

## WHAT IS IDEOLOGY? HOW DOES IT WORK?

Ideology is a vigorously contested concept.[1] All scholars agree, however, that it is not synonymous with just any idea or set of ideas. Although ideas serve as its elements, an ideology consists of certain kinds of ideas spanning a particular realm of reference. In my conceptualization, it denotes *a somewhat coherent and rather comprehensive belief system about social relations.* To say that it is somewhat coherent implies that its components hang together, though not necessarily in a way that would satisfy a logician. To say that it is rather comprehensive implies that it subsumes a wide variety of social categories and their interrelations. Notwithstanding its extensive scope, it tends to revolve about only a few central values, such as individual freedom, social equality, national glory, or social security.

Ideology has four distinct aspects: cognitive, moral, programmatic, and solidary. In its various dimensions, it operates as follows: it structures a person's perceptions and predetermines his understandings of events in the social world, expressing these cognitions in characteristic symbols; it tells him whether the social conduct he "sees" is good, bad, or morally neutral; and it propels him to act in accordance with his cognitions and moral assessments as a committed member of a political action group in pursuit of definite social objectives. Ideologies perform an important psychological service because without them people cannot know, assess, and respond to much of the vast world of social relations. Ideology simplifies a reality too huge and complicated to be comprehended, evaluated, and dealt with in any purely factual, scientific, or other disinterested way.

Every sane adult, unless he is completely apathetic politically, has an ideology. The notion that ideology is only the distorted, fanatical thought of one's intellectual or political opponents cannot be sustained. Of course, every ideology must deal in part with factual, scientific, and other "hard" knowledge, and to the extent that it makes assumptions or claims inconsistent with such well-confirmed, socially tested knowledge, we may properly accuse it of distortion. Nonetheless, all ideologies contain unverified elements, some of which, including their fundamental commitments to certain values, are unverifiable. In relation to those elements, which are neither true nor false, the allegation of distortion has little or no meaning. As Robert K. Merton once exclaimed, "On what grounds may one attribute or refuse 'validity' to ethical norms!" (1937, 501). If someone believes that the protection of individual freedom, the enforcement of social equality, the attainment of national glory, or the provision of social security should be the paramount objective of sociopolitical action, no empirical test can falsify that conviction. Aileen Kraditor has aptly written, "[T]he cause of ideology is not misinformation, to be cured by information" (1988, 97).

Most hypotheses about the sources of ideological commitment are either interest theories or strain theories. In interest theories, people are assumed to pursue wealth or power, and ideologies serve as weapons in the struggle by lending legitimacy to their pursuits. In strain theories, people are assumed to flee from socioeconomic anxieties, and ideologies bring them comfort and fellowship.

Recall that ideology has four aspects: cognitive, moral, programmatic, and solidary. If it had only the first three, we would have no grounds for identifying it as a basis of rational participation in large-group politics. In that event, ideology would allow one to perceive and interpret the social world, to impose moral valuations on it, and to conclude that certain political positions or movements deserve support. Yet one would lack a personal incentive to take any political action because, as Olson (1965) explained, it would be rational to free ride. To join rationally in political action in a large-group context, one must expect a benefit that is contingent on one's own participation. Solidarity, the fourth aspect of ideology is just such a contingent benefit by virtue of its important connection with the maintenance of personal identity.

People acquire and sustain their personal identities within groups by their interaction with other members: first in families, then in various primary and secondary reference groups. The kind of groups to which a person *chooses* to belong is closely connected with the kind of person he takes himself to be—a prime concern to the typical individual. People crave the comfort of association with those they recognize as their "own kind." In the absence of such community membership and involvement in a group's common purposes, people tend to feel alienated and depressed. Aristotle was not joking when he described man as a social animal.

By internalizing the values and precepts of their communities of shared belief, people not only feel better about themselves; they also become trustworthy adherents who will *act* in accordance with their ideology without or even in opposition to external material enticement (Higgs 1987b). Yet such action is completely rational; it need only be seen as a secular application of the calculus expressed in the biblical admonition, "For what shall it profit a man, if he shall gain the whole world, and lose his own soul?" (Mark 8:36). The truth, as Samuel Bowles has succinctly expressed it, is that "people act politically both to *get* things and to *be* someone" (1985, 164, emphasis in original). Indeed, people may act politically to be someone more commonly than they act politically to get things, although the typical economist would be greatly astonished to discover this fact. Expressive motivations surely play a much greater role than classical economic theories of politics have recognized (for discussion of the importance of so-called expressive motivations, see Brennan and Lomasky 1993).

Hence, many people routinely participate in such large-group political actions as voting and giving money or personal services to political pressure groups, and they episodically join in mass endeavors to alter society on a grand scale, sometimes even in violent and risky attempts to overthrow the government. They take these actions not because they are irrational, but because their self-perceived identities are at stake. Not by accident do activists try to shame holdouts by asking rhetorically, "What kind of person are you anyhow?" By acting in concert with others who embrace the same ideology, people enjoy a solidarity essential to the maintenance of their identities. They cannot receive this form of utility without acting; there is no closet solidarity (or, in Brennan and Lomasky's terminology, no expressive utility without actual public expression). To behave differently, a person would have to *be* different; and *being* different would require the internalization of a different ideology.

In sum, ideologies give rise to the personal-political complex of identity, solidarity, and political action in large part because of their inherent moral content. Ultimately, many political actors treat the choice they perceive between right and wrong as more fundamental than the choices they view as purely instrumental.

## THEORIES OF IDEOLOGICAL CHANGE

I now introduce some simple terminology to help us analyze how ideologies change. My basic categories of ideological change distinguish whether it is temporally *steady* or *irregular* and whether it is causally *theory driven* or *event driven.*

The timing category is straightforward and refers to the *pace* at which ideological change takes place, distinguishing even change from erratic change. Many discussions of ideological change presume the former, as if an ideology by its very nature had a sort of inertia that keeps it from changing abruptly; hence slow, gradual change is the only kind possible, in obedience to the motto on the title page of Alfred Marshall's *Principles of Economics:* "Natura non facit saltum" (in English, "nature does not make jumps"). Irregular ideological change, in contrast, denotes a process in which ideology may change slowly or not at all for a while, then more quickly, even abruptly, in a relatively brief episode, perhaps as a result of a great social upheaval, such as war, revolution, or economic cataclysm.

My causal categories pertain to the way in which an ideological change spreads from its original source to the mass public or to a substantial segment of it. In one conception of this transit, which I call "theory driven," it consists of a conveyance through the successive types of actors who contribute to the process of dissemination. This form of transmission often traces a locus of adoption from a Great Thinker to the relatively small but articulate group of intellectuals whom F. A. Hayek ([1949] 1967) labeled the "secondhand dealers" in ideas, thence to a larger group of community opinion leaders, and thence ultimately to a much larger group of ordinary recipients who embrace the new or revamped ideology.

Probably the most famous expression of a theory-driven model of ideological change appears in the final paragraph of John Maynard Keynes's *General Theory of Employment, Interest, and Money:*

> [T]he ideas of economists and political philosophers, both when they are right and when they are wrong, are more powerful than is commonly understood. Indeed the world is ruled by little else. Practical men, who believe themselves to be quite exempt from any intellectual influences, are usually the slaves of some defunct economist. Madmen in authority, who hear voices in the air, are distilling their frenzy from some academic scribbler of a few years back. I am sure that the power of vested interests is vastly exaggerated compared with the gradual encroachment of ideas. Not, indeed, immediately, but after a certain interval; for in the field of economic and political philosophy there are not many who are influenced by new theories after they are twenty-five or thirty years of age, so that the ideas which civil servants and politicians and even agitators apply to current events are not likely to be the newest. But, soon or late, it is ideas, not vested interests, which are dangerous for good or evil. (1936, 383–84)

Hayek could scarcely have agreed more. Indeed, in a 1949 article titled "The Intellectuals and Socialism," published in the *University of Chicago Law Review,* his words almost echoed the words that Keynes had written thirteen years earlier: "What to the contemporary observer appears as the battle of conflicting interests has indeed often been decided long before in a clash of ideas confined to narrow circles" ([1949] 1967, 179).

Ludwig von Mises, in many of his writings, declared his belief that "[w]hat determines the course of a nation's economic policies is always the economic ideas held by public opinion. No government, whether democratic or dictatorial, can free itself from the sway of the generally accepted ideology" (1966, 850). Moreover, in certain passages, Mises maintained the theory-driven view of ideological change in an extraordinarily strong form. "Only very few men," he declared, "have the gift of thinking new and original ideas and of changing the traditional body of creeds and doctrines" (1966, 46).

Hayek had the good fortune to become the eponym for what Milton Friedman and Rose Friedman (1988) describe as a long ideological wave, beginning in the latter part of the twentieth century, in which a "Fabian tide" of interventionism gave way to a "Hayek tide" of opposition to central planning and support for greater economic freedom. Thus, Hayek not only argued in favor of the theory-driven model of ideological change in its Great Thinker variant, but, according to the Friedmans, embodied it as well. (One wonders whether the arguably more influential Milton Friedman was only being modest by naming this alleged phenomenon after Hayek rather than after himself.)

Theory-driven ideological change flows, as it were, straight downhill: from an exalted origin in the pronouncements of a Great Thinker—often expressed in a big book, such as *The Wealth of Nations*, *Das Kapital*, or *The General Theory of Employment, Interest, and Money*—through one or more intermediary groups of intellectually less illustrious disseminators, and on down to the masses, who, it would seem, scarcely have an independent thought, but absorb (or not) whatever washes over them from above. As Hayek put it, "[O]nce the more active part of the intellectuals [that is, the secondhand dealers in ideas] have [*sic*] been converted to a set of beliefs, the process by which these [ideas] become generally accepted is almost *automatic* and *irresistible*" ([1949] 1967, 182, emphasis added).

Perhaps it is to be expected that men such as Mises, Hayek, and Keynes should believe that Great Thinkers play the key role in bringing about ideological change. As Peter Berger and Thomas Luckmann have remarked, "To exaggerate the importance of theoretical thought in society and history is a natural failing of theorizers" (1966, 15). We are well advised, however, to inquire into whether ideological change may have other sources as well and, if so, how such sources relate to the contributions that Great Thinkers make to the process.


## IDEOLOGY AND SOCIAL STRUCTURE

Not much investigation is required to discover that many scholars, even entire disciplines, have disputed what I call the theory-driven model. In 1845, John Stuart Mill astutely remarked that "[i]deas, unless outward circumstances conspire with them, have in general no very rapid or immediate efficacy in human affairs; and the most favourable outward circumstances may pass by, or remain inoperative, for want of ideas suitable to the conjuncture. But when the right circumstances and the right ideas meet, the effect is seldom slow in manifesting itself" ([1845] 1963–91, 370).[2]

The sociology of knowledge, a field of study that took shape largely in Germany and France in the 1920s and 1930s, though its interwar practitioners had much earlier precursors, defines its domain as the relations between social structure and social thought (Merton 1937; Coser 1968). Perhaps its most influential pioneer was Karl Mannheim (1893–1947; about whom, see Shils 1968), whose best-known work is *Ideologie und Utopie* (1929; English translation included in Mannheim 1936). The acknowledged modern giant in this field is the Columbia University sociologist Robert K. Merton (1910–2003), who is best known for his contributions to the sociology of science, although his writing and influence ranged widely (Cole 2004).

Unfortunately, many writers in this field have taken too seriously what Karl Marx had to say about the subject. Marx, of course, maintained the exact opposite of the theory-driven model, espousing instead a paradigmatic version of what I call the event-driven model. As he put it, "It is not the consciousness of men that determines their existence, but on the contrary their social existence determines their consciousness" (from *A Contribution to the Critique of Political Economy* [(1859) 1913], qtd. in Coser 1968, 429). For Marx (at least the earlier Marx), ideology is mere superstructure, its content being entirely dependent on the mode of production, a social complex that comprises the economic production technology and the associated property-rights regime; hence, as technology and property relations change, the ideology, along with everything else in the superstructure, changes accordingly. (Coser points out that Marx and Engels in their later writings "grant[ed] a certain degree of intrinsic autonomy to the development of legal, political, religious, literary, and artistic ideas" and allowed "that the intellectual superstructure of a society was not simply a reflection of the infrastructure but rather could in turn react upon it" [1968, 429].)

Mises naturally disagreed with Marx in this regard, as in virtually all others, and he expressed his disagreement in the form of an adamant denial that social structure affects ideology at all: "society and any concrete order of social affairs are an outcome of ideologies; ideologies are not, as Marxism asserts, a product of a certain state of social affairs" (1966, 187). I do not accept this claim except in the trivial sense that an idea of possibility and an idea of purpose must always precede any specific action. In a broader sense, however, the proposition that an individual's personal experiences and his social circumstances condition to some degree his ideological conceptions seems to me almost self-evident and in accord with a great deal of empirical evidence (Kraditor 1981; Higgs 1987a,

53, 1989b; Siegenthaler 1989; North 2005, 61–62). Therefore, I maintain that we can deny the extreme Marxian proposition without throwing away the sociology of knowledge in toto. (Indeed, Mises himself, in other passages, seems to accept the proposition I am maintaining here; see especially his statements in *Human Action* [1966] on page 46. He maintained only that such "environmental features of human action" [1966, 47] lay outside the pure logic of human action, or praxeology, and within the bounds of historical study, or thymology.)

Among the most instructive modern writers in the sociology of knowledge, Berger and Luckmann develop a multitude of ideas in sensible fashion in their 1966 book *The Social Construction of Reality: A Treatise in the Sociology of Knowledge*. They insist that "the relationship between 'ideas' and their sustaining social processes is always a dialectical one." Expanding on this idea, they write:

> theories are concocted in order to legitimate already existing social institutions. But it also happens that social institutions are changed in order to bring them into conformity with already existing theories, that is, to make them more "legitimate." The experts in legitimation may operate as theoretical justifiers of the *status quo;* they may also appear as revolutionary ideologists. Definitions of reality have self-fulfilling potency. Theories can be *realized* in history, even theories that were highly abstruse when they were first conceived by their inventors.... Consequently, social change must always be understood as standing in a dialectical relationship to the "history of ideas." Both "idealistic" and "materialistic" understandings of the relationship overlook this dialectic, and thus distort history. (1966, 128, emphasis in original)

The sociology of knowledge counsels us to take account of how people's concrete experience of life, with all the peculiarities specific to a particular time and place, may shape their beliefs about social relations, perhaps in ways that are more or less independent of the products of Great Thinkers and the efforts of those who disseminate their theories. Here, everyday life comes to play a potentially important role for both elites and masses.[3]

## THE INFLUENCE OF EVENTS ON IDEOLOGICAL CHANGE

If Burton Folsom is correct in maintaining that "[r]arely do people convert by reading tracts or listening to theories" (1989, 91), and if events as such can affect whether individuals embrace or reject an ideology, then another source of ideological change exists besides the theories that percolate down from Great Thinkers to the masses. Among economists who have recognized this other source, the Friedmans speak of "the climate of intellectual *opinion,* itself generated, at least in part, by contemporaneous social, political, and economic circumstances" (1988, 455, emphasis in original; see also 456, where the Friedmans refer to "the subtle mutual interaction between intellectual opinion, public opinion, and the course of events," and 464, where they conjecture that "the extraordinary force of experience was the major reason for the change" they call the Hayek tide). Of course, no matter how earth-shaking events may be, they do not interpret themselves in ideological terms, so when we speak of the influence of events on ideological change, we mean something qualitatively different from the influence of the articulated ideas that intellectuals employ to express a belief system about social relations: We refer much more to acceptance or rejection, especially among the masses, than to formulation de novo.

To appreciate how events come into play, we need to recognize that in any modern society (except perhaps in a totalitarian society, although probably there, too, in the shadows), more than one ideology exists, so that *ideological competition* occurs all the time. Proponents of rival ideologies take various actions to express their beliefs, sometimes to reassure those of like mind and to keep them in line, but often in the hope of winning converts or, at minimum, of raising doubts among opponents and the undecided. Among the masses especially, the undecided or weakly committed may well constitute a large proportion, so the potential often exists for a minority ideology to gain ascendancy in society if the loosely anchored persons can be pulled over. (Michael Rozeff [2006] calls this idea the "up-for-grabs" hypothesis.) In this quest, ideologues may labor diligently for years, hoping to win converts little by little or to prepare them—to "soften them up," as it were—in anticipation of opportunities to bring them over that may emerge in a future crisis. Friedman and Friedman speak of intellectual opinion as "producing options for adoption when the time is ripe" in a crisis, and they maintain that "[t]he public begins to react to the crisis according to the options that intellectuals have explored, options that effectively limit the alternatives open to the powers that be" (1988, 462, 456).

Thus, the "softening up" aspect of ideological endeavor may have great importance, even though it seems completely futile during the "normal" stretches of social life, when social, economic, political, and ideological relations change slowly, because when the crisis does arrive, its advent creates extraordinary potential for ideological shake-up. Crisis, by its very nature, creates heightened

insecurities and, in extreme cases, widespread bewilderment among the populace. War, revolution, economic collapse, runaway inflation, extreme domestic
disorder—all create new fears, and all tend to discredit established beliefs and
to open new possibilities for the successful propagation of novel understandings, evaluations, and political programs (Higgs 2005, 289–91). After all, whatever the claims that sustained the old order, social arrangements will now be
seen as manifestly "not working any longer" in critical respects. Supporters of
the established order tremble in the face of such adverse, perplexing, but undeniable events; some devotees of orthodoxy lose heart, and some abandon their
old ideology and embrace a competing one. Recall, as an outstanding example,
how many people, both intellectuals and ordinary persons, forsook classical
liberalism and took up some species of collectivism during the Great Depression (see Higgs 1987a, 69–70, 192–93, 292, 313, for documentation, although
I know of no one who disagrees). Friedman and Friedman observe that the
Depression "discredited" and "shattered the public's confidence in private enterprise" (1988, 458, 462).

Precisely such crisis conditions prevailed when, in 1935, Keynes drafted the
passage I quoted earlier about the potency of ideas. With regard to the prospects for adoption of the measures he had tried to justify in his book, he wrote:
"At the present time people are unusually expectant of a more fundamental
diagnosis; more particularly ready to receive it; eager to try it out, if it should be
even plausible" (1936, 383). He seemed to sense the same increased public recep-
tivity to new ideas and new programs that Franklin D. Roosevelt perceived at
the trough of the Great Depression when he declared, "The country needs and,
unless I mistake its temper, the country demands bold, persistent experimenta-
tion. It is common sense to take a method and try it; if it fails, admit it frankly
and try another. But above all, try something" (1933, 51). Only in a crisis, when
previously established convictions have been thrown into doubt, can such blind
and ignorant flailing about strike many people as well-advised policymaking.

Of course, the Roosevelt administration did not seek to try just anything—and such political predisposition is what brings specific ideological
preconditions to the fore. Certain economic theorists like to repeat the old say-
ing "you can't beat something with nothing." By that quip, they mean that an
existing theory's inability to explain certain events is not enough to discredit
it; one must replace it with a more compelling theory (likewise in the sciences
in general, according to the interpretation of paradigm shifts made famous by
Kuhn 1962). The same thing may be said of ideological change. No matter how
frightened and bewildered people may be, no matter how terribly the old arrangements seem to be working, people will abandon their old convictions only

if they have something seemingly better to put in their place. In this light, we see the importance of the "softening-up" phase, when hopeful ideologues cultivate public opinion and prepare it to receive and germinate their brand of seed when the season is propitious. Persuading people to believe a completely novel set of ideas is much more difficult ("why, *that's* unthinkable") than edging a great many confused and fearful individuals over the line—that line itself having been drawn during years or perhaps even decades of patient efforts by missionaries with their voices "crying out in the wilderness," warning people against the false ideological gods they currently worshipped and offering alternative belief systems for them to embrace.

Crisis, however, is not the only occasion when events influence the course of ideological change. Although the events characterized as socioeconomic trends may not be so dramatic, they operate relentlessly and cumulatively, so that over a long period they may bring about a substantial shift in the ideological center of gravity (North 1981, 49–51, 1990, 138; Higgs 1987a, 51–54). The broad societal transformations that we summarize by terms such as *industrialization, urbanization, domestic and international migration, the aging of the population,* and so forth bring about changes in social structure—the composite of social roles being played by persons in the various segments of the population. As the social structure changes, the relative representation in the population changes for persons living in various socioeconomic contexts. In the face of these transformations, we are well advised to consider that, as Thorstein Veblen wrote, "[t]he scheme of thought or of knowledge is in good part a reverberation of the schemes of life" (qtd. in Coser 1968, 432); or, in Mises's words, except for the "very few" who are capable of original thought, a person's "ideology is what his environment enjoins upon him" (1966, 46).

For example, whereas the average American worker as late as the 1870s labored on a farm, and many people in agriculture and elsewhere were self-employed, the great majority of workers in the 1930s were occupied in urban manufacturing, commercial, and service occupations as wage or salary earners. If proposals for, say, government relief of the unemployed had much greater appeal in the 1930s than they had in the 1870s, they did so at least in part because the typical worker in the 1930s faced a much greater risk of unemployment and its attendant loss of income.

Similar observations can be made about any number of other changes in the social structure—for example, about population aging, diminished coherence of the extended family, more frequent divorce, and so forth—that tended to make government provision of a social "safety net" appear more attractive relative to individual or family self-reliance. It seems extremely unlikely that people whose life situations had changed so radically would have maintained all their old ideological convictions. Mises again provides an apt comment: "the common man does choose.... And he is ready to change his ideology and consequently his mode of action whenever he becomes convinced that this would better serve his own interests" (1966, 46).

If people in the late nineteenth and early twentieth centuries gradually came to look more favorably on government promises to deliver social security, they did not do so solely because socialist writers and secondhand dealers in ideas became more successful in persuading them to follow these ideas, but also to some extent because such ideas grew more plausible and enticing as the people's typical socioeconomic condition changed (Higgs 2005, 286–87).[4]

For a schematic representation of the process of ideological change as I have described it, see figure 3.1.

## CONCLUSION

In determining the course of socioeconomic and political change, nothing has greater importance than the dominant ideology. Unfortunately, our understanding of this critical variable, especially our understanding of how it changes over time, remains extremely primitive despite the efforts of some of the finest minds in the human sciences. Perhaps this situation cannot be remedied.

**Figure 3.1**

**Ideology in Relation to Social Structure, Events, and Thinkers**

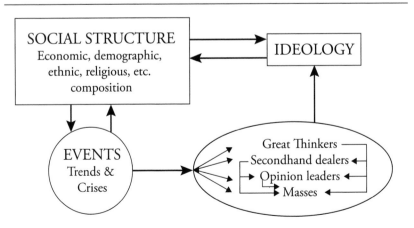

Ideology remains a deeply contested concept, and no matter whose conceptualization we adopt, we still cannot measure it in a way that permits us to trace its precise position over time. Although we may be able to make defensible general statements about the character and pace of ideological change at a specific time and place, such statements themselves will surely attract critics. I have a friend who is a leading figure in something called fuzzy logic (Kosko 1993), and I defer to his superior knowledge of mathematics and engineering, but I have serious doubts that fuzzy sociology of knowledge holds great promise.

Nevertheless, we have little alternative to pushing on. If the sociology of knowledge did not exist, we would have to invent it because (1) beliefs are fundamental to action; (2) belief systems of the sort I call ideology pervade the world of political action and hence fundamentally affect the character of the economic order; and (3) the reciprocal relationship of social structure and social thought seems undeniable. Perhaps we will have to settle for an understanding that falls well short of a general theory, relying instead on an accumulation of careful case studies of specific historical experiences and hoping to identify persistent patterns of interrelations. Moreover, no matter how grandly we frame our theory, we will have to allow for a large measure of stochastic shock—that is, we will have to concede that in the context of human creativity and free will, no theory of ideological change can be fully deterministic. Notwithstanding all of these difficulties, some progress may still be made.

## NOTES

1. In this section, I draw heavily on the more elaborated and extensively documented discussion in Higgs 1987a, 37–43, 54–55.
2. Thanks to Peter Boettke for calling this statement to my attention.
3. In important respects, the reciprocal relations stressed in the sociology of knowledge correspond to the dialectics, or "context keeping," described, recommended, and exemplified in the work of Chris Matthew Sciabarra (2000; see especially the model explicated on 379–83, which Sciabarra ascribes to Ayn Rand). Sciabarra's book, a magnificently detailed and careful work of scholarship, should be required reading for those interested in the interplay of ideas, ideology, social structure, and social action.
4. My most detailed published explication of the historical dynamics of ideological change in the late nineteenth and early twentieth centuries appears in an obscure historical journal and hence has attracted little notice; see Higgs 1989a, esp. 94–100. The article appears in this volume as chapter 4.

## REFERENCES

Berger, Peter L., and Thomas Luckmann. 1966. *The Social Construction of Reality: A Treatise in the Sociology of Knowledge.* Garden City, N.Y.: Doubleday.

Bowles, Samuel. 1985. State Structures and Political Practices: A Reconsideration of the Liberal Democratic Conception of Politics and Accountability. In *Capitalism and Democracy: Schumpeter Revisited,* edited by Richard D. Coe and Charles K. Wilber, 147–90. Notre Dame, Ind.: University of Notre Dame Press.

Brennan, Geoffrey, and Loren Lomasky. 1993. *Democracy and Decision: The Pure Theory of Electoral Preference.* Cambridge, U.K.: Cambridge University Press.

Cole, Jonathan R. 2004. Robert K. Merton, 1910–2003. *Scientometrics* 60: 37–40.

Coser, Lewis A. 1968. Knowledge, Sociology of. In *International Encyclopedia of the Social Sciences,* edited by David L. Sills, 8:428–35. New York: Macmillan and the Free Press.

Folsom, Burton W., Jr. 1989. *Crisis and Leviathan*: Folsom Review. *Continuity: A Journal of History* 13 (spring–fall): 85–91.

Friedman, Milton, and Rose D. Friedman. 1988. The Tide in the Affairs of Men. In *Thinking about America: The United States in the 1990s,* edited by Annelise Anderson and Dennis L. Bark, 455–68. Stanford, Calif.: Hoover Institution Press.

Hayek, F. A. [1949] 1967. The Intellectuals and Socialism. In *Studies in Philosophy, Politics, and Economics,* 178–94. Chicago: University of Chicago Press.

Higgs, Robert. 1987a. *Crisis and Leviathan: Critical Episodes in the Growth of American Government.* New York: Oxford University Press.

———. 1987b. Identity and Cooperation: A Comment on Sen's Alternative Program. *Journal of Law, Economics, and Organization* 3 (spring): 140–42.

———. 1989a. *Crisis and Leviathan:* Higgs Response to Reviewers. *Continuity: A Journal of History* 13 (spring–fall): 92–105.

———. 1989b. Organization, Ideology, and the Free Rider Problem: Comment. *Journal of Institutional and Theoretical Economics* 145 (March): 232–37.

———. 2005. The Ongoing Growth of Government in the Economically Advanced Countries. *Advances in Austrian Economics* 8: 279–300.

Higgs, Robert, and Carl P. Close. 2006. Introduction. In *The Challenge of Liberty: Classical Liberalism Today,* edited by Robert Higgs and Carl P. Close, ix–xxiii. Oakland, Calif.: The Independent Institute.

Keynes, John Maynard. 1936. *The General Theory of Employment, Interest, and Money.* New York: Harcourt, Brace and World.

Kosko, Bart. 1993. *Fuzzy Thinking: The New Science of Fuzzy Logic.* New York: Hyperion.

Kraditor, Aileen S. 1981. *The Radical Persuasion, 1890–1917: Aspects of the Intellectual History and the Historiography of Three American Radical Organizations.* Baton Rouge: Louisiana State University Press.

———. 1988. Unbecoming a Communist. *Continuity: A Journal of History* 12 (fall): 97–102.

Kuhn, Thomas S. 1962. *The Structure of Scientific Revolutions.* Chicago: University of Chicago Press.

Mannheim, Karl. 1936. *Ideology and Utopia: An Introduction to the Sociology of Knowledge.* Translated by Louis Wirth and Edward Shils. New York: Harcourt Brace Jovanovich.

Marshall, Alfred. 1920. *Principles of Economics,* 8th ed. London: Macmillan.

Merton, Robert K. 1937. The Sociology of Knowledge. *Isis* 27 (November): 493–503.

Mill, John Stuart. [1845] 1963–91. The Claims of Labour. In *Collected Works IV: Essays on Economics and Society,* edited by J. M. Robson, 365–89. Toronto: University of Toronto

Press; London: Routledge and Kegan Paul.

Mises, Ludwig von. 1966. *Human Action: A Treatise on Economics*, 3rd rev. ed. Chicago: Contemporary Books.

North, Douglass C. 1981. *Structure and Change in Economic History*. New York: W. W. Norton.

———. 1990. *Institutions, Institutional Change, and Economic Performance*. New York: Cambridge University Press.

———. 2005. *Understanding the Process of Economic Change*. Princeton, N.J.: Princeton University Press.

Olson, Mancur. 1965. *The Logic of Collective Action: Public Goods and the Theory of Groups*. Cambridge, Mass.: Harvard University Press.

Roosevelt, Franklin D. 1933. *Looking Forward*. New York: John Day.

Rozeff, Michael S. 2006. Tyranny of the Status Quo. January 3. Available at: http://www.lewrockwell.com/rozeff/rozeff56.html.

Sciabarra, Chris Matthew. 2000. *Total Freedom: Toward a Dialectical Libertarianism*. University Park: Pennsylvania State University Press.

Siegenthaler, Hansjörg. 1989. Organization, Ideology, and the Free Rider Problem. *Journal of Institutional and Theoretical Economics* 145 (March): 215–31.

Shils, Edward. 1968. Mannheim, Karl. In *International Encyclopedia of the Social Sciences*, edited by David L. Sills, 9:557–62. New York: Macmillan and the Free Press.

Acknowledgments: This chapter was originally prepared for delivery as the Hayek Memorial Lecture at the Austrian Scholars Conference, March 18, 2006, at Auburn, Alabama. I am grateful to the Ludwig von Mises Institute for the invitation to deliver this address. For helpful comments on a previous draft, I thank Peter Boettke and Daniel Klein. Julio Cole helped me track down a source.

## 4

## *Crisis and Leviathan:*
## Review and Response

**PART I: REVIEW BY BURTON W. FOLSOM JR.**

For years liberal historians have described the expanding of the federal government as both benign and inevitable. The benign part is, of course, increasingly
disputed; but the inevitable part is often accepted by both liberals and conservatives. Robert Higgs in a path-breaking book, *Crisis and Leviathan: Critical
Episodes in the Growth of American Government,* describes how and why the
federal government increased its scope and authority during the twentieth century. His thesis is exciting and provocative and deserves wide discussion.

Higgs's argument can be broken into three parts. First, crises were key occasions where federal officials increased their authority in twentieth-century
America. World War I, the Great Depression, and World War II were the three
major crises that Higgs analyzes. In all three cases, crisis meant emergency, and
emergency, so we were told, demanded federal action to control output, to regulate business, and to manipulate markets. Second, Higgs describes a ratchet
effect: after each crisis, some federal powers were returned to private hands. But
a residue remained, and this led to a permanent increase in what Higgs calls Big
Government. Third, the public attitudes, or ideology, toward a mixed economy
changed with each crisis. Many people adopted post hoc ergo propter hoc logic:
we had a crisis, our government tinkered with markets and prices, the crisis
eventually disappeared; therefore, the federal controls solved the crisis.

Higgs starts with Grover Cleveland and the prevailing laissez faire ideology of the late 1800s. When confronted with the depression of 1893, Cleveland
let it run its course. Some wanted him to help boost prices for farmers, set railroad rates for shippers, and create jobs for the unemployed. But he did none of
this. True, Cleveland conceded, per capita income dropped substantially during the crisis, and perhaps one-seventh of the labor force was unemployed. But

using the state to take from one group to give to another was not Cleveland's style. Principle and experience compelled him and others in power to insist that private citizens should spend and invest their own money to spur businesses to bounce back. As Cleveland had said as early as 1887, in his veto of the Texas seed bill, "Federal aid, in such cases, encourages the expectations of paternal care on the part of the Government and weakens the sturdiness of our national character, while it prevents the indulgence among our people of that kindly sentiment and conduct which strengthens the bond of a common brotherhood" (Cleveland 1889, 238).

Cleveland no doubt felt vindicated when the business cycle swung upward after 1896: from 1898 to 1916 real gross national product (GNP) shot up by 46 percent and the crisis of '93 was forgotten. Higgs's point is this: crises do not need to be resolved by government action if the politicians in power (and presumably a large chunk of the electorate) are committed to the ideology of laissez faire.

Higgs sees the Progressive Era (1900–16) as a crucial turning point in tilting the balance of power toward an activist state. Only a slight change was needed because Cleveland's philosophy had at best, during the 1890s, a narrow edge at ballot boxes, in courts, and in Congress.

Why this tilt occurred is hard to explain and does not easily fit with Higgs's emphasis that emergencies are needed to trigger the activist state. Was the growth of statism during the Progressive Era—a period of peace and prosperity—a triumph of ideology over material concerns? From 1900 to 1913, a time of no national emergency, the Supreme Court redefined the Sherman Antitrust Law, and the government prosecuted the Great Northern Railroad and Standard Oil; Congress passed the Hepburn Act, which increased the regulatory powers of the Interstate Commerce Commission; and the states ratified a constitutional amendment permitting a federal income tax. World War I, as Higgs stresses, accelerated these trends: to fight the war, legions of bureaucrats in Washington fixed prices, ran the railroads, distributed fuel, and regulated the factories. To help pay the armies in Washington and in Europe, Congress raised the tax on top incomes from 7 to 77 percent by 1918.

The 1920s saw the "ratchet effect": the crisis was over, and federal powers were trimmed down—but a residue remained, and federal spending was higher after the war than it had been before. Also important to Higgs, the ideology of intervention was entrenched. Most Americans perceived that an active state had been needed to win the war and manage the economy. Therefore, when the Great Depression set in during the 1930s, politicians and their constituents were again ready to crank up the federal machinery to fight it. Many New Deal programs, from the Agricultural Adjustment Administration to the National Recovery Administration, were streamlined from World War I models.

Here is where a discussion of the performance of the federal programs might have been useful. Some of them may have been efficient and needed, but many were disasters. And this should make us wonder why so many people perceived that the active state was the best state—especially during crises—when so many federal regulations and programs were failures. For more than thirty years now, scholars have been documenting that program after program did not perform well. Among the Progressive reforms, for example, the breakup of Standard Oil did not cut oil prices and, in fact, hurt American oil exports (which lost market shares to the Russians).[1] Likewise, the Interstate Commerce Commission's regulation of railroad and shipping rates stifled railroad innovation and hindered foreign trade (Hill 1910, 156–84; Martin 1971). The rare experiments with socialism performed poorly, too: in the 1910s, Congress wasted about $20 million building an armor plant in Charleston, West Virginia, that proved to be totally incapable of competing with U.S. Steel and Bethlehem Steel. Several of the wartime agencies—especially the shipping board—were notoriously inefficient and spent billions of dollars with little to show for it (Hessen 1975, 216–26, 307–10; Folsom 1987, 73–77). If these examples are typical (more research and cost-benefit analysis will be needed to see), and if Higgs is on target about crises, then we have a puzzling situation where poor federal performance increased demand for more federal intervention.

Some Progressives, when confronted with poor federal performance, wanted government to ratchet down more quickly than did others. After the war, for example, many Progressives wanted to keep the high tax rates on large incomes, and, in fact, they succeeded well into the 1920s. But President Wilson and his secretary of the Treasury had discovered that high taxes were supporting boondoggles and stifling investment. The activist state was proving to be inefficient, and Wilson himself, who had wholeheartedly backed federal intervention—even the $20 million armor plant—was letting *experience* change his *ideology*. By December 1919, in his State of the Union Address, Wilson was demanding "economy in government appropriations" at the spending end and lower taxes at the revenue end; the existing high rates were, he now argued, "destructive of business activity and productive of waste and inefficiency" (Wilson 1919). On taxes and efficiency, then, Wilson had ratcheted *completely* down after the war. It was left to Coolidge and his secretary of the Treasury, Andrew Mellon, to push through Congress changes that would take 98 percent of all Americans off the tax rolls and slice the tax on the top incomes from 77 to 25 percent. One irony was that Mellon's low rates generated more government revenue than did the high rates during Wilson's last years. Our economy seems to have benefited during Coolidge's years from the ratcheting down: from 1923 to 1929 we averaged only 3 percent unemployment and 1 percent inflation. Yet, when the Great Depression set in, Hoover and then FDR hiked taxes until they surpassed World War I rates, and revenue again declined (Rader 1971, 415–35; Gwartney and Stroup 1982; Silver 1982, 104–5).

The question then is: Why did Progressive ideology about the active state prevail so resoundingly over experience, at least some of which shows that limited government produces greater economic development? Higgs clearly shows *how* the ideology of statism came to be so dominant. The next question is *why* it did so, when in fact federal performance was often so wretched.

Higgs talks about interest groups, and one refinement of his thesis might be this: interest groups used crises as opportunities to compete for federal aid. When they succeeded, new interest groups then entered the political arena to compete for yet more aid. The ideological line of what should and should not be aided became fuzzy; when it did, what determined the political success of the new interest groups was lobbying skill, not economic performance or even need.

The Great Depression may have been the crucial crisis that gave statism a permanent hold. Hoover first manipulated the tariff, an accepted mode of intervention. Then he borrowed from the World War I experience: price supports for wheat and cotton farmers (the Farm Board) and federal loans to banks and railroads (the Reconstruction Finance Corporation [RFC]). Naturally, other farmers wanted supports, too, and got them; also, complaints soon came in that the Republican heads of the RFC were making most of the loans to Republican heads of business.

New groups entered the federal sweepstakes and demanded winning tickets. World War I veterans, for example, emerged with a unique demand for a special bonus just because they were war vets. Walter Waters, who led the Bonus Expeditionary Force in its march to Washington to lobby Congress in 1932, was frank in his description of his motives. "Headlines told of loans to railroads and to large corporations," Waters said. "I noticed, too, that the highly organized lobbies in Washington for special industries were producing results; loans were being granted to their special interests and these lobbies seemed to justify their existence. Personal lobbying paid, regardless of the justice or injustice of the demand" ([1933] 1969, 9, 11). In 1931, Congress had made a huge advance to the veterans in the form of a low-interest loan, but Hoover and Congress drew the ideological line in 1932, defeating a bill to give a special $2.4 billion bonus to veterans. (Later, however, in 1935, Congress overwhelmingly approved a bonus payment, overriding FDR's veto.)

By 1933, the intervention seems to have reached a threshold beyond which the old ideology of laissez faire could not, in and of itself, be used to block *any* claimants. Then came the deluge. Streaming into Washington came price fixers, electric-power advocates, union organizers, public-works experts, and relief administrators, among others. In one wave of lobbying, Senator Key Pittman of Nevada campaigned for and won a federal price support that tripled the price of silver for western silver miners. As if to underscore Water's observation that "personal lobbying paid [off], regardless of the justice or injustice of the demand," the silver industry, which ranked in size with the Eskimo-pie industry, received more New Deal subsidy dollars than the entire U.S. agriculture industry (Westerfield 1936; Leuchtenburg 1963, 82–84). What was a crisis for some had become a jackpot for others.

The crisis of World War II saw the largest growth of Big Government. Demands for manpower and war material far exceeded those of World War I: Congress and the Supreme Court quickly granted President Roosevelt unprecedented powers to fix prices and wages, regulate production, and draft more than 10 million men into the armed forces. In this environment, Higgs argues, interest groups jockeyed for subsidies and favors. Those with clout, such as the coal miners, challenged the government and won large wage increases. Others, with less power, disobeyed government commands without success—Montgomery Ward, for example, had its mail-ordering business seized. Politically unpopular groups, such as the Japanese Americans, found themselves without civil rights and within relocation camps during the war.

When the war ended, most of the controls came off. Many Americans then saw two things they hadn't seen before: the presence of a $300 billion debt and the absence of unemployment. The full employment was welcomed, of course, and the mounting debt, as the years went on, seemed increasingly harmless. Each year the federal budget would go unbalanced, and the bills would be passed to the next generation. This, perhaps as much as anything else, allowed Americans the luxury of changing their ideology about Big Government. Higgs uses the term *participatory fascism* to describe the U.S. economy since 1945. He is not optimistic about the future, but at least, during the 1980s, we have seen more public criticism of Big Government and more cries for balanced budgets.

Many of Higgs's readers who agree with his attack on Leviathan will wonder what he would do to promote either a strong national defense or traditional moral values. For example, how much dismantling of the national defense can be done without providing incentives to aggressive nations to go to war? Also, shouldn't a government do something to prevent or discourage its citizens from using drugs, having abortions, or selling pornography? In other words, without the government providing a strong defense and some support (actions and words) for traditional values—including the institutions of community, family, and church—can any society endure and prosper? Libertarians and conservatives debate these questions, and the way they are answered will shape strategy of those who want to dismantle Big Government.

*Crisis and Leviathan* qualifies as a great historical work. It has a sound theme—the rise of the federal government—and a clear argument to explain that rise. The scope of the book includes most of the twentieth century, yet Higgs's knowledge and breadth of learning dominate every chapter: he is comfortable describing subtle changes in Supreme Court cases over time, the role of ideology in the behavior of ruling elites, and the interplay of national politics and economic development. Higgs's evidence is compelling, his logic is convincing. The book itself is transforming: it should change the way historians and economists think about the growth of the state and what this development has meant for American life. Where Higgs had gone, others must follow.

Not only is Higgs's argument bold and persuasive, but his focus on crisis and change can be applied to other historical problems. In U.S. social history, for example, World War I marked the first big migration of blacks to the northern cities to work in the factories. This trend accelerated during World War II. The strong, effective presence of blacks in the army and in the factories convinced many after World War II that professional sports—and later schools—had to be integrated. In a similar vein, prohibition and women's suffrage were two explosive social reforms that culminated with the World War I crisis. Prohibition was repealed during the next crisis, the Great Depression, when a new majority became convinced that breweries created more jobs than iniquity. Crises have changed political history, too. World War I ended the loyalty of most German Americans (especially Lutherans) to the Democratic Party. And during the Great Depression, FDR broke the Republican hold on blacks and mobilized urban immigrants behind his crisis reforms. Robert Higgs has tackled a crucial and complex subject and has given us a landmark book to guide us for a long time.

One final note: in world politics in the twentieth century, crisis and ideology have gone hand in hand. Just as crises diminished the sustaining power of laissez faire, crises paved the way for fascism and communism. Not just the Big Government that Higgs describes, but all totalitarian ideologies as well need crises and thrive on them to recruit their believers and sustain their visions. Rarely do people convert by reading tracts or listening to theories. It is when crisis comes that totalitarian ideologies compete with each other and with laissez faire (or democratic capitalism) for the minds and hearts of humanity. Fascism was born in the ruins of World War I in Europe, it came to power during the Great Depression in Germany, and it all but died with the defeat of the Axis powers in World War II. Communism came to power in Russia in World War I, spread its apparatus of parties and spies during the Great Depression, and claimed the votes of one-third of the French and Italians after World War II. Communism offered solutions to the crises of history, which was what many people wanted.[2] It was and is a crisis ideology. Laissez faire, as Higgs has brilliantly shown, has not been a crisis ideology in the twentieth century.

## PART II. RESPONSE TO REVIEWERS BY ROBERT HIGGS

In *Crisis and Leviathan* (hereafter *C&L*), I tried to communicate with several different audiences, including my fellow economists and other social scientists, historians, legal specialists, students, and the general public. I tried to pull together a diverse collection of theoretical and empirical materials into a new interpretive whole. Perhaps, despite my repeated caveats about what I was *not* trying to do, I tried to do too much; or perhaps I simply did not accomplish the chosen, delimited task adequately. No one appreciates better than I the book's imperfections. I was not surprised when reviewers identified various flaws and some critics declared the book lacking in substantial merit. The reader will understand, then, how deeply I appreciate Burt Folsom's laudatory appraisal.

But let us push on. The subject is immense. No one book can cover much of it satisfactorily, and I do not deceive myself that I have said the last word on any part of it. In what follows here, I rejoin the conversation that includes my book and the reviewers' reaction to it. I cannot respond to all or even to a major portion of the questions that have been raised. Nor do I intend to waste the reader's time with a series of denials—nothing is more tiresome than exchanges of the form "yes, you did; no, I didn't." I hope that people will read my book to see for themselves whether the reviewers have been accurate in their accounts of what I wrote. Any author despairs when reviewers overlook or misunderstand the distinctions, qualifications, and subtleties of interpretation he has taken pains to express. Here I confine myself to discussing only a few issues, three that Folsom has brought to the fore and two others that he has mentioned in passing but that other commentators have underscored in their critiques.

## The Progressive Era

Consider first Progressivism. At its heart, despite the diversity of its manifestations, this is the ideology of activist government, especially of activist federal government, that became the dominant ideology of opinion-leading, policymaking elites during the early years of the twentieth century. That dominance—where dominance means only relatively great influence, certainly not the total banishment or disappearance of alternative, competing ideologies—plays a critical role in my account of the ratchet process whereby government grew during the national emergencies from World War I to the present. Unless politically influential elites are predisposed to resort, more or less immediately, to the federal government for resolution of perceived crises, those crises will not set in train the escalation of federal power. Progressivism, then, is an essential precondition for the upswing phase of the ratchet. I considered it essential to my argument, therefore, to document the advent of Progressivism. This documentation was, in one sense, a trivial task. After all, who disagrees?

What I did not do, in part because it was not necessary for my purpose and in part because I did not know how to do it in any event, was to provide a tightly argued and well-documented explanation of why Progressivism became established when it did. Folsom, along with such eminent reviewers as James Buchanan (1988, 227), Joel Silbey (1988, 974), and Aaron Wildavsky (1988, 98), takes me to task for this omission. I agree completely that a full understanding of the growth of American government requires a solution to this puzzle. Although I am still not ready to offer a complete explication of Progressivism—and this is not a proper occasion to do so in any event—I can suggest what I consider fruitful directions for further research and reflection. Some more recently published research has yielded important new findings and insights, contributing to a literature already vast and crying out for synthesis.[3]

Before proceeding, however, some clarification is in order.

First, I never maintained—indeed, I repeatedly denied—that the emergency ratchet process accounts for the entire growth of the federal government during the past century (*C&L*, 4, 18, 28, 33, 60–61). Those who have censured me for maintaining a monocausal Crisis Hypothesis have simply ignored what I wrote. My position is not that national-emergency episodes witnessed or somehow gave rise to all of the growth of the federal government; rather, my position is that these episodes were, as the subtitle of my book indicates, critical in the extended process of governmental expansion. Any account that leaves them out—astonishingly, some econometric attempts to explain the growth of government have actually deleted crisis years from the data set "tested"—or any account that does not place major explanatory emphasis on them fails to capture an essential aspect of the historical dynamics at issue. So, with specific reference to the emergence of Progressivism, the claim that the absence of national emergencies during the Progressive Era undermines my thesis cannot be sustained. I never claimed, nor do I believe, that every aspect of the growth of government or every ideological change is attributable to national emergencies.

Second, several commentators have confused Progressivism as ideology, which was my main focus in the book, with Progressivism as the actual practice of new or extended forms of government intervention in economic life during the decade and a half before World War I. The ascent of an ideology need not occur pari passu with the increase of compatible political practices. In the early twentieth century, Progressive thinking moved somewhat ahead of the events it fostered, although, as always, social experience and social thought were related reciprocally.

Finally, one ought to notice that the people who lived during the Progressive Era had a sense of crisis about their own time, a set of apprehensions related to mass immigration, violent labor relations, erratic macroeconomic performance, and potential class warfare, that many present-day observers have forgotten as they retrospectively pronounce the era, in Folsom's words, "a period of peace and prosperity." Both Theodore Roosevelt and Woodrow Wilson considered the pre–World War I period comparable to the Civil War period in its revolutionary potential, and many contemporaries shared their assessment (Sklar 1988, 350, 360, 395, 439).

With these clarifications in mind, let us consider the underlying causes of the emergence of Progressivism as the dominant ideology.

The heart of the process was the growth of Big Business, known to contemporaries as the Trust Problem. Its origins lay in the mid-nineteenth-century emergence of the interregional railway companies. The large manufacturing and commercial companies that developed during the last quarter of the nineteenth century heightened the public's fears and compounded the political reaction. Trusts, in the strict legal sense, were not the problem. Nor, despite the orthodox claim to the contrary, was the problem large corporate business as such. For political economy, the important development was not that some firms became very big; rather, it was that they did (a great deal of) business in *many states*—sometimes, and increasingly, in many countries. Hence, the giant corporations, which in many cases had been made large in order to exploit new technologies and organizational structures that offered economies of scale and scope, came increasingly into competition with the multitude of established firms serving previously fragmented local or regional markets. Received wisdom notwithstanding, the rise of Big Business produced not monopoly, but rather, certainly in its emergent phase, greatly heightened competition. Countless cozy little markets—places where local suppliers acted pretty much as Adam Smith warned they would—experienced the invasion of "alien" competitors. The octopus arms of big out-of-state corporations reached out to grasp a share of the local markets by offering consumers better products or lower prices. As the national market became more integrated, more and more small firms found themselves blown by what Joseph Schumpeter called the gale of creative destruction. The great merger movement at the turn of the century capped this accelerating development by expanding the number of large firms and significantly augmenting their market shares.

Those threatened by the big interstate suppliers sought protection by appealing to their local and state governments, the usual sources of privilege and succor and the ones from which they could expect the most sympathetic response to their plight. Hence, for this reason, among others, local and state intrusions into market relations grew markedly in the late nineteenth century. Enforcement was erratic, however, because local officials were often corrupt, and laws on the books were frequently ignored or evaded, so one cannot easily assess what all these intrusions really amounted to. Moreover, state interventions, even when strictly enforced, had clear limitations. Each state was, unavoidably, in competition with other states for population, employment, production, and investment. If local controls were too stifling and the big companies unable to bribe local officials into satisfactory accommodations, the companies might simply pick up their resources and go elsewhere, leaving behind unemployment and a diminished tax base. This leverage, known among economists as Tiebout-type competition, helped to contain local de facto protectionism. It also infuriated local competitors and convinced them that only the national government could control companies that operated on a national scale.

At the same time, the managers of the big firms, harassed by dozens of state governments and their rapacious politicos, also began to see the wisdom of federal regulation. Perhaps, they reasoned, they would stand a better chance of escaping the meddlesome, costly, and fluctuating congeries of state and local regulations if they dealt with a single, national, regulatory body. "Variety and conflict of [state] laws," Woodrow Wilson noted in the 1900 edition of his book *The State,* "have brought not a little friction and confusion into our social and business arrangements" (qtd. in Sylla 1986, 15).[4] In addition, a national regulatory agency might be useful in containing the big firms' own internecine competition, making possible the formation of effective, legally secured cartels in industries where even a handful of national competitors generated irresistible rivalry, episodic price wars, and diminished returns on fixed investments. As Martin Sklar has observed, echoing a theme often associated with Gabriel Kolko's *Triumph of Conservatism,* those who controlled the large corporations of course "opposed the old competitive market," and they "favored federal regulations not only to preempt state or local authority but, more positively, to facilitate, legitimize, police, and complement corporate regulation of the market" (1988, 434; see also 56, 316, and passim).

While both small and big businessmen organized and pressed for favorable government interventions, other groups increasingly entered the fray, defensively if not offensively: farm, labor, professional, and academic associations formed and sought expanded government measures. The dominant ideology, a distinctly American version of laissez faire, seemed less and less able to restrain the grasping for economic advantage via the exercise of enlarged government power. Indeed, some scholars maintain that the ideology was entirely a sham even during the era of its apparent dominance. Legal historian Lawrence Friedman, for example, argues that in the late nineteenth century there was no consensus about where to draw the line between the government and the private realm. "Everybody drew a different line, but largely in accord with his own economic interests. Ideology came afterwards, as icing on the cake" (1985, 454).

This claim understates the degree to which an ideology of limited government actually governed the thinking and the actions of politically influential elites in the late nineteenth century (*C&L,* chap. 5) and leads Friedman into self-contradiction;[5] it also reflects a vulgar conception of how ideology becomes involved in conflicts within the political economy.[6] The stark economic reduction reflected in Friedman's views—and in the views of such odd bedfellows as George Stigler and Karl Marx—cannot account for the way people talked, much less for the way they acted. Why, if ideology was nothing more than an afterthought, did all the actors in the political process bother to express themselves in such manifestly ideological terms, making constant appeal to what was right or wrong, fair or unfair, legitimate or illegitimate, virtuous or vicious, consistent or inconsistent with "the public interest"? If naked political (coercive) power determined the outcomes fully, as when a mugger presents his victim with the choice of surrendering his money or his life, and if ideas were just "icing," why did political contestants speak so many thousands of words for every bullet they fired? The correct answer to this question entails recognition that ideology and "interest" are not independent. A major function of ideology, which in my sense of the concept is something every politically active person possesses, is to inform the actor of what his (and others') interest consists in and of how he (and they) may legitimately pursue it (*C&L,* chap. 3, esp. 40–44,

54–55, and 259–60; Higgs 1989; Siegenthaler 1989).

Because ideology and political movements develop reciprocally, the pervasive reactions to the rise of Big Business around the turn of the century gave rise not simply to a proliferation of newly organized interest groups seeking government protection of threatened positions; it also prompted intellectuals, both independents and "hired guns," to develop new rationales for a more activist government. In practice, the process was interactive because just as concrete politicoeconomic events and trends gave rise to new articulations of the "problems" of society and new proposals for their "solution," so also did newly expressed ideas generate and sustain political movements and projects. In this way, Progressivism as ideology developed concurrently with Progressivism as political practice, both of them reflecting the changing structure of socioeconomic opportunities and the hazards created by the rise of Big Business and its repercussions throughout the economy.

### The Power of an Ideology

Folsom finds it puzzling that "so many perceived that the active state was the best state ... when so many federal regulations and programs were failures." Many governmental programs "did not perform well," some were "notoriously inefficient," and "many were disasters." Federal performance was often "wretched." It appears that those who espoused Progressivism blithely ignored experience, from which they should have learned that "limited government produces greater economic development." The question arises, then, Why did people demand new government programs in crises, when experience had already shown that such programs could not perform well even during normal times?

It is a good question, to which I can offer three answers.

First, the effectiveness of the federal programs varied. Although some, such as the Merchant Fleet Corporation created in 1920 to supersede the wartime Emergency Fleet Corporation, were manifest failures and recognized as such by almost everyone, others, such as the federal-state highway construction program, received wide acclaim. Federal immigration restrictions, agricultural research, aids to navigation, and flood-control projects, along with many other programs, also received high marks. So the first difficulty is that experience varied. Because no one was likely to have much reliable information about more than a few of the government's programs, one's judgment about the federal undertakings as a whole was almost certain to be biased. For many citizens, encouraged by favorable propaganda emanating from self-serving government sources, the bias was in a favorable direction.

Second, and more important, people committed to Progressive ideology simply did not—indeed, could not—see the "disasters" that seem so evident to Folsom or others who embrace a different ideology. A basic aspect of ideology is cognitive. An ideology is a belief system that, inter alia, predisposes a person to interpret social "reality" in a certain way. Aileen Kraditor's observation about the Communists applies equally to the Progressives (or to any other species of ideologue): "To assume that such people 'see' the facts as we do is to underestimate the power of ideology to create a whole universe." Kraditor aptly notes that "the cause of ideology is not misinformation, to be cured by information" (1988, 100, 97).

A marvelously apposite illustration of this point is a book by Charles Beard and William Beard, *The American Leviathan,* published (remarkably) in 1930. Charles Beard was certainly among the best-informed people of his time with regard to the political economy. When I first happened upon this book, I feared that he had already invented my wheel, more than fifty years ahead of me. But, no! Although the book, now generally forgotten, constitutes an intelligent and informed survey of the national government and its various activities at length (824 pages), Beard's understanding of the American Leviathan is almost the opposite of mine. Beard and I appreciated many of the same "facts." We both perceived that, already in 1930, the federal government was "a huge complex of wealth, political institutions, military engines, economic undertakings, and technological activities." But whereas I see modern government as, in large part, a means of organized predation, and I applaud almost any action to shrink its swollen mass, Beard supposed that "if governments tried to cling to the functions assigned to them in the eighteenth century, modern societies could scarcely escape disaster." So taken was he by the multifaceted beneficence of the American Leviathan that he dedicated his book "to the thousands of men and women who loyally serve the public on land and sea under the auspices of the Government of the United States" (Beard and Beard 1930, vii, 7, v).

A third reason why Progressives clung to their ideology and its political program even in the face of adverse experience is that Progressivism, like most other ideologies, conceived of the public interest in a way that excluded certain members of society. Any ideology demarcates the "good guys" and the "bad guys." It gives its adherents not only something to love (progress, justice, human brotherhood, etc.), but also someone to hate (monarchy, clergy, capitalists, etc.). Progressive ideology engendered a redistributionist political program, as witnessed especially in the graduated income tax, the Federal Trade Commission, the female-labor and child-labor laws, and many other programs—some of them only ostensibly redistributionist, operating in practice to favor the rich or the established at the expense of the poor or the newcomers. Few people cared about "economic development" in the abstract. If the new federal programs seemed to bring advantage to the causes and groups the Progressives favored, even in a grossly inefficient manner, well, so much the worse for efficiency. They would rather "get in their licks" than enrich the whole society without regard to how the additional wealth might be distributed. (Notice the damning implications of such an attitude for all the proffered "potential compensation" schemes advanced by neoclassical welfare economics [about which, see Lemieux 2006].)

We arrive quite naturally, then, at Folsom's proposals for augmenting my interpretation by an expanded consideration of interest-group politics. I can only concur. Modern politics, at least on domestic questions, is almost entirely interest-group politics. The United States is an enormous country; individuals can scarcely count for anything politically unless they associate themselves with organized groups. Of course, interest groups use crises as occasions for more successfully attaining their goals via the government; *C&L* has a great deal to say about crisis as a pretext for opportunists. Of course, the crisis-prompted enhancement of interest-group politicking encourages others who may have been unorganized or poorly organized to shape up and jump into the ring, for self-protection if nothing else. The lines had become fuzzy by the 1930s, when the veterans joined a vast array of other groups in calling on government for relief, employment, subsidies, and other protections and privileges too numerous to catalog here. Not everyone was yet in the act. The 1960s in particular witnessed another surge of political organization of interest groups previously unorganized or ineffectively organized. For the political zoologist, the proliferation of animals in the jungle during the 1960s was nothing short of magnificent. The consequences of that proliferation for the further politicization of society and the further loss of individual liberty, however, were somewhat less gorgeous.

Once so many organized groups had entered the struggle over political redistribution, other people faced an unpleasant choice. One could remain true to the Old Time Religion, abstaining from acts of predation on others via government and seeking to feather one's nest exclusively through voluntary exchanges in (what was left of) the market. This course of action, however, amounted to what game theorists call the sucker's option because although you might refrain from preying on others, they were not likely to give you the same consideration. Thus, you would bear, through explicit taxation and a plethora of other, less visible costs, your pro rata share of the burden entailed by the largess provided to others, *and* you would fail to get anything back from them; you would not get what modern citizens are inclined to call their "fair share" from the public trough. No one wants to play the sucker, and in the modern American political economy practically everyone is working hard to avoid doing so.

## Analysis or Pessimism?

Folsom notes in passing that I am "not optimistic about the future." Other reviewers dwelt much more on this perceived quality. David Henderson indicted me for "extreme pessimism" (1987, 102), and Walter Wriston characterized my outlook as "a gloomy Spenglerian view of some foreordained future" (1987). In fact, the book contains only about half a page of speculation about the future. Besides disavowing any pretense of foreknowledge, I merely indicated that given the correctness of my analysis, future crises are likely to bring forth the same kind of results that past crises generated—namely, expanded government controls over economy and society at the expense of private rights. Not relishing the prospect, I expressed a hope that my expectation would turn out to be wrong, but insisted that unless the prevailing ideology changed, I could not foresee any other outcome.

I am perplexed by the hypersensitive reaction to this "pessimism." After all, my book is not what the journalists call an "opinion piece." It is a work of analysis and history. As analysis, it might be judged according to whether it is logically consistent, comprehensible, applicable to empirical reality, and perhaps even elegant. As history, it might be judged according to whether its facts are correct, fully documented, placed in proper historical perspective, and undistorted by slanting or critical omissions. But none of this has anything to do with optimism or pessimism. If the analysis is cogent and the facts unexceptionable, then the implications for the future are what they are, and the author's temperament is irrelevant.

Some reviewers have spelled out why they found my outlook excessively gloomy. In their view, I failed to give adequate weight to an alleged revulsion against collectivism during the decade or so prior to the book's publication. Many alluded to the global movements to abandon socialist central planning, to privatize government-owned enterprises, and to permit citizens to exercise more political and civil rights even in such totalitarian nations as China and the Soviet Union. Here in the United States, the critics insisted, deregulation had swept away many of the government controls that had accumulated over the years. Some reviewers, including James Buchanan, charged that I had failed to appreciate important changes in the public's perception of politics: "the collectivist urge," wrote Buchanan, "has surely lost some of its motive force...."

[Hence] future responses to crises may not be unidirectional" (1988, 227).

In my view, the critics placed more weight on these counterclaims than the evidence will support. What was happening in China, the Soviet Union, and other countries, however one characterized it, had little if any connection with changes in the domestic political economy of the United States in the 1980s, or since. In this country—if I may be allowed to compress a great deal into a capsule pronouncement—deregulation was significant, but far from revolutionary. Moreover, although deregulation occurred in some areas (mainly transportation, communication, and certain financial services), increased regulation or manipulation of markets occurred in other areas (international trade and finance, environment, safety, agriculture), not to speak of the enormous taxpayer-financed bailouts of the farm-credit system and the thrift institutions. William Niskanen, an exceptionally well-informed observer, concluded that "the net amount of regulations and trade restraints had increased" since 1980 (1988, 15). At the same time, Paul Weaver judged that the most one could say for Reagan was that "he kept the nation from reverting to liberalism" (1988, 414).

Weaver's statement was actually too generous to Reagan, who could not stop the nation from reverting to liberalism (i.e., Progressivism as it has been known since the 1930s) because the nation, in its political economy viewed as a whole, had never departed from liberalism. As a check on this statement, one can secure an organization chart of the federal government for 1979 and a corresponding chart for 1989. Comparing the two, can one see any evidence that government's scope has been diminished? The Civil Aeronautics Board disappeared, to be sure, but the Department of Veterans Affairs appeared. Bad test? Too simple? Then peruse the *Federal Register* to see whether the government took itself off someone's back. But what about the vaunted tax cuts? In brief, they were an illusion or a hoax. The best simple measure of the nation's tax rate is the proportion of the national product commanded by government spending. Total government expenditures relative to GNP averaged 29.9 percent for 1970–79 and 31.8 percent for 1980–88 (federal spending alone rose from 20.5 percent to 23.2 percent of GNP). No shrinking government there. Nor will any shrinkage be found when one examines the mushrooming totals of federal direct-loan obligations or guaranteed-loan commitments (U.S. Office of Management and Budget 1989, 325–26, 344–45, 361–62).

Even if the so-called Reagan Revolution stands revealed as almost entirely bogus, was there not a dramatic shift of public opinion in favor of the market and against government intervention? Not according to the data obtained from public-opinion surveys. The authors of a 1988 survey of such data were most struck by the stability of the people's ideological self-identification over the preceding decade (Robinson and Fleishman 1988). Examining specific opinions, one finds the following, rather astonishing things, as reported by Tom Smith. In 1985, on the heels of President Reagan's landslide reelection, for example, 46 percent of those polled either favored or expressed indifference toward "control of wages by legislation"; similarly, 59 percent favored "control of prices by legislation"; similarly, 85 percent favored "government financing of projects to create new jobs"; similarly, 90 percent favored "support for industry to develop new products and technology"; similarly, 75 percent favored "support for declining industries to protect jobs." Proportions ranging from 36 percent to 65 percent agreed that government should either own or control the prices and profits of the following industries: electric power, local mass transportation, steel, banking and insurance, and automobiles. At least 95 percent agreed that government has either some or important or essential responsibility for "looking after old people," "seeing to it that everyone who wants a job can have one," "providing good medical care," and "providing adequate housing." At least 73 percent wanted the government to spend more or at least the same amount now being spent on the environment, health, education, retirement benefits, and unemployment benefits; 54 percent wanted the same or greater government spending for culture and arts. Among those polled, 72 percent agreed that taxes on business and industry are either about right or too low (Smith 1987, 413–20). We may all devoutly hope that these data are inaccurate measures of true public opinion, but they are consistent with the data obtained by many other such surveys. If they are the opinions of a nation that has turned away from collectivism, then I am undoubtedly the king of Albania. Or am I simply a "pessimist"?

## History or Polemic?

Folsom speculates that many otherwise sympathetic readers of *Crisis and Leviathan* "will wonder what [Higgs] would do to promote either a strong national defense or traditional moral values." As he suggests, such questions raise the prospect of debates between libertarians and conservatives. He might as well have added that liberals, neoconservatives, and socialists will also object to the polemical thread of libertarianism that runs through the fabric of my book.

For many reviewers, this thread has been sufficient to warrant throwing out the whole cloth. One reviewer faulted the book as "shamelessly pro-market" (Goodsell 1987, 684); another characterized its historical narrative as "little more than the retelling of a libertarian's nightmare" (G. Henderson 1988, 806); a third pointed to its failure to credit a "nobler range of impulses" during past crises (Schambra 1987, 39); and a fourth declared that he was personally "offended" by its characterization of certain government policies and those who supported them (Wildavsky 1988, 100). The reviewer for the *American Spectator* alerted readers that I had taken an "uncompromisingly libertarian perspective on our history," and he exhorted them to "appreciate just how profoundly subversive a doctrine it potentially is" (Schambra 1987, 39).

What I regret most about this kind of objection to the book is that it treats as a pure polemic what is a work of analysis and history that deserves to be judged by the standards appropriate to analysis and history. No one must share my libertarian inclinations, and I scarcely need to be reminded that few people do. But so what? The person who refuses to learn from anyone who does not share his own ideology is sealing himself off from a wealth of knowledge. As for what I personally would do about defense or the preservation of traditional morals or any other public issue, who (besides me) cares? I have views, of course, and their presence between if not on the lines of my book makes them plain enough for anyone interested in them. But if my book was intended as an attempt to "sell" libertarianism, all I can say is that it was a devilishly indirect way to do so.

No one should conclude that I am ashamed of my libertarian principles or unwilling to argue for them. But this is not the place for an extended defense on my ideology. Here, I would simply ask the reader to remember that governments are run by people such as Harry Hopkins and Henry Wallace, Bob Haldeman and John Ehrlichman, Michael Deaver and Edwin Meese, and, more recently, Karl Rove and Dick Cheney—not to mention the intellectual and moral paragons who compose the Congress. Are they the sort of people you want to run your life, or do you think you can do better yourself?

## NOTES

1. Two old and helpful studies are Hidy and Hidy 1955, 130–54, and McGee 1958.
2. This point is tackled in an interesting way in Chambers 1952, esp. 192–93.
3. Besides the sources cited in *C&L,* 293–301, especially the interpretive works by Wiebe, Kolko, Gilbert, Forcey, McCraw, Tariello, Ekirch, and Tipple, my remarks here draw on two books published soon after I had finished writing *C&L:* Livingston 1986 and Sklar 1988.
4. I am indebted to Sylla's paper for part of my present interpretation. A revised, published version of this paper is Sylla 1991. Sklar also notes "the widespread and persistent desire among capitalists for uniform federal standards as against the multiplicity of state laws and jurisdictions, as well as against political tendencies in some states toward stringent anti-corporate polices" (1988, 188).
5. Friedman comes closer to the truth when he notes: "Perhaps the main effect of big government is on the mentality of citizens—on legal culture. In 1900, nobody expected

much out of a national government.... [But] every event of the 20th century seems to conspire to aggrandize the center" (1985, 658).

6. Livingston aptly observes: "the programs and social philosophies of reform-minded businessmen and intellectuals were 'situationally determined,' yet cannot be reduced to expressions of economic function and interest, or be debunked as high-sounding but empty rationalizations for mere greed" (1986, 18).

## REFERENCES

Beard, Charles A., and William Beard. 1930. *The American Leviathan: The Republic in the Machine Age.* New York: Macmillan.

Buchanan, James M. 1988. Review of *Crisis and Leviathan: Critical Episodes in the Growth of American Government,* by Robert Higgs. *Journal of Economic History* 48 (March): 226–27.

Chambers, Whittaker. 1952. *Witness.* New York: Random House.

Cleveland, Grover. 1889. *Public Papers of Grover Cleveland, Twenty-second President of the United States, 1885–1889.* Washington, D.C.: U.S. Government Printing Office.

Folsom, Burton W., Jr. 1987. *Entrepreneurs vs. the State: A New Look at the Rise of Big Business in America, 1840–1920.* Reston, Va.: Young America's Foundation.

Friedman, Lawrence M. 1985. *A History of American Law,* 2d ed. New York: Simon and Schuster.

Goodsell, G. T. 1987. Review of *Crisis and Leviathan: Critical Episodes in the Growth of American Government,* by Robert Higgs. *Choice* (December): 684.

Gwartney, James, and Richard Stroup. 1982. Tax Cuts: Who Shoulders the Burden? *Federal Reserve Bank of Atlanta Economic Review* (March): 19–27.

Henderson, David R. 1987. Review of *Crisis and Leviathan: Critical Episodes in the Growth of American Government,* by Robert Higgs. *Fortune* (August 31): 101–2.

Henderson, Gordon P. 1988. Review of *Crisis and Leviathan: Critical Episodes in the Growth of American Government,* by Robert Higgs. *Journal of Politics* 50 (August): 805–6.

Hessen, Robert. 1975. *Steel Titan: The Life of Charles M. Schwab.* New York: Oxford University Press.

Hidy, Ralph W., and Muriel E. Hidy. 1955. *Pioneering in Big Business, 1882–1911.* New York: Harper and Brothers.

Higgs, Robert. 1987. *Crisis and Leviathan: Critical Episodes in the Growth of American Government.* New York: Oxford University Press.

————. 1989. Organization, Ideology, and the Free Rider Problem: Comment. *Journal of Institutional and Theoretical Economics* 145 (March): 231–37.

Hill, James J. 1910. *Highways of Progress.* New York: Doubleday, Page.

Kraditor, Aileen S. 1988. Unbecoming a Communist. *Continuity: A Journal of History* 12 (fall): 97–102.

Lemieux, Pierre. 2006. Social Welfare, State Intervention, and Value Judgments. *The Independent Review* 11 (summer): 19-36.

Leuchtenburg, William E. 1963. *Franklin D. Roosevelt and the New Deal, 1932–1940.* New York: Harper and Row.

Livingston, James. 1986. *Origins of the Federal Reserve System: Money, Class, and Corporate Capitalism, 1890–1913.* Ithaca, N.Y.: Cornell University Press.

Martin, Albro. 1971. *Enterprise Denied: Origins of the Decline of American Railroads 1897–*

*1917.* New York: Columbia University Press.

McGee, John S. 1958. Predatory Price Cutting: The Standard Oil Case. *Journal of Law and Economics* 1 (October): 137–69.

Niskanen, William A. 1988. Reflections on Reaganomics. In *Assessing the Reagan Years,* edited by David Boaz, 9–15. Washington, D.C.: Cato Institute.

Rader, Benjamin G. 1971. Federal Taxation Policy in the 1920's: A Re-examination. *Historian* 33 (May): 415–35.

Robinson, John P., and John A. Fleishman. 1988. The Polls—a Report. Ideological Identification: Trends and Interpretations of the Liberal-Conservative Balance. *Public Opinion Quarterly* 52 (spring): 134–45.

Schambra, William. 1987. Review of *Crisis and Leviathan: Critical Episodes in the Growth of American Government,* by Robert Higgs. *American Spectator* (July): 38–39.

Siegenthaler, Hansjörg. 1989. Organization, Ideology, and the Free Rider Problem. *Journal of Institutional and Theoretical Economics* 145 (March): 215–31.

Silbey, Joel. 1988. Review of *Crisis and Leviathan: Critical Episodes in the Growth of American Government,* by Robert Higgs. *Journal of American History* 75 (December): 974.

Silver, Thomas B. 1982. *Coolidge and the Historians.* Durham, N.C.: Carolina Academic Press.

Sklar, Martin J. 1988. *The Corporate Reconstruction of American Capitalism, 1890–1916: The Market, the Law, and Politics.* New York: Cambridge University Press.

Smith, Tom W. 1987. The Polls—a Report: The Welfare State in Cross-National Perspective. *Public Opinion Quarterly* 51 (fall): 413–20.

Sylla, Richard. 1986. The Progressive Era and the Political Economy of Big Government. Unpublished paper presented to the Pacific Institute and Liberty Fund Conference on Crisis and Leviathan, October 9–12.

———. 1991. The Progressive Era and the Political Economy of Big Government. *Critical Review* 5 (fall): 531–57.

U.S. Office of Management and Budget. 1989. *Budget of the United States Government, Fiscal Year 1990: Historical Tables.* Washington, D.C.: U.S. Government Printing Office.

Waters, Walter W. [1933] 1969. *B.E.F.: The Whole Story of the Bonus Army.* New York: Arno Press.

Weaver, Paul H. 1988. The Intellectual Debate. In *Assessing the Reagan Years,* edited by David Boaz, 413–21. Washington, D.C.: Cato Institute.

Westerfield, Ray. 1936. *Our Silver Debacle.* New York: Ronald Press.

Wildavsky, Aaron. 1988. Review of *Crisis and Leviathan: Critical Episodes in the Growth of American Government,* by Robert Higgs. *Public Choice* 59: 97–100.

Wilson, Woodrow. 1919. Woodrow Wilson's Seventh State of the Union Address. Available at: http://en.wikisource.org/wiki/Woodrow_Wilson's_Seventh_State_of_the_Union_Address.

Wriston, Walter R. 1987. Review of *Crisis and Leviathan: Critical Episodes in the Growth of American Government,* by Robert Higgs. *Wall Street Journal,* June 24.

Acknowledgments: This chapter was published originally as an article in *Continuity: A Journal of History,* no. 13 (spring/fall 1989): 85–105. It appears here (in revised form) with the permission of *Continuity's* editor Burton W. Folson, Jr.

# 5

## What Got Us Into and Out of the Great Depression?

When scholars consider what pushed the United States into and out of the Great Depression, they usually begin their analysis in, or shortly before, 1929 and end it in 1941 or thereabouts. Moreover, they presuppose that the event to be explained is a twelve-year series in which annual real output invariably fell short of the economy's capacity to produce and that, within this time span, the determinants of each year's substandard performance consisted of contemporaneous or shortly preceding conditions and events.

This approach tends to mislead us in two important ways. First, it fails to give adequate weight to the events of 1914–29 that served as preconditions for the onset of the Depression and help us to understand why governments responded to it as they did and thereby exacerbated it; that is, scholars too often fail to appreciate that "[t]he origins of the Great Depression lie largely in the disruptions of the First World War" (Temin 1989, 1). Second, the usual analysis mistakenly takes for granted that the Great Depression ended in 1941 or thereabouts and was superseded by a business-cycle boom, often called "wartime prosperity," whereas, in reality, the war years themselves were not a time of genuine prosperity. An adequate understanding of the Great Depression requires that we view it as contained within a longer series of political and economic events—an Age of Endless Emergencies from 1914 to 1945, or, in Peter Temin's words, "one long conflict with an uneasy truce in the middle" (1989, 1).[1] In this light, we perceive World War I to have been the mother of all the great politicoeconomic disasters during a period of more than thirty years and in many ways beyond it, even to our own times.

My overall interpretation of these events proceeds along the following lines. The actions taken and the policies adopted by the warring governments in World War I destroyed the foundations of a highly successful economic order in which all the economically advanced countries had participated for several decades before 1914. After the armistice, the Treaty of Versailles put in place defective and unsustainable economic arrangements, which the leading economic powers sought to keep afloat during the 1920s. The policies they adopted in an attempt to patch this system, along with other ill-chosen policies, produced one crisis after another and set the stage for the economic downturn that began in mid-1929. In the United States, as elsewhere, the government responded to the economic bust with a series of policy actions that only exacerbated it, plunging the world economy into the greatest economic catastrophe of modern times. After the economy hit bottom in 1933, the government continued to treat the disease with an outpouring of snake-oil cures that seriously hampered spontaneous recovery, although some improvement occurred in spite of the government's actions. After World War II began in 1939, if not earlier, U.S. government leaders turned their attention away from domestic economic nostrums and toward mobilization of the economy for future participation in the war. From mid-1940 until the latter part of 1945, the government imposed a command economy, setting aside essential elements of a genuine market order. "Wartime prosperity," however, is a myth: the war merely replaced the economic suffering of the 1930s with a new form of privation, in many ways a worse form. Only in 1945–46, with the end of the war and the reconversion of the command economy to a more market-directed economic order, did genuine prosperity resume and persist.

## THE OLD ECONOMIC ORDER AND ITS DESTRUCTION BY WORLD WAR I

No one ever depicted the old economic order any better than John Maynard Keynes, who wrote in *The Economic Consequences of the Peace:*

> What an extraordinary episode in the economic progress of man that age was which came to an end in August, 1914! The greater part of the population, it is true, worked hard and lived at a low standard of comfort, yet were, to all appearances, reasonably contented with this lot. But escape was possible, for any man of capacity or character at all exceeding the average, into the middle and upper classes, for whom life offered, at a low cost and with the least trouble, conveniences, comforts, and amenities beyond the compass of the richest and most powerful monarchs of other ages. The inhabitant of London could order by

telephone, sipping his morning tea in bed, the various products of the whole earth, in such quantity as he might see fit, and reasonably expect their early delivery upon his doorstep; he could at the same moment and by the same means adventure his wealth in the natural resources and new enterprises of any quarter of the world, and share, without exertion or even trouble, in their prospective fruits and advantages; or he could decide to couple the security of his fortunes with the good faith of the townspeople of any substantial municipality in any continent that fancy or information might recommend. He could secure forthwith, if he wished it, cheap and comfortable means of transit to any country or climate without passport or other formality, could dispatch his servant to the neighboring office of a bank for such supply of the precious metals as might seem convenient, and could then proceed abroad to foreign quarters, without knowledge of their religion, language, or customs, bearing coined wealth upon his person, and would consider himself greatly aggrieved and much surprised at the least interference. But, most important of all, he regarded this state of affairs as normal, certain, and permanent, except in the direction of further improvement, and any deviation from it as aberrant, scandalous, and avoidable. The projects and policies of militarism and imperialism, of racial and cultural rivalries, of monopolies, restrictions, and exclusion, which were to play the serpent to this paradise, were little more than the amusements of his daily newspaper, and appeared to exercise almost no influence at all on the ordinary course of social and economic life, the internationalization of which was nearly complete in practice. (1920, 10–12)

As Keynes's depiction suggests, the main pillars of the old order were unrestricted international travel, trade, and investment; the monetary system known as the gold standard; and reliable but limited government. Under this regime, international trade, mass migration, and investment flourished; nations developed their economic activities in accordance with their comparative advantages; and the people of all the participating countries improved their economic well-being beyond any standard previously achieved by the masses or, in certain regards, even by the upper echelon of society.

With the onset of the Great War, the warring governments pulled down each of these pillars. Blockades, naval warfare, and shipping shortages impeded international trade; foreign investments were cashed in to pay for munitions; the belligerent nations fell back into greater self-sufficiency and hence into diminished real income; the gold standard was suspended (wholly by the European belligerents, partly by the United States), and the national monetary authorities brought about the creation of enormous amounts of new fiat money unredeemable for gold, silver, or other commodities at fixed rates (again, the United States was a partial exception because it maintained domestic [but not foreign] convertibility), causing tremendous reductions in money's purchasing power.

Moreover, during the war the governments on both sides abandoned old limitations of their economic intervention and put in place various forms of "war socialism," a species of central economic planning and resource allocation that gave highest priority to the state's own demands and restricted the citizens' traditional economic and civil rights. These governments drafted millions of men into involuntary service in the armed forces, seized hugely increased amounts of taxes, and generally rode roughshod over the old economic order of private-property rights, contractual freedom, and extensive personal liberties. If the war itself was a catastrophe, senselessly slaughtering men by the millions and bringing about great suffering for hundreds of millions of others, the economic measures that governments adopted to reallocate resources to war purposes were nearly as disastrous, going far toward wrecking everything that had been built up at such great sacrifice during the previous century of economic progress.

When the armistice took effect on November 11, 1918, the belligerent nations of Europe were economically almost prostrate. Their labor forces and capital stocks had been depleted greatly, their domestic economic organization distorted grotesquely, and their old arrangements for international cooperation by means of trade and investment shattered.

## FROM THE ARMISTICE TO 1929

To make matters worse, the Versailles Treaty, signed in 1919, required that Germany make huge reparation payments to France, Great Britain, Italy, and Belgium. To earn the wherewithal to make these transfers, Germany needed to sell great amounts of its goods abroad, but doing so was nearly impossible, given its own economic devastation and its direct loss of important territories and other resources to the victorious powers—not to mention the barriers other countries erected to protect their own producers from foreign competition.

It soon became clear that the stipulated reparations would be paid only if Germany borrowed large amounts from other countries, and the only lenders capable of providing sufficient funds were the Americans. Therefore, arrangements were made whereby in effect the Germans borrowed from the Americans and then handed over much of the proceeds to the French and the British, who in turn sent some of the money back to the United States to repay loans received during the war.[2]

This scheme held so little charm for the Germans, who got nothing out of it but more debt, that they resorted to engineering a hyperinflation of the German currency in 1922 and 1923 to ease the government's fiscal woes. Unfortunately for the German people—especially middle-class people, who held monetary assets such as bonds, insurance policies, and bank accounts—this inflationary eruption proved devastating, not only to the economy, but in the longer term to the moral fortitude of the bourgeoisie, who felt that the rug had been pulled out from under frugal, respectable people. No one described this devastation better than Thomas Mann, who wrote:

> there is neither system nor justice in the expropriation and redistribution of property resulting from inflation.... [O]nly the most powerful, the most resourceful and unscrupulous, the hyenas of economic life, can come through unscathed. The great mass of those who put their trust in the traditional order, the innocent and unworldly, all those who do productive and useful work, but don't know how to manipulate money, the elderly who hoped to live on what they earned in the past— all these are doomed to suffer. An experience of this kind poisons the morale of a nation. ([1942] 1977, 166)

By creating disaffection with the Weimar Republic, the hyperinflation helped to prepare fertile ground for the growth and eventual triumph of Hitler's party.

After the hyperinflation was stopped, new international lending arrangements were hastily concocted, but each such Band-Aid served only as a temporary means of staunching the bleeding. The reparations regime was simply not viable in the long run; the only question was precisely how it would break down and what would replace it. From 1919 onward, the German government "struggled ceaselessly for the reduction and elimination of its reparations obligations" (Temin 1989, 30). After the Germans defaulted in 1923 and the French army occupied the Ruhr district in response, the payments were rescheduled in 1924, scaled down in 1929, then delayed and ultimately, after Hitler came to power in 1933, repudiated along with every other German obligation under the Versailles Treaty.

At the same time that the economically advanced countries were dealing with the reparations problem, they were striving to reconstruct the international financial regime that they had wrecked during the war by suspending the gold standard and issuing vast quantities of fiat money. The general assumption was that the European nations ought to return to the gold standard, and one by one they did so during the latter half of the 1920s. The monetary system to which they "returned," however, was not the old prewar gold standard, but a "gold-exchange" standard that lacked essential attributes of the old system, such as circulating gold coins and domestic convertibility. Murray Rothbard called it "a bowdlerized and essentially sham version of that venerable standard" (1998, 123; see also Timberlake 2007 ). Unlike the classical system, it was subject to constant "management" by central bankers who sought to achieve new goals, such as price stability or a low rate of unemployment.

When Great Britain finally resumed international convertibility of the pound sterling into gold in 1925, it made a serious mistake by setting the official value of the pound at the old, prewar parity. Because of the rise in prices that had occurred in Britain during the war, however, the pound in free exchange was no longer worth as much relative to the U.S. dollar as it had been worth before the war. By officially overvaluing the pound (at £1 = \$4.86, when the prevailing free-market rate was in the neighborhood of \$4.40), the British made their export products—goods priced in terms of the pound sterling—relatively expensive and hence difficult to sell overseas. British export industries, such as coal, steel, textiles, and shipbuilding, suffered accordingly, and workers in those industries, traditionally reluctant to go far afield in search of jobs, endured high rates of unemployment. Many workers subsisted on the infamous "dole." The British economy languished, and investment funds tended to flow out of the country, especially to the United States, putting even more pressure on the overvalued pound.

To help the British succeed in their resumption of gold convertibility, central bankers in the United States, led by Benjamin Strong, governor of the Federal Reserve Bank of New York, undertook to pursue monetary policies that would reduce interest rates in the United States, thereby diminishing the relative attractiveness of U.S. investments for British investors and causing them to reduce the pressure they would otherwise put on the pound's exchange value by trading pounds for dollars (Rothbard 1998, esp. 120–21).

These U.S. policies, however, also had other effects on the domestic economy. The "momentous decision of forcing a regime of cheap money," as Lionell Robbins described it (qtd. in Temin 1989, 19), caused the U.S. money stock to grow faster than it otherwise would have grown, kept interest rates lower than they otherwise would have been, and thereby encouraged domestic investors to make certain investments—in structures and other long-lived producer goods—that they otherwise would not have made. In short, U.S. monetary policies, aimed at assisting the British monetary authorities, had the effect of bringing about "malinvestments" in the United States and thereby distorting the structure of the capital stock in an unsustainable fashion (because investments in structures and other long-lived capital goods ultimately prove economically unwarranted when they are made in response to artificially low interest rates, and such projects will go bankrupt).

U.S. central bankers also began to worry in the late 1920s that by keeping interest rates artificially low, their policies were feeding a frenzy to buy corporate shares and creating a stock-market bubble destined to pop with destructive effects on the real economy. Accordingly, in 1928 and more so in 1929, they moved away from their "cheap money" policies, adopting new policies of higher interest rates and exerting direct pressure on commercial banks to stem what they viewed as "speculative excesses" and diversions of bank loans from economically sound purposes. Most economists now believe that this change of monetary policy triggered the U.S. economic downturn that occurred in mid-1929 and the stock-market crash that followed later in the year. Others believe that the prior ("cheap money") policies presaged the downturn because the malinvestments that those policies fostered would have to be liquidated sooner or later by means of bankruptcies and reallocations of resources to more sustainable uses, a process marked by economic disruptions and transitional unemployment.

## THE GREAT CONTRACTION, 1929–1933

The economy's initial recession, whatever its trigger, need not have become a disaster. Many downturns had occurred previously in U.S. economic history, and nearly all of them had been fairly shallow and soon were followed by recovery and continued growth. The depression of the mid-1890s was the most severe macroeconomic bust prior to 1929. In previous economic downturns, however, hardly anyone had expected the government to take vigorous action to bring about recovery. In the nineteenth century, most people believed that the government neither knew how nor possessed the constitutional authority to act effectively as an economic savior. They appreciated that "[r]ecessions unhampered by government interventions almost invariably work themselves into recovery within a year or so" (Rothbard 1998, 151).

By the end of the 1920s, however, many informed observers had come to believe that the economy had entered a "new era" in which government and business leaders understood how to counteract any recession that might occur before it turned into a catastrophe. Unfortunately, the knowledge they imagined themselves to possess in this regard was, for the most part, nothing more than an example of what F. A. Hayek later called the pretense of knowledge—the conviction that government planners, including the monetary authorities, know how to make the world a better place than it would be if people were simply left to their own devices.[3]

Moreover, by 1929, the dominant ideology had changed substantially. Many opinion leaders and large segments of the general public were embracing the Progressive faith in activist government. To make matters even worse, the economics profession for the most part had come to believe that the government could and should intervene actively in economic life (Rockoff 1998). These ideological and intellectual changes came as music to the ears of many politicians, who welcomed a plausible excuse to enlarge their powers and to turn the exercise of those enlarged powers to their own advantage. Organized special interests also seized on the new ideas and attitudes as pretexts for the creation of the pensions, subsidies, insurance benefits, protections from competition, bailouts, and other privileges they sought from the government.

As officials at all levels responded to the newly strengthened demands that government "do something" in late 1929 and afterward, the government adopted an enormous number and variety of interventionist measures, spanning every industry, region, and demographic group in the country. Many of these measures simply reestablished under new names the measures that had been used during the war, on the ill-considered ground that these policies and programs had proved successful in a previous emergency (war), so they would prove successful again during the existing emergency (economic depression). As President Hoover himself declared, "We used such emergency powers to win the war; we can use them to fight the depression" (qtd. in Rothbard 2000, 323; for many examples of such reapplications during Roosevelt's presidency, see Leuchtenburg 1964). So, for example, the defunct War Finance Corporation was revived in 1932 and called the Reconstruction Finance Corporation.

Because the government's economic rescue programs often worked at cross-purposes or interfered with the successful operation of the private competitive economy, they exacerbated the downturn between 1929 and 1933, making it deeper than it otherwise would have been, and slowed the economy's recovery after 1933, so that even when the government began to shift the economy onto a war footing in mid-1940, full recovery had not yet been attained. (The official unemployment rate in 1940 was 14.6 percent, but if we count persons enrolled in government emergency employment programs as employed, the unemployment rate was 9.5 percent.) In short, the government's cures made the disease much worse and slowed the patient's natural recovery. No wonder the authors of a recent book on the Great Depression blame government officials for "an incredible sequence of policy errors that generated a cataclysmic event reaching around the entire globe" (Hall and Ferguson 1998, xii).

The dimensions of the disaster were shocking. For nearly four years, with only brief and abortive reversals, the economy fell deeper and deeper into the trough. By 1933, real gross domestic product (GDP) had declined by 30 percent. Production of consumer durables fell by 50 percent, producer durables by 67 percent, new construction by 78 percent, and gross private domestic investment by almost 90 percent. The real value of U.S. exports and imports dropped by nearly 40 percent. The unemployment rate reached nearly 25 percent, and perhaps one-third of those still working in 1933 were laboring only part-time. Prices fell on average by about 23 percent. Banks failed in waves, and by the end of 1933 nearly ten thousand of them had gone under. In 1931, 1932, and 1933, the after-tax profits of all corporations added up to less than zero. Rental and proprietary income dropped by more than 60 percent. The stock market hit bottom in 1932, having lost more than 80 percent of its value during the preceding three years. Farm-product prices fell by more than 50 percent; net income of farm operators declined by nearly 70 percent; and thousands of farmers surrendered their homes and farms to mortgage lenders and tax collectors. Three states—Arkansas, Louisiana, and South Carolina—and approximately thirteen hundred municipalities defaulted on their debts, and many other states and local governments verged on default. The sky, it seemed, really had fallen.

Conditions need not have become so desperate, and on their own they would not have done so. The collapse was worsened by a succession of powerful pushes from government policies ostensibly aimed at alleviating it or some aspect of it. Among the most harmful of these counterproductive policies was the Smoot-Hawley Act of 1930, which "raised tariff rates on imports to the highest levels in the nation's history" and set in motion a tariff war, a trade-constricting sequence of action and reaction around the trading world (Chandler 1970, 12–13). In late 1929, President Hoover urged employers to maintain real-wage rates despite the plummeting decline in demand for their products. Many of the larger employers did so in 1930 and into 1931 and, as a result, unemployment increased much faster than it otherwise would have (Rothbard 1972, 128-30;

2000, 210-14, 245-46; Vedder and Gallaway 1997, 74–97). The Revenue Act of 1932, which became fully effective in 1933, "provided the largest percentage tax increase ever enacted in American peacetime history," administering a stunning blow to already-struggling businesses and households (Chandler 1970, 125, see also 139–40).

Perhaps worst of all, at the Federal Reserve System, which had been created in 1913 to provide emergency liquidity to commercial banks during financial panics, officials stood by while banks failed by the thousands, bizarrely convinced that in the circumstances they had done all that they could and should do to prevent the banking system's collapse. As a result, the money stock (M2 measure) fell by 32 percent between June 1929 and June 1933. As banks failed and depositors clamored to withdraw their funds and to augment their cash holdings, financial stringency took an enormous toll on businesses and households throughout the country. The vaunted "lender of last resort" had failed spectacularly to perform its designated function, with enormous consequences not only for the banks that relied on it to supply emergency reserves, but for everybody. As Gottfried Haberler concludes, "there can be no doubt that the collapse of the banking system, the bankruptcy of many thousand banks, and the inept and overly timid monetary policy which permitted the money stock to shrink by about one-third was to a large extent responsible for the disaster" (1976, 31–32).

Owing to the foregoing policies and many others that might be mentioned if space permitted, the economic downturn that began in 1929 turned out to be not just another recession, but a catastrophe.

## THE GREAT DURATION

Economists, following the usage of Milton Friedman and Anna Schwartz in their classic study *A Monetary History of the United States, 1867–1960,* call the economic collapse in the United States between 1929 and 1933 the Great Contraction. In my own writings, I have added two similar terms to refer to other aspects of the Great Depression—the Great Duration and the Great Escape. The former denotes the Depression's exceptional length, from 1929 to 1941 (when the societal disaster did not actually end, but merely changed its form, as I describe later). The Great Duration is as puzzling as the Great Contraction, and in some ways even more so. No previous economic bust had persisted nearly so long. The second-worst one, in the mid-1890s, lasted less than half as long. Except for France, where political conflicts stymied recovery, no other major industrial country took as long as the United States to escape from the Great Depression; all the others had recovered well before World War II began. What accounts for the Great Duration?

In brief, the Depression's exceptional length is attributable to the same general cause that explains the Great Contraction's exceptional severity: a series of ill-chosen government policies. These policies disrupted and distorted the operation of the competitive economy, created paralyzing fear in the minds of its most essential investors and businessmen, and gummed the gears of the economy's normal recuperative processes. After some headway had been made toward recovery between 1933 and 1937, new government policies—collecting new taxes, encouraging aggressive labor unionization, and, especially, abruptly doubling bank reserve requirements—knocked the economy into a serious depression within a depression, setting full recovery back by at least another two years.

Nearly all of the counterproductive policies adopted from 1933 to 1938 reflected the triumph of Progressive ideology and political self-serving over the application of economic rationality to improve economic conditions on a wide scale—which is to say that these policies, regardless of their creators' beliefs or assurances, were not actually in the public interest. It was a great misfortune for the American people that the New Dealers "turned away from the market toward a managed economy and democratic socialism" (Temin 1989, 97) and that they embraced above all "the conviction that government must play an active role in the economy" (Brinkley 1995, 10). In practice, this conviction was equivalent to the belief that a bull elephant must play an active role in the China shop.

When Franklin D. Roosevelt took office in March 1933, the economy was in the ditch. His first official act was to issue an executive order to close all the commercial banks in the country, thereby bringing economic activity almost to a complete standstill. By that time, after nearly four years of relentlessly deteriorating economic performance, almost everyone was clamoring for some kind of economic salvation from the federal government. The supplicants did not agree about the form this salvation should take; indeed, all sorts of schemes and proposals blossomed like the proverbial thousand flowers to which Chairman Mao referred during the Cultural Revolution. As John T. Flynn described the scene, "Washington was now full of Great Minds and Deep Thinkers—youthful pundits from Harvard and Yale and Princeton and especially Columbia, with charts and equations; cornfield philosophers from Kansas and California and, of course, the unconquerable champions of all the money theories, including free silver, paper money and inflation. There were advocates of the 30-hour week and of every variety of plan for liberating the poor from their poverty and the rich from their riches" ([1948] 1949, 10–11). Everyone demanded immediate help of some kind, and many petitioners verged on desperation.

In this charged atmosphere, politicians found themselves in paradise because they could easily rationalize on grounds of "national emergency" their creation of a host of policies to appease countless organized special-interest groups and then reap the return on the political "exchange," whether it took the form of votes in the next election or cash in a plain brown wrapper. Politicians who normally might have blocked one another's schemes now found it expedient to organize enormous "logrolls," rewarding every clamoring special-interest group at once. "The crisis," historian John Garraty has written, "justified the casting aside of precedent, the nationalistic mobilization of society, and the removal of traditional restraints on the power of the state, as in war, and it required personal leadership more forceful than that necessary in normal times" (1973, 932). In short, as Roosevelt and the Democrats in Congress perceived the situation, it required FDR's New Deal.

Which is what it promptly got—good and hard. No summary can do justice to the astonishing breadth of the legislative outpouring during Roosevelt's first term, especially during the congressional sessions of 1933 and 1935, from "a Congress made dizzy by the swiftness and variety and novelty of the demands" the administration sent to Capitol Hill (Flynn [1948] 1949, 11). Jim Powell (2003) has written an entire book to line up the numerous studies that show, in the words of the book's subtitle, "how Roosevelt and his New Deal prolonged the Great Depression." These measures included abandonment of the gold standard; confiscation of everyone's monetary gold, and abrogation of all gold clauses in contracts, including the government's own contracts; breakup of some of the nation's strongest banks by mandating the separation of commercial and investment banking; enactment of a series of soak-the-rich tax laws that discouraged entrepreneurship and capital accumulation and doubled federal taxes as a proportion of gross national product (GNP) between 1933 and 1940; operation of huge make-work programs that served as vote-buying schemes for Democrats and diverted millions of workers from productive private employment; supply reductions and price increases of farm products at a time when millions of poor families were struggling to afford food and clothing; federal government entry into competition with private entrepreneurs in the production and distribution of electricity; establishment of a Ponzi scheme known as Social Security that raised taxes and discouraged private saving; promotion of labor-union monopolies in the sale of labor services, thus pushing affected wages above competitive market levels and increasing costs for struggling businesses; suppression of competition in a wide range of industries, from petroleum production to coal mining to ordinary retailing, thus allowing sellers to charge increased prices for a great variety of products, notwithstanding consumers' diminished incomes; and general subversion of private-property rights in ways too numerous to specify. The Roosevelt administration taxed, spent, borrowed, regulated, insured, subsidized, and confiscated on a scale never before seen in the United States in peacetime.

No wonder the recovery was so slow: goaded by special interests and intellectual crackpots and sustained by the public's desperate cry for salvation, the government had placed itself, in effect, in a state of war against the great cooperative order of the people's productive efforts and arrangements, sanctifying its destructive efforts with hot-air claims about the achievement of "relief, recovery, and reform." Powell concludes: "[t]he New Dealers really came to believe that their knowledge, combined with political power, could cure the problems of the world. They thought that by issuing executive orders, passing laws, raising taxes, and redistributing money, they could make society better" (2003, 270).

During the first two years of Roosevelt's presidency, which historians call the First New Deal, the administration tried to work with nearly all organized political interest groups, including important business groups, such as the Chamber of Commerce and the National Association of Manufacturers. Indeed, the keystone of the First New Deal—the harebrained scheme to cartelize every industry in the country under the terms of the National Industrial Recovery Act—was the brainchild primarily of those business interests (Hawley 1966; Shaffer 1997, 77–104). "It would have been impossible," Flynn observed, "to invent a device more cunningly calculated to obstruct the revival of business than this half-baked contrivance" ([1948] 1949, 48). Having surveyed the evidence of the National Recovery Administration's operation and effects, Gene Smiley concurs that "[a]ll the initiatives created under the 'enlightened management' of the NRA were inimical to recovery" (2002, 102). As this scheme degenerated into multidimensional squabbling and enforcement difficulties on the way to its death at the hands of the Supreme Court in the spring of 1935, and as Roosevelt came under increasing fire from goofy-left challengers such as Huey Long and Upton Sinclair, he decided to change course, switching his emphasis toward more collectivist, anticapitalist policies during the so-called Second New Deal, which spanned the years from 1935 to 1938 or 1939, when the New Deal in any form had run out of steam.

During the Second New Deal, the president, cheered on by a coterie of enthusiastically anticapitalist advisers—many of them the youthful acolytes of Louis Brandeis and Felix Frankfurther—frequently lashed out at businessmen and investors, demonizing them as "economic royalists" and blaming them for sabotaging the economy's recovery. "Roosevelt's opinions at this moment," Flynn wrote, "were generally that big business was immoral, that the poor were not getting a fair break and that the depression was the result of the sins of business and that business must be punished for these sins" ([1948] 1949, 101).[4] Pushing such collectivist measures as the Social Security Act and the National Labor Relations Act, the administration embraced "that easy, comfortable potpourri of socialism and capitalism called the Planned Economy which provided its devotees with a wide area in which they might rattle around without being called Red" (Flynn [1948] 1949, 75). Accepting the Democratic nomination for the presidency in 1936, Roosevelt gave a speech that "was widely regarded as essentially a formal declaration of war against the free enterprise system" (Smiley 2002, 114). The *Washington Post* called it "the sort of speech which paves the way for fascism" (qtd. in Best 1991, 132).

Although this strategy proved successful politically—FDR was reelected by a landslide in 1936—it had a disastrous effect on the recovery. By creating heightened fears about the security of private-property rights, it led investors to refrain from making enough long-term investments to propel the economy back to full prosperity. As Flynn observed, "[t]he great investment industries were idle" more than seven years after the onset of the Depression, and "[w]ithout the revival of investment there could be no revival of the economic system" ([1948] 1949, 99). A leading businessman, Lamont du Pont, described the prevailing state of uncertainty that investors faced in 1937: "Uncertainty rules the tax situation, the labor situation, the monetary situation, and practically every legal condition under which industry must operate. Are taxes to go higher, lower or stay where they are? We don't know. Is labor to be union or non-union? ... Are we to have inflation or deflation, more government spending or less? ... Are new restrictions to be placed on capital, new limits on profits? ... It is impossible to even guess at the answers" (qtd. in Krooss 1970, 200).[5] Also in 1937, even the Milquetoast Treasury secretary Henry Morgenthau pumped up his courage enough to challenge the president by insisting, "What business wants to know is: are we headed toward Socialism or are we going to continue on a capitalist basis?" (qtd. in Flynn [1948] 1949, 119).[6]

After several years of sponsoring the cartelization of U.S. industry across the board, the president abruptly decided to embark on a "trust-busting" jihad in late 1937, even as economic conditions began to slide into the depression within a depression (Hawley 1966). This radical reversal of course only gave businessmen a new reason to worry about the future. Indeed, as *The Economist* observed on November 6, the president's policy "might almost have been a concerted program to discourage capital investment" (qtd. in Best 1991, 180). Historian Gary Dean Best concludes: "Instead of improving business sentiment, Roosevelt seemed intent on stamping out any confidence that might remain" (1991, 180). After net investment had totaled *minus* $18.3 billion for the years from 1931 to 1935—that is, gross investment fell short of compensating for depreciation by that amount—it revived to positive amounts in 1936 and 1937, only to fall back into the negative range in 1938 before resuming its recovery. For the eleven-year period from 1930 through 1940, net private investment totaled *minus* $3.1 billion, and only in 1941 did annual net investment finally exceed the 1929 amount. No economy can prosper when it goes more than ten years without adding to its capital stock, and economists of various schools agree that the failure of private investment to recover accounts in great part for the Great Duration.

Table 5.1 lists some of the more important laws enacted during the New Deal that threatened the security of private-property rights, thereby creating what I call "regime uncertainty" and causing investors to refrain from risking their money in long-term investments in such uncertain circumstances.

The regime-uncertainty hypothesis also gains support from public-opinion surveys conducted in the 1930s among businessmen as well as among the general public and from evidence drawn from the financial markets.[7] Even as late as November 1941, a *Fortune* poll of business executives found that almost 93 percent of the respondents expected the postwar regime to be one that would further attenuate private-property rights to a greater or lesser degree, and more than 40 percent of them expected a regime in which the government would dominate the economy (Higgs 2006a, 18). Between 1934 and 1936, yields of longer-term corporate bonds increased sharply, relative to the yield on a bond with one year to maturity, manifesting an increased risk premium that investors required on longer-term investments. By 1936, bonds with five years to maturity had a yield that was *three times* that of a bond with one year to maturity. The yield multiple was more than four for a bond with ten years to maturity, five for a bond with twenty years to maturity, and more than five for a bond with thirty years to maturity. Between the first quarter of 1941 and the first quarter of 1942, however, these bond-yield spreads (risk premia) dropped precipitously, and by early 1943 they had returned to their 1934 levels (Higgs 2006a, 23–24). These bond-yield data show that investors' confidence in their ability to appropriate the longer-term interest payments and principal repayments promised by the country's most secure corporations plummeted between early 1934 and early

### Table 5.1  Selected Acts of Congress Substantially Attenuating or Threatening Private Property Rights, 1933–40

| Year | Congressional Acts |
|------|--------------------|
| 1933 | Agricultural Adjustment Act |
|      | National Industrial Recovery Act |
|      | Emergency Banking Relief Act |
|      | Banking Act of 1933 |
|      | Federal Securities Act |
|      | Tennessee Valley Authority Act |
|      | Gold Repeal Joint Resolution |
|      | Farm Credit Act |
|      | Emergency Railroad Transport. Act |
|      | Emergency Farm Mortgage Act |
|      | Home Owners Loan Corporation Act |
| 1934 | Securities Exchange Act |
|      | Gold Reserve Act |
|      | Communications Act |
|      | Railway Labor Act |
| 1935 | Bituminous Coal Stabilization Act |
|      | Connally ("Hot Oil") Act |
|      | Revenue Act of 1935 |
|      | National Labor Relations Act |
|      | Social Security Act |
|      | Public Utilities Holding Company Act |
|      | Banking Act of 1935 |
|      | Emergency Relief Appropriations Act |
|      | Farm Mortgage Moratorium Act |
| 1936 | Soil Conservation and Domestic Allotment Act |
|      | Federal Anti-Price Discrimination Act |
|      | Revenue Act of 1936 |
| 1937 | Bituminous Coal Act |
|      | Revenue Act of 1937 |
|      | National Housing Act |
|      | Enabling (Miller-Tydings) Act |
| 1938 | Agricultural Adjustment Act |
|      | Fair Labor Standards Act |
|      | Civil Aeronautics Act |
|      | Food, Drug, and Cosmetic Act |
| 1939 | Administrative Reorganization Act |
| 1940 | Investment Company Act |
|      | Revenue Act of 1940 |
|      | Second Revenue Act of 1940 |

1936, as the Second New Deal came into prominence. Confidence remained at an extremely low level from 1936 through the first quarter of 1941, after which it improved rapidly, despite the country's becoming a declared belligerent in the greatest war of all time. This evidence testifies to the terrifying effect the Second New Deal had on investors as well as to the stultifying effect it had on the recovery of private investment and therefore on the recovery of the entire economy, whose growth depended critically on such revitalized investment.

## FROM THE NEW DEAL TO ENGAGEMENT IN THE WAR

In 1937, the New Deal began to peter out, as the president alienated many people, even fellow Democrats, by his attempt to pack the Supreme Court and especially as the depression within the depression set in, canceling much of the previous four years' gain; the official rate of unemployment in 1938 was 19 percent. In Congress, disaffected southern Democrats and northern Republicans formed a "conservative coalition" powerful enough to block most attempts to enact new legislation along New Deal lines.

As the president's political prospects waned domestically, he turned his attention increasingly to the world scene, where a resumption of the war in Europe seemed imminent and, in September 1939, actually occurred. Notwithstanding proclaimed U.S. neutrality, the president immediately took sides with the British, and he worked assiduously, if deviously, for the next two years to maneuver the overwhelmingly reluctant American people into supporting U.S. engagement in the war against Germany. By conducting economic warfare against Japan, a German ally, the Roosevelt administration expected that these provocative actions might incite a Japanese attack and thereby open a "back door" to enter the war in Europe.[8]

The Roosevelt administration accordingly undertook to mobilize the economy for war. The U.S. armed forces were small and the country's munitions industries ill developed, though both were potentially very large. The buildup of the armed forces themselves accelerated after enactment of a conscription bill in September 1940. A substantial obstacle to the military-industrial buildup, however, took the form of businessmen's reluctance to enter into arms contracts with the government. After years of being browbeaten and vilified, many of them did not trust the government to treat them fairly and honestly. Hence, "private industry was, on the whole, profoundly reluctant to invest in new [war-related] plants" (Brinkley 1995, 182; for details, see Higgs 2006a, 36–38).

Having no good alternative to placating the suspicious businessmen—after all, New Deal lawyers and economists did not know how to produce steel, copper, aluminum, and the countless other products essential to the operation of the war machine—the administration proceeded to make its peace with them.

> Both the attitude and policies of the Roosevelt administration toward business during the New Deal years were reversed when the president found new, foreign enemies to engage his attention and energies. Antibusiness advisers were replaced by businessmen, pro-labor policies became pro-business policies, cooperation replaced confrontation in relations between the federal government and business.

> Probably no American president since, perhaps, Thomas Jefferson ever so thoroughly repudiated the early policies of his administration as Roosevelt did between 1939 and 1942. (Best 1991, 222)

In mid-1940, Henry Stimson, a lion of the northeastern Republican establishment, was made secretary of war, and publisher Frank Knox, who had been the Republican vice presidential candidate in 1936, was made secretary of the navy. (Note, however, that "[b]oth Stimson and Knox were eager and ardent supporters of Roosevelt's war policy" [Flynn (1948) 1949, 208].) A multitude of businessmen—more than ten thousand by mid-1942—often working without compensation or as dollar-a-year men, soon joined the ranks of the government's bureaucracy in preparing the economy for effective participation in the war (Brinkley 1995, 190). Several important laws were enacted or amended to shift the risks of building up the munitions industries from private investors to the taxpayers.[9]

This war-induced reconciliation between the government and the businessmen would eventually prove essential in making possible a resumption of economic prosperity, but such a resumption could not occur *during* the war because all efforts were turned in those years toward producing military goods and placing large, well-equipped armed forces in the theaters of war. New homes, new cars, new refrigerators, and even a decent men's dress shirt would have to wait.

## THE MYTH OF WARTIME PROSPERITY

The standard story, of course, is that the war itself brought back prosperity, that by 1941 or at the latest 1942 the Great Depression had ended. Although perhaps understandable—even at the time many people thought along these lines—this view is completely mistaken. It fails to appreciate that the economy during 1941 and 1942 became a command economy and that it continued to operate as such until the reconversion that began in the second half of 1945 and was not completed until, probably, early in 1947 or thereabouts. In a command economy, many standard economic concepts, such as gross domestic product (GDP), lose their meaning because they are no longer moored to the realities of voluntary choices within the competitive price system. Even "employment" and "unemployment" lose their usual meaning when the labor market operates under the cloud of massive conscription and extraordinary manpower controls.

Therefore, the most often cited evidence of wartime prosperity, the nearly complete disappearance of unemployment, does not signify "full employment" in the usual sense. In 1940, the unemployment rate (according to the Darby concept, which, unlike the official measure [14.6 percent in 1940], does not count those enrolled in government emergency employment programs as unemployed) was 9.5 percent. During the war, the government pulled the equivalent of 22 percent of the prewar labor force into the armed forces. Voilà, the unemployment rate dropped to less than 2 percent. This disappearance of unemployment reflected not, as Keynesians would have it, the beneficial effects of huge government budget deficits or, as monetarists would have it, the beneficial effects of huge increases in the stock of money. Instead, the disappearance of unemployment reflected overwhelmingly the direct and indirect effect of the gigantic military conscription: more than 10 million men were drafted, and many others were induced to join the armed forces before being drafted in hopes of avoiding service in the infantry. Throwing people into the army to cure unemployment is scarcely what we have in mind when we speak of creating prosperity.

It is true, of course, that measured GDP increased greatly during the war, which would seem to indicate economic recovery. However, when we break down the wartime increase in output, we see that it consists entirely of war goods and services; indeed, private consumption and investment declined after 1941 and did not regain their prewar levels until 1946. In short, the wartime "miracle of production" consisted entirely of guns and ammunition—hardly the stuff of genuine prosperity, unless B-17s, machine guns, aircraft carriers, and A-bombs epitomize the substance of the good life.[10]

In sum, although people were employed at a high rate (millions of them involuntarily) during the war and produced military goods and services galore, the war years were not a time of genuine economic prosperity. Many civilian goods, such as automobiles and important consumer durable goods, were not produced at all or were produced only in sharply reduced amounts owing to government prohibitions; and scores of ordinary nondurable goods, such as gasoline, tires, clothing, shoes, canned foods, and meats, were in short supply and subject to rationing. Every facet of economic life, from the speed limits on the highways to the availability of women's hosiery, was subject to extraordinary regulations and controls. We may say that the Depression continued from 1941 to 1945, or we may say that a different kind of economic privation occurred in those years. In no event, however, may we say that the war years were a time of genuine economic prosperity.

## THE GREAT ESCAPE

Having considered the Great Contraction and the Great Duration, we come now to the Great Escape, the end of a sixteen-year period of economic privation—twelve during the Depression proper and four during the war. In one great, glorious push in late 1945 and throughout 1946, the American people returned to something that deserves to be called normal prosperity, the kind they had enjoyed during the 1920s and earlier times. The ease and success of the economic reconversion deserve to be regarded as little short of miraculous, although, strange to say, economists and economic historians have scarcely paused to notice this astonishing event and even when they have taken notice of it, they have not understood it properly.

During the war, the newly ascendant Keynesian economists had feared that when the war ended and government spending diminished drastically, the economy would plunge back into depression (they did not, as I do, understand the war years themselves to be merely a different kind of depression). However, when the government cancelled the bulk of the munitions contracts, released more than 10 million servicemen from the armed forces, and eliminated most of the controls and regulations put in place during the war, mass unemployment did not develop. Indeed, despite the unprecedented rapid reallocation of resources, the unemployment rate rose only to 4 percent in 1947 and 1948. Moreover, as production for military purposes dropped to a much smaller amount, private output leaped upward, rising between 1945 and 1946 by 30 percent, a rate of increase never equaled before or since.

This nearly miraculous economic recovery, *which decisively refuted the Keynesian theory used then and later to explain the apparent economic boom during the war* (though hardly anybody took notice of that refutation), reflected in great part the substantial lessening of the regime uncertainty that had impeded recovery between 1935 and 1940. During the war, the most zealous New Dealers had been removed from the government or pushed onto the periphery of policymaking; "a massive shift of power [occurred] within the federal government away from liberal administrators and toward corporate interests" (Brinkley 1995, 118, see also 145). Dollar-a-year men and military officers had ruled the roost of the wartime command economy, directing all efforts toward feeding the war machine. By their influence in the upper reaches of the wartime bureaucracy and by their reestablished prestige in the eyes of the public, businessmen and investors had greatly diminished the threats they had perceived to private-property rights in the latter half of the 1930s. As Alan Brinkley has noted, "The wartime experience muted liberal hostility to capitalism and the corporate world" (1995, 7). In 1946, with Roosevelt dead, the New Deal in retreat, and most wartime controls eliminated or soon to be scrapped, investors came out in force. To be sure, the federal government had become and would remain a much more powerful force with which business would have to reckon. Nevertheless, the government no longer appeared to possess the terrifying potential that businesspeople had perceived before the war. For investors, the nightmare was over. For the economy, once more, real prosperity was possible.

## NOTES

1. Temin calls it "the Second Thirty Years' War" (1989, 10).
2. See the delightfully incomprehensible diagram of these financial flows reproduced in Eichengreen 1995, 225.
3. Hayek concluded: "The recognition of the insuperable limits to his knowledge ought indeed to teach the student of society a lesson in humility which should guard him against becoming an accomplice in men's fatal striving to control society—a striving which makes him not only a tyrant over his fellows, but which may well make him the destroyer of a civilization which no brain has designed but which has grown from the free efforts of millions of individuals" (1978, 34).
4. Flynn added that "[t]here is no evidence that Roosevelt ever put his finger on the real causes that make the free private enterprise system fail to work."
5. Hall and Ferguson write: "the uncertainty experienced by the business community as a result of the frequent tax law changes (1932, 1934, 1935, 1936) must have been enormous. Since firms' investment decisions very much depend on being able to plan, an increase in uncertainty tends to reduce investment expenditures" (1998, 147).
6. For contemporary testimony documenting the fear and uncertainty that Roosevelt's policies instilled in businessmen and investors, see Best 1991.
7. For presentation and analysis of this evidence in the context of a complete exposition of the "regime uncertainty" hypothesis, see Higgs 2006a, 3–29.

8. For massive documentation, see Barnes 1953. A brief account appears in Higgs 2006b.
9. For a full analysis of this development, see Higgs 2006a, 37–56.
10. For extensive documentation of the claims made in this section, see Higgs 2006a, 3–123.

## REFERENCES

Barnes, Harry Elmer, ed. 1953. *Perpetual War for Perpetual Peace: A Critical Examination of the Foreign Policy of Franklin Delano Roosevelt and Its Aftermath.* Caldwell, Idaho: Caxton Printers.

Best, Gary Dean. 1991. *Pride, Prejudice, and Politics: Roosevelt versus Recovery, 1933-1938.* New York: Praeger.

Brinkley, Alan. 1995. *The End of Reform: New Deal Liberalism in Recession and War.* New York: Knopf.

Chandler, Lester. 1970. *America's Greatest Depression, 1929–1941.* New York: Harper and Row.

Eichengreen, Barry. 1995. *Golden Fetters: The Gold Standard and the Great Depression, 1919–1939.* New York: Oxford University Press.

Flynn, John T. [1948] 1949. *The Roosevelt Myth.* Garden City, N.Y.: Garden City Books.

Friedman, Milton, and Anna Jacobson Schwartz. 1963. *A Monetary History of the United States, 1867–1960.* Princeton, N.J.: Princeton University Press.

Garraty, John A. 1973. The New Deal, National Socialism, and the Great Depression. *American Historical Review* 78 (October): 907–44.

Haberler, Gottfried. 1976. *The World Economy, Money, and the Great Depression, 1919–1939.* Foreign Affairs Study no. 30. Washington, D.C.: American Enterprise Institute for Public Policy Research.

Hall, Thomas E., and J. David Ferguson. 1998. *The Great Depression: An International Disaster of Perverse Economic Policies.* Ann Arbor: University of Michigan Press.

Hawley, Ellis W. 1966. *The New Deal and the Problem of Monopoly: A Study in Economic Ambivalence.* Princeton, N.J.: Princeton University Press.

Hayek, F. A. 1978. The Pretence of Knowledge. In *New Studies in Philosophy, Politics, Economics, and the History of Ideas,* 23–34. Chicago: University of Chicago Press.

Higgs, Robert. 1987. *Crisis and Leviathan: Critical Episodes in the Growth of American Government.* New York: Oxford University Press.

———. 2004. The Mythology of Roosevelt and the New Deal. In *Against Leviathan: Government Power and a Free Society,* 33–40. Oakland, Calif.: The Independent Institute.

———. 2006a. *Depression, War, and Cold War: Studies in Political Economy.* New York: Oxford University Press for The Independent Institute.

———. 2006b. How U.S. Economic Warfare Provoked Japan's Attack on Pearl Harbor. *The Freeman* 56 (May 2006): 36–37.

Keynes, John Maynard. 1920. *The Economic Consequences of the Peace.* New York: Harcourt, Brace and Howe.

Krooss, Herman E. 1970. *Executive Opinion: What Business Leaders Said and Thought on Economic Issues, 1920s–1960s.* Garden City, N.Y.: Doubleday.

Leuchtenburg, William E. 1964. The New Deal and the Analogue of War. In *Change and Continuity in Twentieth-Century America,* edited by John Braeman, Robert H. Bremner, and Everett Walters, 81–143. Columbus: Ohio State University Press.

Mann, Thomas. [1942] 1977. The Witches' Sabbath. In *Inflation,* by Michael Jefferson, Thomas Mann, Walt Rostow, and Andrew Dickson White. London: John Calder.

Powell, Jim. 2003. *FDR's Folly: How Roosevelt and His New Deal Prolonged the Great Depression.* New York: Crown Forum.

Rockoff, Hugh. 1998. By Way of Analogy: The Expansion of the Federal Government in the 1930s. In *The Defining Moment: The Great Depression and the American Economy in the Twentieth Century,* edited by Michael D. Bordo, Claudia Goldin, and Eugene N. White, 125–54. Chicago: University of Chicago Press.

Rothbard, Murray. 1972. Herbert Hoover and the Myth of Laissez-Faire. In *A New History of Leviathan: Essays on the Rise of the American Corporate State,* edited by Ronald Radosh and Murray N. Rothbard, 111–45. New York: E. P. Dutton.

———. 1998. The Gold-Exchange Standard in the Interwar Years. In *Money and the Nation State: The Financial Revolution, Government, and the World Monetary System,* edited by Kevin Dowd and Richard H. Timberlake, Jr., 105–65. New Brunswick, N.J.: Transaction.

———. 2000. *America's Great Depression.* 5th ed. Auburn, Ala.: Ludwig von Mises Institute.

Shaffer, Butler. 1997. *In Restraint of Trade: The Business Campaign Against Competition, 1918–1938.* Lewisburg, Penn.: Bucknell University Press.

Smiley, Gene. 2002. *Rethinking the Great Depression.* Chicago: Ivan R. Dee.

Temin, Peter. 1989. *Lessons from the Great Depression.* Cambridge, Mass.: MIT Press.

Timberlake, Richard H. 2007. Gold Standards and the Real Bills Doctrine in U.S. Monetary Policy. *The Independent Review* 11, no. 3 (winter): 325-54.

Vedder, Richard K., and Lowell E. Gallaway. 1997. *Out of Work: Unemployment and Government in Twentieth-Century America.* Updated ed. New York: New York University Press for The Independent Institute.

Acknowledgments: This chapter was originally prepared for a Durell Program colloquium at Hillsdale College, "The Role of Markets and Governments in Pursuing the Common Good," October 27–29, 2006. It is published here (in revised form) with the approval of Hillsdale College.

# 6

## The United States Won the World Wars, but Americans Lost

With fire and sword the country round
  Was wasted far and wide,
And many a childing mother then,
  And new-born baby died;
But things like that, you know, must be
  At every famous victory.
    —Robert Southey (1774–1843), "The Battle of Blenheim"

General Thomas Power, commander in chief of the Strategic Air Command (SAC) from 1957 to 1964 and director of the Joint Strategic Target Planning Staff from 1960 to 1964, ranked near the top of the U.S. armed forces waging the Cold War. An ardent warrior, he did not subscribe to the Aristotelian maxim of moderation in all things. In 1960, while being briefed on counterforce strategy, he reacted petulantly to the idea of exercising restraint in the conduct of nuclear war: "Restraint!" he retorted. "Why are you so concerned with saving *their* lives? The whole idea is to *kill* the bastards.... Look. At the end of the war, if there are two Americans and one Russian, we win!" (qtd. in Kaplan [1983] 1991, 246). Everyone who knew Power seems to have thought he was crazy.

Even the man he replaced as SAC commander, General Curtis LeMay, regarded him as unstable—and everybody knew that LeMay himself was, as *Dr. Strangelove*'s Group Captain Lionel Mandrake would have put it, "as mad as a bloody March hare." After LeMay left his command at SAC, he became vice chief of staff of the air force in 1957 and chief of staff in 1961. He is most often remembered as a tireless advocate of an all-out nuclear first strike on the Soviet Union and its allies and as the most likely inspiration for General Buck Turgidson in *Strangelove*. Either Power or LeMay might have served as a model for the

*Strangelove* character General Jack D. Ripper, whose own nuclear first strike on the Ruskies came straight out of the LeMay-Power playbook.

It is chilling to recall that such men once held—and may still hold—the fate of the world in their hot hands. In Power's day, heaven be thanked, the top civilian leaders had slightly more sense than the top military leaders, but in more recent times sensible civilian leaders have become almost nonexistent, and now men such as Dick Cheney, Donald Rumsfeld, and their zealous, bloodthirsty subordinates vividly attest to F. A. Hayek's observation that "the worst get on top" (1944, 134).

## WINNING

Whatever else one might say about our glorious leaders, one must admit that they have had, just as the current gang claims to have, a dedication to "winning" the wars they set out to fight. In his 2006 State of the Union address, President George W. Bush spoke repeatedly of "victory," especially in the ongoing "long war" that "we did nothing to invite" against terrorists who espouse "radical Islam." Undismayed by the fresh carnage and further devastation that each new day brings to the people of Iraq, the president assured his listeners that "[w]e're on the offensive in Iraq, with a clear plan for victory. . . . [W]e are in this fight to win, and we are winning."[1] Indeed, winning a war strikes most people as a splendid idea until they stop to think about it.

Given an option to fight and win a war à la Thomas Power, however, with just two Americans and one Russian (or Iraqi or Iranian or Chinese or other foreign devil du jour) left alive at the end, sane people recoil. Such winning seems all too clearly absurd. As we back away from this reductio ad absurdum to consider less extreme conceptions of "winning the war," a great deal of the senselessness continues to cling to the notion as long as we insist on an honest account of what actual war and winning involve.

The main reason for people's confusion on this account pertains to their reification or anthropomorphization of the collectives—the clans, tribes, nation-states, or coalitions of such groups—whose violent conflict defines the war. Lost in the fog of war-related thought is the concrete, unique, individual person. Hardly anyone seems capable of talking about war except by marshalling such collectivistic linguistic globs as *we, us,* and *our,* in opposition to *they, them,* and *their.* These flights of fight-fancy always pit our glob against their glob, with ours invariably prettied up as the good against the bad, the free men against the enslavers, the believers against the infidels, and so forth—on one side God's chosen, on the other side the demons of hell.[2]

Of course, which is which depends entirely on the side people happen to find themselves on, usually as a result of some morally irrelevant contingency, such as birthplace, family migration, or a line that distant diplomats once drew on a map (De Jasay 1998; Calhoun 2000). More than fifty years ago, sociologist George A. Lundberg observed that despite "the cavalier fashion in which 'statesmen' revise boundaries, abolish existing nations, and establish new ones,... the demarcations thus arrived at thereupon become sacred boundaries, the violation of which constitutes 'aggression,' an infringement on people's 'freedom'" (1953, 581). It is almost as if human beings clamored to slay one another on behalf of little more than historical accidents and persistent myths. French philosopher Ernest Renan aptly characterized a nation as "a group of people united by a mistaken view about the past and a hatred of their neighbors" (qtd. in Bronner 1999, 6).

A widespread inclination to think in terms of the group, rather than in terms of the distinct individuals who compose it, plays directly into the hands of violent, power-hungry leaders. Without that popular inclination, the leaders' capacity to wreak destruction would be reduced nearly to the vanishing point, but with it the sky's the limit—or maybe it's not the limit now that space-based weapons are all the rage in the military-industrial-congressional complex. Nothing promotes the sacrifice of the individual to the alleged "greater good of the whole" as much as war does. On this ground, government leaders successfully levy confiscatory taxes, impose harsh regulations, seize private property, and even enslave their own country's citizens to serve as soldiers and to kill or be killed in hideous ways.

Sometimes, as in the aftermath of World War I, people have the wit to recognize, with the benefit of hindsight, that the alleged "greater good" for which so many individuals' lives have been sacrificed and so many individuals' wealth and well-being have been squandered actually consists of little more than their leaders' foolishness and vanity. They finally grasp that they were told, as Wilfred Owen expressed it in a timeless poem, "the old lie: dulce et decorum est pro patria mori."[3]

On other occasions, however, people never come to that realization, preferring to live with a mythical justification for their losses. Even now, after more than sixty years have passed in which people have had ample opportunity to see through the official lies and cover-ups, the myth of World War II as "the good war" (in the United States) or "the Great Patriotic War" (in Russia) remains robust.

Bill Bonner has written recently that as we contemplate people's capacity for swallowing such myths, "we pause and we wonder":

> We take our man as we find him, but we cannot quite believe he is the dumb ox he appears to be. There were more than five million armed men at any given time in the Red Army. They could have turned on their incompetent and merciless leaders if they had wanted to. Instead, they lined up and marched to their own slaughter, many of them, perhaps the majority, believing that it would help make the world a better place.

> Even now ... they sit around shabby old soldiers' homes and congratulate themselves. They beat the fascists! They saved the Proletarian Revolution! Thus, they lived almost their entire lives under the heel of an even more delusional and murderous regime, but didn't seem to notice. (2006)

Their allies, the Americans, helped them directly and indirectly to preserve Stalin's regime, suffering more than a million casualties while effectively delivering a substantial share of humanity into the loving arms of Communist overlords not only in the USSR and eastern Europe, but also in China and its environs, where defeat of the Japanese Empire, which had served as a bulwark against communism in Asia, opened the doors to Mao Tse-tung's victory and to Communist takeovers in North Korea and southeast Asia. Notwithstanding these realities, Americans proudly identify their effort as "the good war" (Terkel 1984) and fancy that it was fought by "the greatest generation" (Brokaw 1998), secure in the conviction that simply because it brought down the Nazis in Germany, it must have made the whole world a better place.

Once memories of the War Between the States had faded, the mythologization of war came more easily to Americans because all our wars from the Spanish-American War on down to the current wars in Afghanistan and Iraq have been fought on other people's soil. As the poet Samuel Taylor Coleridge (1772–1834) expressed in "Fears in Solitude,"

> Secure from actual warfare, we have loved
> To swell the war-whoop, passionate for war!
> Alas! for ages ignorant of all
> Its ghastlier workings, (famine or blue plague,
> Battle, or siege, or flight through wintry snows,)

We, this whole people, have been clamorous
For war and bloodshed; animating sports,
The which we pay for as a thing to talk of,
Spectators and not combatants!

No American can recall in sorrow and bitterness the wartime devastation of Philadelphia or Chicago because it never happened; devastation is what Americans dispense to the residents of Tokyo or Dresden or Fallujah. In an immensely important sense, our wars have long seemed to be, in their worst aspect, somebody else's problem, something that happens "over there."

If Ambrose Bierce could observe a century ago that "war is God's way of teaching Americans geography," one shudders to imagine what he might say today.[4] Guadalcanal, Tarawa, Saipan, Peleliu, Iwo Jima, Okinawa—in 1940, probably not even one American in a hundred had ever heard of these remote places where tens of thousands of young American men and many more Japanese would soon lose their lives. Our good fortune in not having to fight wars on our own territory has been real and important, but it ought not to blind us to the great variety of genuine losses that we have sustained notwithstanding our capacity to make all our wars since 1865—apart from the sporadic clashes between whites and Indians—take the form of "foreign wars."

For one thing, many Americans have gone "over there" and done some definite dirty work. Let's be honest, war is always dirty work, no matter how hyped up we might get about its seeming necessity. In this regard, World War II, the so-called good war, might have been the dirtiest work of all. American forces abroad slaughtered not only multitudes of enemy soldiers, including prisoners and the wounded (Higgs 2006a), but also hundreds of thousands (maybe more) of noncombatants—men, women, and children, most notably in the terror bombing of German and Japanese cities.

Curtis LeMay had an important hand in this evil work, as commander of the B-29 forces that laid waste to scores of Japanese cities. Speaking of his flyers' devastation of Tokyo with incendiary bombs, LeMay declared: "We knew we were going to kill a lot of women and kids when we burned that town. Had to be done" (qtd. in Lindqvist 2000, 109). Oh, did it really? Brigadier General Bonner Fellers, an aide to General Douglas MacArthur, called the March 10, 1945, raid on Tokyo "one of the most ruthless and barbaric killings of noncombatants in all history" (qtd. in Sato 2002). As a result of the U.S. air attacks on Japanese cities, "civilian casualties exceeded 800,000, including 300,000 dead," by the end of July 1945, and more than 8 million people had been left homeless (Falk 1995, 1078). Unsated by this orgy of savagery, the Americans went on, completely unnecessarily, to annihilate scores of thousands of hapless Hiroshima and Nagasaski residents with atomic bombs.[5]

These events were not losses for the Germans and the Japanese only. The men who carried out these barbarous acts also sacrificed their decency and a vital part of their humanity. War brings many of its participants to such tragic ends. Only a deranged man can live complacently with the knowledge that he has committed such heinous acts. To a greater or lesser degree, however, every war encompasses an enormous mass of such indecencies. Soldiers may excuse themselves on the ground that they are "just following orders" or, if they are especially naive, that they are acting heroically in defense of all that is good and great about their own country. Kept in combat long enough, however, nearly everyone who is not a natural-born killer becomes either psychologically disabled or absolutely cynical in a single-minded quest to survive (Grossman 1996, 43–50).

Government leaders and their blindly nationalistic followers invariably tolerate and even glorify many of the bestialities perpetrated during warfare and elevate the perpetrators to the status of heroes, but these ignoble rituals of apotheosis ring hollow when placed alongside the raw realities of the conduct of warfare and its typical outcomes. Looking back on fifteen years of warfare and its aftermath, William Henry Chamberlin wrote, "It was absurd to believe that barbarous means would lead to civilized ends" (1953, 519).[6] It is no less absurd today.

In the past century in the United States, the two world wars required the greatest degree of mobilization and therefore entailed the heaviest losses for individuals both on the battlefield and on the home front, notwithstanding that this country is said to have "won" both wars.

## WORLD WAR I

Although American casualties in the Great War did not loom large in comparison with those of the other major belligerents, they must have seemed more significant to each of the 116,516 men who died as a result of their service and to their wives and sweethearts, mothers and fathers, sisters and brothers, among others. In addition, 204,002 men sustained nonmortal wounds, and an undetermined number had their minds rearranged for the worse—"shell shock" was the common name for battle-induced psychic derangements in that war (casualty data from U.S. Bureau of the Census 1975, 1140). All these individuals, vaguely denominated "casualties" in military parlance, paid the heaviest price, but many other Americans—in some respects, all Americans—also bore substantial costs.

World War I changed the character of the American political economy for the worse in ways too numerous to describe fully here. Before the war, federal revenues had never exceeded $762 million in a fiscal year; during the 1920s they were never less than $3,640 million annually. Before the war, federal expenditures had exceeded $747 million in a fiscal year only twice, in 1864 and 1865; during the 1920s they were never less than $2,857 million annually. Although part of the increase in the volume of fiscal activities reflected price inflation, which in itself was the product of the government's war finance, the bulk of it was real. The public debt ballooned from slightly more than $1 billion before the war to more than $25 billion at its end. Income tax rates were pushed up enormously during the war, and although they were reduced somewhat in the 1920s, they never again receded to the prewar level or even close to it.[7]

Many aspects of "wartime socialism" left enduring legacies. The War Food Administration became the model for the New Deal's agriculture program, which, despite countless changes to and fro during the subsequent decades, continues to plague consumers and taxpayers today. The Railroad Administration gave way to a virtual nationalization of the railroad industry in 1920. The Shipping Board inaugurated the government's involvement in and regulation of the ocean shipping industry, which have continued ever since 1916. After the war, the War Finance Corporation continued to operate until 1925, came back to life as the Reconstruction Finance Corporation in 1932, and ultimately transmogrified into the Small Business Administration in 1953, misallocating resources by means of its extensions of subsidized credit and other interventions. The War Industries Board roared back to life in 1933 as the disastrous National Recovery Administration, which unsettled the entire economy at the depths of the Great Depression with a muddleheaded program to cartelize every industry in the country, thereby making a mighty contribution to prolonging the Depression. Although the Supreme Court struck down this loony experiment in 1935, the National Recovery Administration then fragmented into a variety of interventionist components, such as the National Labor Relations Board, that have persisted for decades.

Space here does not permit me to continue this doleful recitation. Suffice it to say that the war's consequences in fostering freedom-squashing, prosperity-destroying federal interventions in the economy have no equal in U.S. history. People typically think that this sort of government policy began for the most part in the 1930s, but almost everything the New Dealers did along these lines amounted to the revival of a precedent set in World War I.

The war's constitutional legacies also took big bites out of American liberties. In virtually every case, the Supreme Court upheld the extraordinary powers that the government had exercised during the war. Highly significant was the blessing the Court gave to military conscription. Chief Justice Edward White could not take seriously the idea that the draft constituted involuntary servitude and was therefore proscribed by the Thirteenth Amendment. He declared that the Court was "unable to conceive upon what theory the exaction by government from the citizen of the performance of his supreme and noble duty of contributing to the defense of the rights and honor of the nation, as the result of a war declared by the great representative body of the people, can be said to be the imposition of involuntary servitude" (*Arver v. United States,* 245 U.S. 366 [1918] at 390).

While the Court was smashing individual liberty under the iron heel of "the great representative body of the people"—the same gang that Mark Twain had described more accurately as "America's only native criminal class"—the justices did not hesitate to give their approval to the government's rampant wartime assaults on the freedoms of speech, press, and assembly, many of these outrages being the offspring of the Espionage Act (1917) and its notorious amendment the Sedition Act (1918). The justices also validated the government's wartime takeovers of the railroads, telephone and telegraph lines, and oceanic cables. They sustained wartime rent controls. Everything, so far as the Court was concerned, was fair game. Said the chief justice, "[T]he complete and undivided character of the war power of the United States is not disputable" (*Northern Pacific Railway v. State of North Dakota,* 250 U.S. 135 [1919] at 149).

In later times, Franklin D. Roosevelt and other presidents would boldly seek, gain, and exercise quasi-wartime powers triggered solely by their declaration of a national emergency, even when the country was not at war, thereby cloaking their crimes with a mantle of pseudolegal legitimacy. Owing to the consolidation of the various war-spawned assaults on liberty, now codified in the National Emergencies Act (1976) and the International Emergency Economic Powers Act (1977), nearly all economic liberties in this country exist at the sufferance of the president. If he decides to take over the economy, he possesses ample statutory power to do so.

Perhaps equally disastrous in their implications for the future were the war's ideological legacies. Because wartime economic-management schemes did not have much time to operate during the short U.S. engagement as an active belligerent, they could not reveal fully how badly they were working. When the war ended, their managers, not surprisingly, announced that the programs had been splendid successes, critically important in equipping the Allies to defeat the Hun. Bernard M. Baruch, the chairman of the War Industries Board and a wealthy gray eminence for a large stable of Democratic politicians, did much to promote this myth and to attain its incorporation into received wisdom. Moreover, the hordes of businessmen who had played roles in the government's wartime economic planning emerged from the experience with, as a contemporary writer described it, "a sort of intellectual contempt [for] the huge hit-and-miss confusion of peace-time industry ... [and with] dreams of an ordered economic world" (Clarkson 1923, 312). In other words, they came away from the war with a bad case of what F. A. Hayek (1989) famously called "the fatal conceit," the fallacious idea that central planners can produce a better social outcome than can the free market. These same misguided men would reappear in later crises to perpetrate additional assaults on liberty.

## WORLD WAR II

The Big One took a far greater human toll on Americans than had the previous world war. The 405,399 deaths loomed largest, for the deceased themselves and for all those who knew and cared about them as individuals. The number of seriously wounded amounted to 670,846, many of them suffering total disability for life (casualty data from U.S. Bureau of the Census 1975, 1140).

Approximately 25–30 percent of the casualties were psychological cases—victims of "combat fatigue," as it was dubbed this time around. In the fighting at Okinawa, for example, American mental casualties accumulated to 26,221 out of the total of 65,641 dead and wounded (Adams 1994, 95). In the entire war, more than a million men "suffered psychiatric symptoms serious enough to debilitate them for some period" (Roeder 1993, 16), and "by V-J Day, 504,000 Americans soldiers, enough for 50 divisions, had been lost to emotional collapse" (Shapiro 1998). Some were psychologically disturbed for life. Others, seemingly having gone back to normal, endured mental tics and phobias for the rest of their lives, often treating their conditions with copious doses of alcohol or narcotics. Approximately 75,000 men were listed as missing in action. Most of them, says historian Michael Adams, "had been blown into vapor" (1994, 105).

So repulsive were the sights, sounds, and smells of actual combat that the government heavily censored what the folks at home were permitted to see or hear of them. If many of the soldiers, sailors, and airmen ultimately came home and appeared fairly normal, chances are that they were among the great majority who, though serving in the armed forces, never got very close to harm's way or stayed there for long—laborers, clerks, technicians, mechanics, trainers, supply troops, and millions of others who constituted the big "tail" behind the relatively small fighting "tooth." A minority of the men, most prominently the infantrymen and in a different way the bomber crews over Europe, bore the brunt of the sustained horror and paid the most awful price. Recognizing their position as sacrificial lambs, condemned to remain at terrible risk until they were killed or seriously wounded, or until the war ended, the infantrymen came to despise their numerous comrades who stayed safely behind the lines as well as the people who remained back home in a regular job.

On the home front, with World War I already in the books, the men who ran the political economy during World War II could not do much that was genuinely original, but they did almost everything on a vastly greater scale. The Wilson administration had built up military and naval forces of some 4 million men, including 2.7 million draftees, by the end of 1918. Roosevelt and his lieutenants commanded more than 12 million in 1945 and during the course of the war drafted some 10 million of the 16 million who served at some point. In prosecuting the war, the government spent approximately ten times more than it had spent on World War I, and it imposed much more comprehensive and longer-lasting economic controls.[8]

Federal outlays increased from $9.5 billion in fiscal year 1940 to $92.7 billion in fiscal year 1945, at which time they amounted to almost 44 percent of officially measured gross national product (GNP). To get the wherewithal for this huge gush of spending, the government proceeded, as it had during 1917 and 1918, to impose new taxes, to increase the rates of existing taxes, and to lower the income thresholds above which people were required to pay income taxes. Annual excise tax revenue more than tripled between 1940 and 1945. Employment tax revenue more than doubled. The major sources of increased tax revenue, however, were individual and corporate income taxes. The latter zoomed from $1.0 billion in 1940 to $16.4 billion in 1945, the greater part of that sum representing an "excess-profits" tax, and the former jumped from $1.1 billion to more than $18.4 billion. Before the war, fewer than 15 million individuals had to file an income tax return; in 1945, approximately 50 million had to do so. Not only did most income earners have to pay, but they also had to pay at much higher rates: the bottom bracket rose from 4.4 percent on income in excess of $4,000 in 1940, to 23 percent on income in excess of $2,000 in 1945. The top rate became virtually confiscatory: 94 percent on income in excess of $200,000. In one mighty wartime push, the government had completed the transformation of the income tax from a "class tax" to a "mass tax," which it would remain ever afterward. Moreover, payroll withholding of income taxes, which the government imposed midway through the war, also remained an essential component of the great federal revenue-reaping machine. Notwithstanding the stupendous increase in taxation, the government's tax revenues amounted to less than half of its outlays, and it had to borrow the rest (with essential assistance from Federal Reserve System officials, who conducted monetary policies so as to place a floor under government bond prices and hence a ceiling on interest rates). As a result, the national debt swelled from $54 billion in 1940 to $260 billion in 1945.

Entire volumes would be required just to summarize all the economic controls the government imposed: price, wage, and rent controls; materials allocations; shutdown orders, some of which applied to entire industries (e.g., civilian automobile production, gold mining); employment controls; allocations of transportation services; rationing of many consumer goods (e.g., shoes, clothing, meats, fats, canned goods, gasoline, tires); consumer credit controls; and countless others.

Vastly more outrageous than any economic control was the forced relocation of more than 110,000 persons of Japanese ancestry, two-thirds of them U.S. citizens, who were herded at gunpoint from their homes in the coastal regions of California, Oregon, and Washington into camps in desolate areas of the West, surrounded by barbed wire and guarded by armed troops. Although not one of these people received due process of law, the Supreme Court, dominated at that time by justices who saw no limits to FDR's war powers, could find nothing unconstitutional in the government's actions.

Nor could the justices bring themselves to strike down any of the government's arbitrary and capricious economic regulations. Of course, with the precedent of World War I decisions in its hip pocket, the Court had no interest in hearing constitutional challenges to military conscription. This judicial stance was more than convenient for the government because, as Justice Hugo Black wrote, employing the logic that would guide the Court throughout the war, "Congress can draft men for battle service. Its power to draft business organization to support the fighting men who risk their lives can be no less" (*United States v. Bethlehem Steel Corp.*, 315 U.S. 289 [1942] at 305). As presidential powers rose to unprecedented heights, Roosevelt's appointees on the Court nodded approvingly.

Perhaps even more consequential than the war's constitutional legacies were its effects on the country's dominant ideology. As World War I had done, only more so, the Big One produced a prominent move toward acquiescence in and often affirmative demand for collectivism. Not only did the masses now look more expectantly to the federal government for salvation from life's troubles, large and small, but the leadership of the business class also came finally to make a complete peace with the government it had long seen as a nuisance and a menace. The war brought not only countless regulations and demands for reports in octuplicate to the government's control agencies, but also a deluge of government contracts, the fulfillment of which earned the typical contractor extraordinary profits with little or no risk (Higgs 2006b, 54). Thousands of leading businessmen had served in the government as dollar-a-year men. From this experience they took away not so much a lesson in the ponderous irrationalities of government bureaucratic action as an appreciation that government can provide a bottomless reservoir of subsidies, cozy deals, and other benefits. The experience, wrote Calvin Hoover, "conditioned them to accept a degree of governmental intervention and control after the war which they had deeply resented prior to it" (1959, 212). In short, the war had broken them to the yoke, either coercing them or co-opting them to comply with the government's schemes—indeed, holding out the prospect that they might have a hand in guiding those schemes if they behaved themselves. The old business-class hostility toward government eventually faded into a pale semblance of its former self. As Herbert Stein commented in the 1980s, after having observed the process at close quarters for nearly half a century, businessmen "had learned to live with and accept most of the regulations." Disturbed only by new and unfamiliar regulations, "they regard the regulations they are used to as being freedom" (1984, 84).

## WAR IS THE MOTHER OF TYRANNY

Stein's comment, which might aptly be applied far more generally, captures the essence of how the American people transformed their society from one in which, circa 1910, people enjoyed a great many freedoms to one in which, circa 1950, they had lost many of their former freedoms, perhaps irretrievably. Nothing propelled that process more powerfully than the two world wars—along with the New Deal, of course, but that crisis response itself involved little more than the revitalization, expansion, and elaboration of measures first taken during World War I and so must be understood as causally linked to the nation's participation in that war. The upshot in all cases is that whenever the government went to war, whether the war was real or metaphorical, it went to war against the liberties of its own citizens.

Of course, it invariably justified these assaults on liberty by characterizing them as necessary and merely temporary means of preserving the people's liberties in the longer run—in General George C. Marshall's words, making "sacrifices today in order that we may enjoy security and peace tomorrow" (qtd. in Neumann 1953, 549).[9] The claim was either a mistake or a lie, however, because the U.S. government did not need to go to war, not even in the world wars, to preserve its people's essential liberties and their way of life. Neither Kaiser Wilhelm's forces nor Hitler's—and certainly not Japan's—had the capacity to deprive Americans of their liberties, to "take over the country," to "destroy our way of life," or to do anything of the sort. This country has always contained persecuted minorities, and it still does, but since 1789 the only government on earth that has had the power to crush the American people's liberties across the board has been the government of the United States.

U.S. participation in World War I was the classic instance of self-interested elites' whipping up a war and a megalomaniacal president's carrying it into effect. As Walter Karp (1979) and other historians have shown, the upper-crust, Anglophile, northeastern movers and shakers—leading figures in what Murray Rothbard dubbed the Morgan ambit—maneuvered the psychically twisted, would-be world saver Woodrow Wilson into seeking U.S. entry into the war. Wilson, in turn, on completely spurious grounds, stampeded the overwhelmingly opposed populace into the war against their better judgment. Once war had been declared, the government used a combination of relentless propaganda and Draconian coercive measures to beat down active opponents and to stir up a generalized frenzy of chauvinism—One Hundred Percent Americanism, as its devotees called it.

Within a few years, most people came back to their senses, but by then the harm had been done. U.S. participation in the war brought about many inauspicious, irreversible, politicoeconomic developments within the United States. More important, it contributed decisively to the creation of a worldwide complex of interrelated ethnic, political, and economic disequilibria whose resolution would entail many of the great horrors of the following century, including World War II, communism's geopolitical triumphs, the Cold War, and endless troubles in the Middle East (Fromkin 1989; Fleming 2003; Powell 2005). So visible were the war's poisonous fruits that soon after it ended, most Americans vowed they would never take part in such an idiotic and destructive escapade again. Unfortunately, within a generation they permitted themselves to be lured into an even more horrific charnel house.

Roosevelt idolaters and the jingoes of all parties have always maintained that the United States went to war altruistically to save the Jews of Europe from the monster Hitler and to stop Japan's horrible aggression in East Asia, especially in China. A fair reading of the evidence supports neither claim.

As for the European Jews, the U.S. government did not go to war to save them; once in the war, it did not conduct its military operations in a manner designed to save them, and, most important, it did not actually save them. Approximately 80 percent of them were killed (Holocaust historian Raul Hilberg's estimate cited in Russett 1972, 42).

The U.S. government can claim some credit for stopping Japan's aggression against the Chinese, of course, owing to its defeat and occupation of Japan, even though the same result might well have been achieved by peaceful means: "in the year before Pearl Harbor the Japanese were willing to abandon their expansionist program if they could be provided some face-saving formula, but this the United States persistently refused to grant" (Chamberlin 1953, 516). In any event, however, one must bear in mind what came next. With Japan no longer acting as a powerful counterforce to the Chinese and Russian Communists in East Asia, the North Koreans and the Chinese soon fell victim to Communist totalitarianism—a far worse fate than integration into Japan's Greater East Asia Co-Prosperity Sphere would have been.

As for the idea that Japan launched an unprovoked "sneak attack" on the United States and thereby "started the war," I can only say that anyone who believes this simplistic contention needs to learn more about the Roosevelt administration's actions in the years leading up to the Japanese attack. Long before the bombs and torpedoes rained down on the Pacific fleet conveniently concentrated at Pearl Harbor, the United States had become an active, if undeclared, belligerent against Germany, cooperating closely with and providing vital supplies to the British, the French (until late June 1940), and the Soviets (after late June 1941).

Moreover, the Roosevelt administration had imposed a series of increasingly stringent economic and financial sanctions on Japan, culminating in joint U.S.-British-Dutch economic embargoes that placed a strangle hold on the natural-resource-deficient Japanese economy. Finally, the U.S. government presented an unnecessary and completely unacceptable ultimatum that "called for complete Japanese withdrawal from China and Indochina, for Japan to support only the Nationalist government of China, with which it had been in conflict for four years, and to interpret its pledges under the Tripartite [Germany, Italy, and Japan] Pact and the [Cordell] Hull program so that Japan would be bound to peace in the Pacific and to noninterference in Europe, while the

United States should be free to intervene in Europe" (Morgenstern 1953, 346). By these measures, among many others, the U.S. government provoked (and, having broken the Japanese diplomatic and naval communication codes, knew full well that it was provoking) the desperate Japanese to attack U.S.-controlled islands in the Pacific as well as the Asian colonies of Roosevelt's European co-conspirators in these hostile actions.[10]

Whether the U.S. government's publicly pronounced rationales for entering the wars should be viewed as self-serving falsehoods or as mere mistakes, however, the ultimate outcome of waging the wars was the same. As William Graham Sumner wisely wrote, "It is not possible to experiment with a society and just drop the experiment whenever we choose. The experiment enters into the life of the society and never can be got out again" (1934, 2:473). Thus, although the wars eventually ended, society never reverted to the status quo ante bellum. Every year, on Veterans Day, orators declare that our leaders have gone to war to preserve our freedoms and have done so with glorious success, but the truth is just the opposite. In ways big and small, direct and indirect, crude and subtle, war—the quintessential government activity—has been the mother's milk for the nourishment of a growing tyranny in this country, and it remains so today.

## NOTES

1. Speech is available at http://www.whitehouse.gov/news/releases/2006/01/20060131-10.html.
2. Vice President Henry A. Wallace, characterizing World War II as "a fight between a free world and a slave world," declared: "We shall cleanse the plague spot of Europe, which is Hitler's Germany, and with it the hellhole of Asia—Japan. No compromise with Satan is possible." One ought to bear in mind, however, that Wallace also said, "The object of this war is to make sure that everybody in the world has the privilege of drinking a quart of milk a day" (qtd. in Chamberlin 1953, 498–99). Similarly, the Ayatollah Khomeini declared: "If one allows the infidels to continue playing their role of corrupters on Earth, their eventual moral punishment will be all the stronger.... To allow the infidels to stay alive means to let them do more corrupting.... War is a blessing for the world and for every nation. It is Allah himself who commands men to wage war and kill" (qtd. in Katz 2006).
3. Wilfred Owen, "Dulce et Decorum Est," written 1917, published posthumously in 1921. Available at http://www.warpoetry.co.uk/owen1.html.
4. Bierce quotation available at http://en.wikiquote.org/wiki/Ambrose_Bierce.
5. For a thorough debunking of claims for the military necessity of dropping the atomic bombs, see Raico 2001, 577–86.
6. Strange to say, Chamberlin later became a fanatical Cold Warrior (see Raimondo 2000, 75–76).

7. Factual information about World War I given in this paragraph and the remainder of the section are drawn from Higgs 1987, 123–58, and the sources given there, and from Higgs 2005 and the sources given there.

8. Factual information about World War II given in this paragraph and the remainder of the section are drawn from Higgs 1987, 196–236, and the sources given there, and from Higgs 2005 and the sources given there.

9. On the occasion of this particular remark, Marshall was speaking specifically in support of the European Recovery Program, which became known as the Marshall Plan, but the spirit of his statement animated the justifications advanced for all of the government's assaults on the people's liberties.

10. Historians agree that U.S. cryptographers had indeed already solved the Japanese diplomatic code. For extensive evidence that they had also solved the Japanese naval code well before the attack on Pearl Harbor, see Stinnett 2000.

## REFERENCES

Adams, Michael C. C. 1994. *The Best War Ever: America and World War II.* Baltimore: Johns Hopkins University Press.

Bonner, Bill. 2006. Ivan's War. February 11. Available at: http://www.lewrockwell.com/bonner/bonner196.html.

Brokaw, Tom. 1998. *The Greatest Generation.* New York: Random House.

Bronner, Ethan. 1999. Israel: The Revised Edition. *New York Times Book Review,* November 14.

Calhoun, Laurie. 2000. Just War? Moral Soldiers? *The Independent Review* 4, no. 3 (winter 2000): 325–45.

Chamberlin, William Henry. 1953. The Bankruptcy of a Policy. In *Perpetual War for Perpetual Peace: A Critical Examination of the Foreign Policy of Franklin Delano Roosevelt and Its Aftermath,* edited by Harry Elmer Barnes, 483–554. Caldwell, Idaho: Caxton Printers.

Clarkson, Grosvenor B. 1923. *Industrial America in the World War: The Strategy behind the Lines, 1917–1918.* Boston: Houghton Mifflin.

De Jasay, Anthony. 1998. Is National Rational? *The Independent Review* 3, no. 1 (summer 1998): 77–89.

Falk, Stanley L. 1995. Strategic Air Offensives. In *The Oxford Companion to World War II,* edited by I. C. B. Dear and M. R. D. Foot, 1066–79. New York: Oxford University Press.

Fleming, Thomas. 2003. *The Illusion of Victory: America in World War I.* New York: Basic Books.

Fromkin, David. 1989. *A Peace to End All Peace: Creating the Modern Middle East, 1914–1922.* New York: Henry Holt.

Grossman, Dave. 1996. *On Killing: The Psychological Cost of Learning to Kill in War and Society.* Boston: Little, Brown.

Hayek, F. A. 1944. *The Road to Serfdom.* Chicago: University of Chicago Press.

———. 1989. *The Fatal Conceit: The Errors of Socialism.* Chicago: University of Chicago Press.

Higgs, Robert. 1987. *Crisis and Leviathan: Critical Episodes in the Growth of American Government.* New York: Oxford University Press.

———. 2005. *Government and the Economy: The World Wars.* Independent Institute Working Paper no. 59. Oakland, Calif.: Independent Institute. Available at: http://www.independent.org/pdf/working_papers/59_government.pdf.

———. 2006a. Atrocities in the "Good War": A Tract for Today. June 19. Available at: http://www.lewrockwell.com/higgs/higgs45.html.

———. 2006b. *Depression, War, and Cold War: Studies in Political Economy.* New York: Oxford University Press for The Independent Institute.

Hoover, Calvin B. 1959. *The Economy, Liberty, and the State.* New York: Twentieth Century Fund.

Kaplan, Fred. [1983] 1991. *The Wizards of Armageddon.* Stanford, Calif.: Stanford University Press.

Karp, Walter. 1979. *The Politics of War: The Story of Two Wars Which Altered Forever the Political Life of the American Republic (1890–1920).* New York: Harper and Row.

Katz, Ira. 2006. A Simple Solution. February 11. Available at: http://www.lewrockwell.com/katz/katz15.html.

Lindqvist, Sven. 2000. *A History of Bombing.* Translated by Linda Haverty Rugg. New York: New Press.

Lundberg, George A. 1953. American Foreign Policy in the Light of National Interest at the Mid-century. In *Perpetual War for Perpetual Peace: A Critical Examination of the Foreign Policy of Franklin Delano Roosevelt and Its Aftermath,* edited by Harry Elmer Barnes, 555–625. Caldwell, Idaho: Caxton Printers.

Morgenstern, George. 1953. The Actual Road to Pearl Harbor. In *Perpetual War for Perpetual Peace: A Critical Examination of the Foreign Policy of Franklin Delano Roosevelt and Its Aftermath,* edited by Harry Elmer Barnes, 315–406. Caldwell, Idaho: Caxton Printers.

Neumann, William L. 1953. Postscript: Some Notes for Future Historians on the Truman Foreign Policies. In *Perpetual War for Perpetual Peace: A Critical Examination of the Foreign Policy of Franklin Delano Roosevelt and Its Aftermath,* edited by Harry Elmer Barnes, 542–54. Caldwell, Idaho: Caxton Printers.

Powell, Jim. 2005. *Wilson's War: How Woodrow Wilson's Great Blunder Led to Hitler, Lenin, Stalin, and World War II.* New York: Crown Forum.

Raico, Ralph. 2001. Harry S. Truman: Advancing the Revolution. In *Reassessing the Presidency: The Rise of the Executive State and the Decline of Freedom,* edited by John V. Denson, 547–86. Auburn, Ala.: Ludwig von Mises Institute.

Raimondo, Justin. 2000. *An Enemy of the State: The Life of Murray N. Rothbard.* Amherst, N.Y.: Prometheus Books.

Roeder, George H., Jr. 1993. *The Censored War: American Visual Experience during World War Two.* New Haven, Conn.: Yale University Press.

Russett, Bruce M. 1972. *No Clear and Present Danger: A Skeptical View of the U.S. Entry into World War II.* New York: Harper Torchbooks.

Sato, Hiroaki. 2002. Great Tokyo Air Raid Was a War Crime. *Japan Times,* September 30.

Shapiro, Bruce. 1998. Lugging the Guts into the Next Room. *Salon,* July 30. Available at http://www.salon.com/media/1998/07/30media.html.

Stein, Herbert. 1984. *Presidential Economics: The Making of Economic Policy from Roosevelt to Reagan and Beyond.* New York: Simon and Schuster.

Stinnett, Robert B. 2000. *Day of Deceit: The Truth about FDR and Pearl Harbor.* New York: Free Press.

Sumner, William Graham. 1934. *Essays of William Graham Sumner.* Edited by Albert G. Keller and Maurice R. Davie. New Haven, Conn.: Yale University Press.

Terkel, Studs. 1984. *The Good War: An Oral History of World War II.* New York: New Press.

U.S. Bureau of the Census. 1975. *Historical Statistics of the United States, Colonial Times to 1970.* Washington, D.C.: U.S. Government Printing Office.

Acknowledgments: Thanks to Michael Moore (no, not *that* Michael Moore, but the former editor of the *Bulletin of the Atomic Scientists*) for helping me track down the original source of the quotation from Thomas Power and to editor Stephen Cox for permission to reuse material that appeared first in my article in the April 2006 issue of *Liberty* magazine.

# 7

## Government and the Economy in the United States Since World War II

When World War II ended in the late summer of 1945, the United States entered a new era in its economic and political history. During the preceding sixteen years, the American people had endured twelve years of economic depression, then four years of wartime economic privation and regimentation. Those sixteen years had composed a seemingly endless era of national emergency, to which governments at all levels, but most strikingly at the federal level, had responded in unprecedented ways. Consequently, as the postwar era began, the size, scope, and power of governments in the United States greatly exceeded their magnitudes in the "good old days" before the onset on the Depression. Although some emergency measures had already been terminated or soon would be, many persisted, sometimes under a new name or lodged in a different agency. In countless ways, an era of permanent Big Government had arrived.

Nowhere was the role of government magnified more than in international affairs. The United States had traditionally pursued a relatively modest foreign policy, complying for the most part with Washington and Jefferson's advice to steer clear of entangling alliances and especially of the endless quarrels among the great European powers. The United States had gained overseas colonies during the Spanish-American War and then fought a brutal war against Filipino insurgents, and Woodrow Wilson's intervention in World War I had constituted a highly significant deviation from the country's traditional foreign policy. Nevertheless, on the eve of World War II the great majority of Americans favored a policy of neutrality, peaceful commerce with all nations, and avoidance of military interventions abroad. Engagement in the war, however, shattered the old convictions and arrangements irreparably.

The United States emerged from World War II as the world's richest and most militarily powerful country, and its leaders immediately decided to follow a long-term policy of global military engagement in pursuit of perceived "national security." In 1947, President Harry S Truman declared what would become known as the Truman Doctrine, an open-ended pledge to assist virtually any government threatened by Communists, whether from within or without. To secure the U.S. position in Europe, the U.S. government devised the Marshall Plan and entered into the North Atlantic Treaty, the first formal U.S. alliance since the one with France during the American Revolution. In 1948 the Berlin crisis; in 1949 the Communist victory in China, the Soviet nuclear test, and the establishment of the North Atlantic Treaty Organization (NATO); and in 1950 the outbreak of the Korean War—all tipped the balance permanently in favor of a policy of active global containment and deterrence of the USSR. Henceforth, for the next four decades, there would be no distinct peacetime and wartime, but instead a continuing Cold War punctuated by episodes of all–too–hot conflict in Korea, in Vietnam, and, on a smaller scale, in many other places. The end of the Cold War did nothing to alter the broad contours of U.S. foreign policy, which continued to favor global interventionism and, most recently, has been broadened even further by the concept of preventive war and the commitment to a "global war on terror," accompanied by U.S. invasions and occupations of Afghanistan and Iraq and much saber rattling against those who are "not with us" (Higgs 2005b). Maintenance of the postwar warfare state has had tremendous repercussions on all aspects of American life—economic, political, social, and cultural (Sherry 1995; Leebaert 2002).

The postwar U.S. government, paralleling its vastly enlarged tasks as an international power wielder, inherited from the New Deal and the wartime command economy a panoply of greatly expanded activities at home, especially in managing the domestic economy. Formalizing acceptance of its newly embraced role as permanent economic overseer, the government enacted the Employment Act of 1946, which declared "that it is the continuing policy and responsibility of the Federal Government to use all practicable means ... to promote maximum employment, production, and purchasing power" ("Employment Act of 1946," 514–15). Thus did the federal government undertake as a permanent policy the prevention of macroeconomic malfunctions such as the Great Depression. Henceforth, "doing something" would be official policy, although the precise nature of the "something" would vary with political circumstances and calculations. The chosen action would often entail spending huge sums of money, which the government would obtain by continuing to operate the "mass tax" system created to secure funds during the war (Higgs 1987, 229–31; Twight 2002, 87–131) and by resorting to chronic borrowing of enormous amounts.

In the postwar era, the Constitution no longer served as it once had to constrain the public's hunger for the redistribution of income and wealth or the politicians' ambitions for power. As constitutional scholar Edward S. Corwin wrote, the country for the first time in U.S. history did not return to a "peacetime Constitution" after the war. The Supreme Court's decisions during the war had embedded even deeper in the U.S. system of government the revolutionary changes first validated during the late 1930s. Corwin noted that the Court's wartime pronouncements brought into greater prominence all of the following:

> (1) the attribution to Congress of a legislative power of indefinite scope; (2) the attribution to the President of the power and duty to stimulate constantly the positive exercise of this indefinite power for enlarged social objectives; (3) the right of Congress to delegate its powers *ad libitum* to the President for the achievement of such enlarged social objectives...; (4) the attribution to the President of a broad prerogative in the meeting of "emergencies" defined by himself and in the creation of executive agencies to assist him; (5) a progressively expanding replacement of the judicial process by the administrative process in the enforcement of the law—sometimes even of constitutional law. (1947, 179).

Thus, in the postwar era, the traditional system of constitutional checks and balances served far less to restrain the growth of government than it had during the first century and a half of U.S. history.

These constitutional changes reflected dramatic ideological changes brought about during the period of recurrent national emergencies (1914–45). Amid the storms of two world wars and a deep, lengthy depression, long-standing beliefs in individual responsibility and free markets had lost much ground. In their stead, people had embraced a faith in the government's capacity to provide security, not only against foreign threats but also against workaday economic hazards, such as unemployment or low earnings during the working-age years and insufficient income during old age. With the passage of time, Americans would look to government for more and more sorts of security—protection from the risk of workplace accidents, from race or sex discrimination, from the adverse side effects of drugs, from environmental pollution, and so on (see Twight 2002; and for many details and intelligent discussion of the dominant, security-obsessed ideology of the postwar era, see McClosky and Zaller 1984, Page and Shapiro 1992).

With the public clamoring for governmentally guaranteed security in all areas of life and with neither the dominant ideology nor the Constitution serving to constrain the growth of government, the political system opened wide to all those capable of organizing to express their special-interest demands. More and more previously unorganized groups formed political organizations, movements, and coalitions. Eventually almost every cause or group, except individual taxpayers and consumers in general, had a voice in the state capitals and Washington, D.C., demanding largess, subsidies, privileges, insurance coverage, bailouts, protections from competition, and other favors. Legislators were happy to trade such favors for votes; politicians who declined to do so lost out in the political competition to those who would. This system of interest-group liberalism—known also as social democracy, democratic socialism, or participatory fascism—naturally fostered a continuous growth of government in many different dimensions.

## THE WARFARE STATE

From 1950 to the late 1960s, the dominant Cold War ideology and a bipartisan consensus on defense and foreign policy, focused on global containment of communism and deterrence of a Soviet attack on the United States or its allies, gave nearly unchallenged support to the unprecedented allocation of resources to the "peacetime" military establishment (Neu 1987, 91–92, 100–101; Rockman 1987, 18, 28–29).[1] Though weakened under the strains of the Vietnam War controversy and its political aftermath, both the ideology and the consensus persisted, but was now subject to considerable fraternal squabbling, notably in Congress (Ambrose 1985, 221–22 and passim). President Ronald Reagan's rhetorical hostility toward the Soviet Union's "evil empire" and the hawkish posture of his administration, especially during the first term, gave renewed luster to the tarnished Cold War ideology and preserved its vitality until the USSR left the scene.

The ideological climate was important, indeed essential, in maintaining high levels of resource allocation for defense, but it was not sufficient. Ordinary citizens, almost none of whom had any direct contact with Communists menacing the United States, easily came to suspect that maintaining the nation's security did not require such vast expenditures and that military interests, especially the uniformed services and the big weapons contractors, were using bogus threats as a pretext for siphoning off the taxpayers' money. Frequent newspaper and television reports of waste, fraud, mismanagement, and bribery fostered the public's tendency, absent a crisis, to doubt what the defense authorities said. The underlying Cold War ideology, however, created the potential for political leaders periodically to arouse the public's slumbering apprehensions.

Episodic crises offset the tendency of the background threat to lose its potency in sustaining public support for high levels of military spending. Some crises delivered themselves—for example, when the North Koreans crossed the thirty-eighth parallel in 1950 and when the Soviets invaded Afghanistan at the end of 1979—but ordinarily world events did not present such clear-cut cases, and the national-security managers had to take matters into their own hands.

Accordingly, the authorities alerted the public to a series of ominous "gaps" (Weiner 1990, 19–45). Just after World War II, U.S. leaders exaggerated Soviet force levels and offensive capabilities (Kolodziej 1966, 77). Then came a bomber gap in the mid-1950s and a missile gap between 1958 and 1961, followed within a few years by an antimissile gap and a first-strike missile gap. All were revealed in due course to have been false alarms. Meanwhile, the American people received an almost wholly fictitious account of an incident in the Gulf of Tonkin in 1964, after which Congress gave its blessing to what soon became a major war (Page and Shapiro 1992, 227–28). Subsequent gaps were alleged with regard to bombers (again), thermonuclear megatonnage, antisubmarine capabilities, and missile throw weights. An influential group of Republican hawks, calling themselves the Committee on the Present Danger, declared the 1970s to have been a "decade of neglect" that opened a dangerous "window of vulnerability." According to Secretary of Defense Caspar Weinberger, an "enormous gap" had "emerged since 1970 between the level of Soviet defense activities and our own," though fortunately the Reagan administration was "manag[ing] to close much of this gap" (1987, 17). Economist Franklyn D. Holzman has argued that the alleged defense spending gap of the 1970s was illusory, the product of faulty methods of estimation whose adoption represented a "deliberate attempt [by the Central Intelligence Agency, the Defense Intelligence Agency, and possibly the administration] to mislead our policy makers and the public" (1992, 34). Still, as the Cold War passed through its twilight years, government officials warned that the country faced a Star Wars gap that could be closed only by spending vast amounts of money.

Although not every gap scare led directly to a corresponding U.S. response, the drumbeat succession of such episodes helped to sustain an atmosphere of tension and insecurity that fostered the maintenance of an enormous ongoing arms program. Claims about gaps placed the burden of argument on relatively ill-informed opponents of military spending who were already vulnerable to charges of insufficiently robust patriotism or even worse transgressions. During the Cold War, the government adopted a rigorous cult of secrecy. Although some secrecy served a legitimate military purpose, much of it merely protected U.S. policy makers from the public whose interest they ostensibly served. As one analyst observed, "[W]hat no one knows, no one can criticize" (Sapolsky 1987, 122). When the government released information, it did so in a way that served its own interests and embarrassed its critics (Page and Shapiro 1992, 172–284, 367–72).

When the national-security elite lacked persuasive strategic rationales to present to the public, they could only draw on the pool of patriotism, but that pool was not a bottomless reservoir, and without replenishment in a form that the public could imbibe, it tended to run dry. As the balance of public opinion became strongly negative, that dissatisfaction worked its way through political processes, reaching both Congress and the administration, to affect the allocation of resources to the military establishment (Higgs and Kilduff 1993). Such negative feedback occurred strongly during the latter stages of both the Korean War and the Vietnam War. The drawn out, inconclusive character of the U.S. occupation of Afghanistan and especially of Iraq has elicited a typical decay of public support for continuation of these ill-fated adventures, but the George W. Bush administration has chosen so far (as of December 2006) to pronounce that all will be well if only the American people will "stay the course" (Higgs 2006b).

The biggest problem for the defense authorities has arisen from that inevitable duo, death and taxes—the most evident manifestations of the costs of extensive commitments of resources to military purposes. Of the two, death is the more important. John Mueller fitted statistical models to public-opinion data gathered during the Korean War and the Vietnam War and found that in both cases "every time American casualties increased by a factor of 10, support for the war dropped by about 15 percentage points" in the polls (1973, 60–61). R. B. Smith reported public-opinion data showing that "complaints about taxes were high during the two limited wars and increased as the wars progressed" (1971, 250). Discontent with U.S. engagement in the Asian wars fostered Dwight D. Eisenhower's electoral victory in 1952 and led to Lyndon B. Johnson's decision not to seek reelection in 1968.

Immediately after World War II, military spending fell sharply: in inflation-adjusted dollars, it dropped by nearly 90 percent between fiscal years 1945 and 1948, after which it rebounded substantially, rising by almost 50 percent during the next two years as the Truman administration sought to rebuild the military establishment in order to back up its foreign policy of resisting and containing the USSR and its satellites on a global scale (see table 7.1). A far greater change occurred, however, after the outbreak of the Korean War: real defense outlays jumped by 220 percent between fiscal years 1950 and 1953. The bulk of that increase, though, went not to fight the war in Korea, but to strengthen overall U.S. forces and to deploy many of them around the world, especially in western Europe and Japan. Although military spending shrank somewhat after the 1953 armistice in Korea, it remained thereafter much greater—by some 200 percent—than during the late 1940s.

Atop the permanent Cold War plateau of military spending, three distinct upsurges came and went. During the early years of the twenty-first century, a fourth upsurge began whose peak, at the time of this writing, remains impossible to forecast, although the real dollar increase of nearly 50 percent during the five years from fiscal 2001 to 2006 approaches the Carter-Reagan increase of nearly 60 percent during the eleven fiscal years from 1978 to 1989. The upsurge of the early 1950s was the biggest in either percentage terms or relative to the size of the federal budget or the overall economy (see table 7.1). The Vietnam War brought about an upsurge of 44 percent between fiscal years 1965 and 1968. After each upsurge, spending fell back toward or even slightly below the level of the Cold War plateau. In fiscal year 2001, a decade after the breakup of the USSR, however, real military outlays were as great as they had been during the height of the Cold War in the late 1950s and early 1960s, even though the United States no longer had any current or potential military rival in sight (Higgs 2001). U.S. invasions of Afghanistan in 2001 and Iraq in 2003, followed by military occupation and ongoing combat operations against resistance forces in those countries, have fostered greatly increased arms spending. Owing to the upsurge after 2001, real national defense outlays in fiscal year 2007 will exceed those of any other year since World War II.

The immense military spending during the sixty years after World War II has fostered the operation of a new politicoeconomic arrangement, which assumed its modern form during the early 1940s (see Higgs 1993), the military-industrial-congressional complex. Before leaving the presidency in 1961, Dwight D. Eisenhower warned in his farewell speech to the American people against "the military-industrial complex," which he characterized as the "conjunction of an immense military establishment and a large arms industry" and whose influence, he feared, posed dangers to "our liberties or democratic processes" (Eisenhower [1961] 1973, 653). Beginning in the 1960s and gaining impetus during the 1970s and 1980s, congressional involvement in the details of the operations of this complex grew ever greater, as members of Congress sought to turn military-industrial funding and operations to their own political advantage

## Table 7.1 National Defense Outlays, Fiscal Years 1945–2006

| Fiscal Year | National Defense Outlays (Billions of FY 2000 Dollars) | Percent of Federal Budget | Percent of All Net Government Budgets | Percent of GDP |
|---|---|---|---|---|
| 1945 | 775 | 89.5 | 82.1 | 37.5 |
| 1946 | 406 | 77.3 | 65.2 | 19.2 |
| 1947 | 113 | 37.1 | 27.3 | 5.5 |
| 1948 | 87 | 30.6 | 19.9 | 3.5 |
| 1949 | 124 | 33.9 | 23.0 | 4.8 |
| 1950 | 130 | 32.2 | 21.8 | 5.0 |
| 1951 | 212 | 51.8 | 34.8 | 7.4 |
| 1952 | 397 | 68.1 | 50.5 | 13.2 |
| 1953 | 416 | 69.4 | 52.2 | 14.2 |
| 1954 | 382 | 69.5 | 50.0 | 13.1 |
| 1955 | 320 | 62.4 | 43.2 | 10.8 |
| 1056 | 298 | 60.2 | 41.0 | 10.0 |
| 1957 | 304 | 59.3 | 40.2 | 10.1 |
| 1958 | 300 | 56.8 | 38.3 | 10.2 |
| 1959 | 298 | 53.2 | 36.4 | 10.0 |
| 1960 | 300 | 52.2 | 35.1 | 9.3 |
| 1961 | 302 | 50.8 | 33.8 | 9.4 |
| 1962 | 316 | 49.0 | 32.9 | 9.2 |
| 1963 | 309 | 48.0 | 32.0 | 8.9 |
| 1964 | 315 | 46.2 | 30.8 | 8.5 |
| 1965 | 292 | 42.8 | 27.8 | 7.4 |
| 1966 | 323 | 43.2 | 28.4 | 7.7 |
| 1967 | 383 | 45.4 | 30.3 | 8.8 |
| 1968 | 420 | 46.0 | 31.3 | 9.4 |
| 1969 | 400 | 44.9 | 29.4 | 8.7 |
| 1970 | 375 | 41.8 | 27.0 | 8.1 |

| Fiscal Year | National Defense Outlays (Billions of FY 2000 Dollars) | Percent of Federal Budget | Percent of All Net Government Budgets | Percent of GDP |
|---|---|---|---|---|
| 1971 | 341 | 37.5 | 23.7 | 7.3 |
| 1972 | 310 | 34.3 | 21.7 | 6.7 |
| 1973 | 279 | 31.2 | 19.9 | 5.8 |
| 1974 | 267 | 29.5 | 18.7 | 5.5 |
| 1975 | 263 | 26.0 | 16.9 | 5.5 |
| 1976 | 253 | 24.1 | 15.7 | 5.2 |
| 1977 | 251 | 23.8 | 15.8 | 4.9 |
| 1978 | 251 | 22.8 | 15.4 | 4.7 |
| 1979 | 257 | 23.1 | 15.5 | 4.6 |
| 1980 | 267 | 22.7 | 15.4 | 4.9 |
| 1981 | 282 | 23.2 | 15.9 | 5.1 |
| 1982 | 307 | 24.8 | 16.9 | 5.7 |
| 1983 | 331 | 26.0 | 17.8 | 6.1 |
| 1984 | 334 | 26.7 | 18.1 | 5.9 |
| 1985 | 357 | 26.7 | 18.1 | 6.1 |
| 1986 | 381 | 27.6 | 18.4 | 6.2 |
| 1987 | 387 | 28.1 | 18.2 | 6.1 |
| 1988 | 393 | 27.3 | 17.6 | 5.8 |
| 1989 | 399 | 26.5 | 17.0 | 5.6 |
| 1990 | 383 | 23.9 | 15.3 | 5.2 |
| 1991 | 334 | 20.6 | 13.2 | 4.6 |
| 1992 | 354 | 21.6 | 13.7 | 4.8 |
| 1993 | 340 | 20.7 | 13.0 | 4.4 |
| 1994 | 323 | 19.3 | 12.1 | 4.0 |
| 1995 | 306 | 17.9 | 11.1 | 3.7 |
| 1996 | 289 | 17.0 | 10.5 | 3.5 |
| 1997 | 288 | 16.9 | 10.3 | 3.3 |
| 1998 | 283 | 16.2 | 9.9 | 3.1 |
| 1999 | 284 | 16.2 | 9.7 | 3.0 |
| 2000 | 295 | 16.5 | 9.8 | 3.0 |

| Fiscal Year | National Defense Outlays (Billions of FY 2000 Dollars) | Percent of Federal Budget | Percent of All Net Government Budgets | Percent of GDP |
|---|---|---|---|---|
| 2001 | 298 | 16.4 | 9.6 | 3.0 |
| 2002 | 329 | 17.3 | 10.3 | 3.4 |
| 2003 | 365 | 18.7 | 11.3 | 3.7 |
| 2004 | 397 | 19.9 | 12.0 | 3.9 |
| 2005 | 420 | 20.0 | 12.2 | 4.0 |
| 2006 | 443 | 19.8 | 12.3 | 4.1 |

SOURCE: U.S. Department of Defense, Office of the Under Secretary of Defense (Comptroller) 2006, 206–7, 216–17

(Higgs 1989, 31)—hence the congressional component of the military-industrial-congressional complex.

Besides funding gigantic military-industrial operations, the government also funded for military purposes a huge part of the most advanced scientific and technological research and development in the postwar United States, which led Eisenhower to warn also against the "danger that public policy could itself become the captive of a scientific-technological elite" (Eisenhower [1961] 1973, 654; for data and an astute analysis, see Butos and McQuade 2006). To some extent, all of Eisenhower's fears proved justified, although historians and other observers continue to debate the extent to which, and the precise manner in which, the nation's permanent military mobilization shaped its social, political, technological, and economic institutions and conduct (Sherry 1995; Friedberg 2000; Leebaert 2002; Higgs 2006a). No one can deny, however, the vast repercussions of such militarily motivated enactments as the Interstate Highway Act of 1956, which provided the basic plan for building the National System of Interstate and Defense Highways (Patterson 1996, 274), and the National Defense Education Act of 1958, which gave the federal government another big foot in the door of higher education (Twight 2002, 143–54)—both following hard on the heel of the first big foot, the GI Bill of 1944, itself a consequence of mass militarization.

Of all the government's military measures, none loomed larger in its effect on the American people's personal liberties than the military draft, a system of compulsory service employed during both world wars and extended repeatedly during the Cold War until the Nixon administration sponsored its ultimate abandonment in 1973. Over the years, millions of young men suffered involuntary induction into the military services, usually the army, and millions of others lived in fear that they might be snared and so often took otherwise undesirable actions to reduce their risk of conscription, such as relocation to foreign countries or extended enrollment in college or seminary. Hundreds of thousands of draftees lost their lives in the U.S. wars of the twentieth century. Although in most respects the government has grown more powerful and intrusive during the postwar era, the abolition of the draft constitutes a tremendous advance of liberty.

## THE WELFARE STATE

Despite the widespread belief that prior to the New Deal the United States had a brutal laissez-faire economy, the roots of the modern welfare state stretch far back in American history.[2] Local governments always provided a modicum of relief for the destitute who had no one to help them. After the War Between the States, the federal government extended its veterans' pension system to cover hundreds of thousands of former Union soldiers and their dependents. In the early twentieth century, the states adopted workmen's compensation systems to insure workers against workplace injuries (Fishback and Kantor 2000), and almost all states paid stipends to impoverished widows with young children.

These "mother's pensions" merged into Aid to Dependent Children (later called Aid to Families with Dependent Children, or simply "welfare") when the Social Security Act became law in 1935. That landmark federal statute also provided government assistance to the blind and the aged poor; state administered unemployment insurance (subject to federal requirements); and old-age and (after a 1939 amendment) survivors pensions. So, by the beginning of the postwar era, the United States already had a fairly well-developed welfare state, although at that time it served relatively few beneficiaries and cost relatively little—not until 1960 did annual Social Security payments exceed $10 billion (see table 7.2). During the 1950s, 1960s, and 1970s, members of Congress turned Social Security into a fabulous vote-buying scheme, repeatedly raising the amounts of existing benefits, expanding the types of benefits (for example, adding disability insurance in 1956), and easing the eligibility requirements for receiving benefits. In addition, minimum wages and prescribed working conditions, first provided by permanent federal law in 1938, fleshed out the postwar welfare state. Much more important, the GI Bill enacted in 1944 provided a variety of benefits—including educational stipends and loan guarantees for the purchase of homes, farms, and businesses—to millions of World War II veterans and set an irresistible precedent for Congress.

The first fifteen years of the postwar era brought relatively few new welfare-state measures, as the country seemed content for the most part to digest the many legacies of the New Deal and the war, but with the succession of the ambitious New Dealer Lyndon B. Johnson to the presidency in late 1963, the drive to expand the welfare state became prominent again. The election of 1964 brought into office a large, extraordinarily statist Democratic majority in Congress. Keynesian economists assured the public that they could fine-tune the economy, taking for granted a high rate of economic growth from which the government could reap a perpetual "fiscal dividend" to fund new programs. John Kenneth Galbraith, Michael Harrington, and other popular social critics condemned the failures of the market system and ridiculed its defenders. The public seemed prepared to support new measures to fight the "War on Poverty," establish "social justice," and end racial discrimination—thus making a move toward the Great Society (Matusow 1984; Higgs 1987, 246–51).

Congress loosed a legislative flood by passing the Civil Rights Act of 1964. Among other things, this landmark statute set aside long-established rights of private property and of free association in an attempt to quash racial discrimination. The ideal of a color-blind society died an early death, however, succeeded within a few years by "affirmative action," an array of official preferences for members of designated racial and sex categories enforced by an energetic Equal Employment Opportunity Commission and sympathetic federal judges (Glazer 1975; Sowell 1984, 38–42). Eventually the antidiscrimination laws seriously threatened even the basic rights of free speech, a free press, and the practice of religion long guaranteed by the First Amendment (Bernstein 2003). In the same spirit, the government also enacted the Equal Pay Act in 1963, ostensibly guaranteeing women equal pay for equal work, and the Age Discrimination in Employment Act in 1967, making a similar guarantee to older workers.

Congress proceeded to pass a variety of statutes that injected the federal government more deeply into education, job training, housing, and urban redevelopment. The Food Stamp Act of 1964 gave rise to one of the government's most rapidly growing benefit programs: in 1969, fewer than 3 million persons received the stamps, and federal outlays for the program totaled $250 million; in 1981, 22 million persons received the stamps, and federal outlays for the program totaled $11 billion (Browning and Browning 1983, 128). The Community Action Program aimed to mobilize the poor and to raise their incomes. When Congress appropriated $300 million to create community action agencies, a wild scramble to get the money ensued, led by local politicians and, in some cities, by criminal gangs—as vividly portrayed in Tom Wolfe's tragicomic tale

## Table 7.2 Government Expenditures, Total and Selected Components, Fiscal Years 1948–2005 (billions of current dollars)

| Fiscal Year | Total Govt | Defense and International | Federal Payments to Individuals | | State and Local from Own Sources (except net interest) |
| --- | --- | --- | --- | --- | --- |
| | | | Social Security and Medicare | Other | |
| 1948 | 44.0 | 13.7 | 0.5 | 8.5 | 14.0 |
| 1949 | 55.5 | 19.2 | 0.6 | 9.5 | 16.5 |
| 1950 | 62.0 | 18.4 | 0.7 | 12.9 | 19.2 |
| 1951 | 66.4 | 27.2 | 1.5 | 8.8 | 20.7 |
| 1952 | 90.1 | 48.8 | 2.0 | 8.9 | 22.2 |
| 1953 | 99.7 | 54.9 | 2.6 | 8.3 | 23.3 |
| 1954 | 96.7 | 50.9 | 3.3 | 9.3 | 25.5 |
| 1955 | 97.6 | 45.0 | 4.3 | 10.0 | 28.7 |
| 1956 | 102.2 | 44.9 | 5.4 | 9.8 | 31.1 |
| 1957 | 111.4 | 48.6 | 6.5 | 10.5 | 34.2 |
| 1958 | 120.8 | 50.2 | 8.0 | 12.9 | 37.7 |
| 1959 | 134.0 | 52.2 | 9.5 | 13.2 | 41.0 |
| 1960 | 135.8 | 51.1 | 11.4 | 12.8 | 42.6 |
| 1961 | 145.1 | 52.8 | 12.2 | 15.3 | 46.4 |
| 1962 | 157.9 | 58.0 | 14.0 | 14.9 | 49.8 |
| 1963 | 165.7 | 58.7 | 15.5 | 15.5 | 53.1 |
| 1964 | 177.7 | 59.7 | 16.2 | 16.0 | 57.7 |
| 1965 | 181.9 | 55.9 | 17.1 | 16.0 | 62.3 |
| 1966 | 204.2 | 63.7 | 20.3 | 16.8 | 68.3 |
| 1967 | 234.2 | 77.0 | 24.5 | 18.7 | 75.5 |
| 1968 | 263.5 | 87.2 | 28.4 | 21.4 | 83.9 |
| 1969 | 279.7 | 87.1 | 33.0 | 24.2 | 94.9 |
| 1970 | 298.3 | 86.0 | 36.4 | 28.4 | 101.0 |
| 1971 | 325.4 | 83.0 | 42.6 | 38.0 | 113.8 |

| Fiscal Year | Total Govt | Defense and International | Federal Payments to Individuals | | State and Local from Own Sources (except net interest) |
|---|---|---|---|---|---|
| | | | Social Security and Medicare | Other | |
| 1972 | 354.1 | 84.0 | 47.7 | 45.3 | 121.0 |
| 1973 | 376.2 | 80.8 | 57.2 | 47.5 | 128.2 |
| 1974 | 416.5 | 85.1 | 65.7 | 54.7 | 146.0 |
| 1975 | 499.9 | 93.6 | 77.7 | 76.2 | 166.8 |
| 1976 | 556.8 | 96.1 | 89.6 | 91.0 | 182.6 |
| 1977 | 607.5 | 103.6 | 104.5 | 92.5 | 194.7 |
| 1978 | 670.6 | 112.0 | 116.7 | 95.0 | 209.7 |
| 1979 | 738.4 | 123.8 | 130.8 | 103.1 | 234.6 |
| | | | | | |
| 1980 | 853.5 | 146.7 | 151.0 | 127.5 | 265.6 |
| 1981 | 963.8 | 170.6 | 179.1 | 146.1 | 290.9 |
| 1982 | 1058.0 | 197.6 | 203.1 | 155.3 | 318.4 |
| 1983 | 1145.9 | 221.8 | 224.0 | 172.9 | 342.5 |
| 1984 | 1215.6 | 243.3 | 237.0 | 164.8 | 368.8 |
| 1985 | 1347.4 | 268.9 | 256.1 | 171.9 | 409.7 |
| 1986 | 1429.3 | 287.5 | 270.7 | 181.2 | 452.5 |
| 1987 | 1486.6 | 293.6 | 285.0 | 186.9 | 491.2 |
| 1988 | 1582.2 | 300.8 | 302.5 | 199.0 | 524.1 |
| 1989 | 1699.4 | 313.1 | 324.4 | 212.8 | 562.9 |
| | | | | | |
| 1990 | 1862.1 | 313.1 | 353.8 | 231.8 | 615.6 |
| 1991 | 1984.0 | 289.1 | 380.7 | 271.2 | 662.3 |
| 1992 | 2082.9 | 314.5 | 414.3 | 315.3 | 699.6 |
| 1993 | 2137.4 | 308.3 | 444.8 | 340.0 | 724.1 |
| 1994 | 2220.7 | 298.7 | 476.2 | 348.4 | 754.5 |
| 1995 | 2318.3 | 288.5 | 510.1 | 367.1 | 800.5 |
| 1996 | 2319.0 | 279.2 | 538.1 | 374.5 | 829.6 |
| 1997 | 2475.5 | 285.7 | 569.4 | 384.2 | 874.0 |
| 1998 | 2558.7 | 281.6 | 586.2 | 395.3 | 906.7 |
| 1999 | 2672.1 | 290.1 | 595.2 | 406.2 | 973.1 |

| Fiscal Year | Total Govt | Defense and International | Federal Payments to Individuals | | State and Local from Own Sources (except net interest) |
|---|---|---|---|---|---|
| | | | Social Security and Medicare | Other | |
| 2000 | 2834.0 | 311.7 | 621.0 | 433.2 | 1049.8 |
| 2001 | 2986.9 | 321.4 | 666.1 | 462.0 | 1121.4 |
| 2002 | 3209.9 | 370.9 | 704.6 | 536.6 | 1184.8 |
| 2003 | 3410.5 | 426.1 | 743.3 | 588.1 | 1230.1 |
| 2004 | 3589.5 | 482.8 | 787.2 | 609.8 | 1274.9 |

SOURCE: U.S. Office of Management and Budget 2006, 314.

*Mau-Mauing the Flak Catchers* (1970). In 1965, misrepresenting its efforts as part of the War on Poverty, Congress effected a huge and enduring federal intrusion into basic public education—traditionally a local government matter—by enacting the Elementary and Secondary Education Act (see Twight 2002, 154–64).

In 1965, Congress added Medicare to the Social Security system, insuring medical care for everyone older than sixty-five years of age. Simultaneously, Medicaid, a cooperatively administered and financed (state and federal) program, assured medical care for welfare recipients and the medically indigent. These programs were not exactly what they were represented to be. "Most of the government's medical payments on behalf of the poor compensated doctors and hospitals for services once rendered free of charge or at reduced prices," historian Allen Matusow has observed. "Medicare-Medicaid, then, primarily transferred income from middle-class taxpayers to middle-class health-care professions" (1984, 231–32).

The federal government's health programs also turned out to be fiscal time bombs. Between 1970 and 2005, Medicare outlays (excluding premiums paid by beneficiaries) increased from $7.1 billion to $336.9 billion and federal Medicaid outlays from $2.7 billion to $181.7 billion. Like Social Security's old-age pensions, federal health programs grew at a rate that could not be sustained indefinitely. All federal health programs together consumed 7.1 percent of total federal outlays (equivalent to 1.4 percent of gross domestic product [GDP]) in 1970 and 24.7 percent of total federal outlays (equivalent to 5.0 percent of GDP) in 2005 (U.S. Office of Management and Budget 2006, 317). Yet in the face of that rapid growth and undeterred by massive federal deficits stretching as far as the eye could see, Congress and President George W. Bush added in 2003 an enormously expensive prescription-drug benefit to the Medicare system, a benefit whose cost is certain to exceed even the already huge projected amounts before long.

Other Great Society measures to protect people from their own incompetence or folly included the Cigarette Labeling and Advertising Act of 1965, the Fair Packaging and Labeling Act of 1966, the Child Protection Act of 1966, the National Traffic and Motor Vehicle Safety Act of 1966, the Flammable Fabrics Act of 1967, and the Consumer Credit Protection (Truth-in-Lending) Act of 1968.

After Richard Nixon became president, highly significant measures continued to pour forth from the federal government, expanding the welfare state even further. In this category belong such statutes as the Occupational Safety and Health Act of 1970, the Consumer Product Safety Act of 1972, the Equal Employment Opportunity Act of 1972, and the Employee Retirement Income Security Act of 1974. (Many other new laws, greatly expanding the reach of federal regulations, are mentioned in the next section.)

Although the growth of the scope of the welfare state slowed after the mid-1970s, it did not stop, and the Reagan administration certainly did not reverse it, as conservative Republican legend maintains. More recent statutes along these lines include the Nutrition Labeling and Education Act of 1990, the Americans with Disabilities Act of 1990, and the Civil Rights Act of 1991, among many others. In any event, the existing welfare state has taken on such vast dimensions that even if no new programs were added, the growing cost of the existing programs cannot be sustained over the long term. Before long, something will have to give.

In the mid-1940s, Bertrand de Jouvenel wrote, "The essential psychological characteristic of our age is the predominance of fear over self-confidence.... Everyone of every class tries to rest his individual existence on the bosom of the state and tends to regard the state as the universal provider." This protection, however, costs the public far more than the high taxes required to fund its provision: "if the state is to guarantee to a man what the consequences of his actions shall be, it must take control of his activities ... to keep him out of the way of risks" ([1945] 1993, 388–89). Just as de Jouvenel foresaw, after World War II the demand for government protection in the United States rose to new heights, while the corresponding loss of individual liberties proceeded apace.

## REGULATIONS AND SUBSIDIES

Ever since the establishment of the British colonies in North America, governments here have regulated or subsidized certain economic and social activities in various ways and to various degrees, the details differing from place to place and changing from time to time. In the nineteenth century, nearly all such regulation and subsidization took place at state and local levels, and governments at those levels have continued to involve themselves actively right up to the present day. Only in the late nineteenth century did the federal government begin to intervene in important, enduring ways (aside from the de facto subsidies associated with tariff protection and sometimes with military procurement). Thereafter, during "normal" times the federal government gradually added to the scope of its interventions. Moreover, each great crisis of the first half of the twentieth century—the two world wars and the Great Depression—became yet another occasion for abrupt government expansion and intervention. As a result, by the beginning of the postwar era, federal regulators had entrenched themselves in agriculture and food processing; banking and finance; corporate and industrial organization and trade practices; airline, railroad, and highway transportation; telecommunications and radio broadcasting; oil and gas production and distribution; electricity transmission; coal mining; maritime shipping; labor-management relations; pharmaceutical innovation and marketing; international trade and finance; and many other areas of economic life. One might have thought that the scope of regulation and subsidization in the late 1940s was more than sufficient in what was still described (incorrectly) as capitalism or a market economy, but evidently the politically potent actors thought otherwise because despite a few significant reversals (most of them in the late 1970s and early 1980s), the scope of regulation and subsidization continued to grow during the following half-century. Anyone who believes that the current U.S. economic system is accurately described by the term *capitalism* or *market system* needs to take a closer look at the current *Code of Federal Regulations*.

After the Korean War began, the federal government reinstituted many of the same sorts of economic controls it had imposed during World War II—controls over industrial production, wages, prices, credit, shipping, and the allocation of raw materials—but this time the controls did not bind as tightly, apply as comprehensively, or last as long as before. Most of them were permitted to lapse when the war ended in 1953 or even before it ended (Williams 1954, 64–66; Higgs 1987, 244–46), although some, such as the Defense Production Act of 1950, remained on the statute books as a framework for future mobilizations (and to facilitate continued subsidies to selected defense contractors).

During the decade coinciding with the presidential terms of Dwight D. Eisenhower and John F. Kennedy, the United States enjoyed a respite from the imposition of significant new federal regulations of economic activities. The next decade, however, coinciding with the presidential terms of Lyndon B.

Johnson and Richard M. Nixon, brought forth a deluge of new regulations comparable only to the flood during the heyday of Franklin D. Roosevelt's New Deal. Certain elements of this outpouring—new regulations aimed at stopping discrimination based on race, sex, age, or disability and at protecting consumers and workers—have been noted already in the preceding section, but many other elements are notable as well, chief among them being wage-and-price controls and environmental regulations.

The new era of environmental regulation began with passage of the National Environmental Policy Act in 1969—the authority for requiring the preparation and approval of a detailed "environmental impact statement" for federal construction projects or private projects subject to any form of federal permission. The environmental-impact-statement process immediately became a substantial source of delay, cost escalation, and exasperation for developers. In 1970, President Nixon created the Environmental Protection Agency (EPA) to set and enforce environmental standards, consolidating into a single agency some fifteen different federal programs then dealing with air and water pollution, waste disposal, and radiation. The EPA acquired sharper teeth from the enactment of the Clean Air Act Amendments of 1970 (and later amendments as well); the Water Pollution Control Act of 1972 (and later amendments to it); the Toxic Substances Control Act of 1976; and the Comprehensive Environmental Response, Compensation, and Liability Act (often called the Superfund law) of 1980, among other statutes. The EPA quickly became one of the most intrusive and controversial of all federal regulatory agencies, and it has remained so to the present day. If big corporations have the Commerce Department and labor unions have the Labor Department, then environmental organizations have the EPA. None of these developments took place, of course, without great, ongoing, ideological, political, and legal debate and struggle.

Nixon, by his willingness to sign so many significant regulatory acts, displayed his political hallmark: though supposedly a conservative, he was, above all, an opportunist. Nothing illustrates that opportunism better, however, than his imposition of mandatory wage-price controls, a definite conservative anathema, in August 1971. Twenty-five years later Herbert Stein, a member and later chairman of Nixon's Council of Economic Advisers, characterized the adoption of Nixon's New Economic Policy, whose centerpiece was the wage-price controls, as utterly heedless of long-term considerations. Recalling the meetings at which the plan was laid, Stein wrote: "Even after 25 years I am amazed by how little we looked ahead during that exciting weekend at Camp David, when we (the president, really) made those big decisions." Everybody seems to have assumed without discussion that after a ninety-day wage-and-price freeze, the government would somehow ease back to a regime of flexible prices. However, "[a]s it turned out, we were in the price and wage control business not for 90 days but for nearly 1,000. [Moreover,] [w]e were in the business of controlling energy prices for much longer" (Stein 1996; for a full account of this episode, see Stein 1984, 133–207).

If Nixon could not be bothered to look ahead, he surely had a keen view of, if not an obsession with, the past. He believed he had lost the presidential election in 1960 because Eisenhower's administration failed to generate favorable macroeconomic conditions on the eve of the election, and he was determined not to repeat that mistake in 1972. His calculations and machinations proved astute, no matter how wrongheaded they were with regard to serving the general interest. The public, as always, reacted with great approval to the initial imposition of wage-price controls, as indicated by favorable opinion polls, by a soaring stock market, and most of all by Nixon's landslide reelection. Although Nixon ultimately suffered ignominy when he was driven from office by hostile reaction to his Watergate gambit, his far more damaging economic mismanagement, in contrast, never caused him any personal or political harm whatsoever.

The wage-price controls passed through several phases of greater or lesser stringency until finally, with relief all around, they were allowed to lapse in the spring of 1974. While they remained in force, however, they gave rise to significant distortions in the allocation of resources and hence to economic inefficiency. They also created congenial conditions for the adoption of unusually bad monetary policies by the Federal Reserve System, which produced rates of inflation not seen since the 1940s and not squeezed back to tolerable levels until the early 1980s, after the failure of the Carter administration's sham anti-inflation program, the so-called wage-price guidelines (see Higgs 1979a, 1979b, 1980, 1981). Of course, the Nixon wage-price controls did not actually prevent inflation—only changes in the underlying supply of or demand for money can affect money's true exchange value—but they did suppress the manifestation of the actual inflation and produce the politically profitable appearance of temporary success.

The most important legacy of Nixon's wage-price controls was the government's energy-price controls and allocations that persisted long after the comprehensive price controls expired. When the first energy crisis struck, the administration was looking forward to disengagement from its no-longer-useful price controls, but given the lingering presence of those controls, the Arab oil embargo and the Organization of Petroleum Exporting Countries price hikes of late 1973 and early 1974 quickly led in many areas to shortages that were rationed for the most part by the customers' waiting in the infamous gas lines. The inconvenience and uncertainty proved to be more than the public could bear and, in William E. Simon's words, "collective hysteria" arose. "The political heat was on both Congress and the executive to solve the problem overnight" (Simon 1979, 54).

To deal with the crisis, the president created by executive order the Federal Energy Office (which by statute later became the Federal Energy Administration and later still the Department of Energy) and named Simon to head it. Overnight, Simon became the "energy czar," authorized by Nixon "to decide everything and to decide it rapidly." The president equated the energy crisis to a wartime situation and likened Simon's job to that of Albert Speer, Hitler's minister of arms and munitions during World War II. Finding the government's energy allocation procedures tangled and ineffective, Simon and his assistants worked frantically for months to channel existing supplies to the areas with the most desperate shortages. Although some improvements were eventually made and the gas lines shortened and began to disappear by the spring of 1974, the whole arrangement remained fundamentally defective. Simon concluded: "There is nothing like becoming an economic planner oneself to learn what is desperately, stupidly wrong with such a system" (1979, 50, 55).

The energy situation did not improve as Congress passed ever more complicated energy legislation in the mid-1970s. Another crisis inevitably struck, and early in 1979 the gas lines reappeared. The Energy Department's erratic efforts to fix the problem only made it worse (Chapman 1980; Glasner 1985, 130–37). Only after Ronald Reagan assumed the presidency and scrapped all oil-price controls was the mess permitted to clean itself up through market processes. Even then, however, a complex system of price controls for natural gas lingered for more than a decade until complete decontrol of wellhead gas prices took effect at the beginning of 1993, terminating a forty-year experiment in the federal regulation of natural-gas prices that had produced nothing but market distortions and some wholly avoidable energy crises (see Bradley 1995 for many historical details about and insightful analysis of the energy industries and their regulation).

Passing along its own parallel track of perceived crises and government response via the enactment of new and more stringent regulatory statutes, the Food and Drug Administration (FDA) became steadily more powerful during the postwar era, exercising regulatory control over goods that account for approximately 25 percent of all consumer spending—processed foods, pharmaceuticals, medical devices, and cosmetics, among other products. Created in its modern form by a 1938 statute, the agency gained major new powers in the aftermath of the thalidomide tragedy by enactment of the so-called Kefauver-Harris Amendments to the Food, Drug, and Cosmetic Act in 1962. These amendments gave the agency much greater control over drug-testing procedures, and its exercise of these powers slowed down the rate of pharmaceutical innovation considerably and blocked the marketing of new drugs that might have saved thousands of lives and alleviated the suffering of millions (see Gieringer 1985; Higgs 1994a, 1995, 2004). Despite the devastating results of its actions, the FDA continued to maintain a sterling public reputation, in no small part because of its own ceaseless public-relations efforts, along with the courts' deference to it and an ability to play congressional politics as well as anybody. It also succeeded in gaining ever more power by lobbying for the enactment of new legislation (for example, the Medical Device Amendments of 1976 and the Safe Medical Devices Act of 1990) and by continually "pushing the envelope" of its existing regulatory authority (Higgs 1995, 2–4). Even when it came under attack by conservative members of Congress in the mid-1990s, the agency succeeded in shaping the resulting legislation—the FDA Modernization Act of 1997—so that the bureaucracy lost little, if any, of its essential power over the many products and activities it regulates.

The FDA's having to fend off powerful critics in the mid-1990s reminds us that from time to time the victims of government regulation do rise up against it, and occasionally they succeed in slaying a dragon. The most notable counterattack occurred in the late 1970s and early 1980s, when a slew of deregulatory statutes gained enactment. The upshot was the reduction or elimination of several forms of economic regulation that had been in place since the 1930s or even longer. In 1978, Congress passed the Airline Deregulation Act, providing for the gradual deregulation of commercial airlines. In accordance with this statute, the Civil Aeronautics Board ceased allocating domestic routes in 1981, stopped regulating fares in 1983, and closed up shop entirely in 1985—an exceedingly rare occurrence in the world of regulation. Airline passengers gained major benefits from the board's disappearance, which opened up competition. A cluster of statutes between 1976 and 1984 reduced the extent of the government's regulation of transportation by railroads, trucks, and buses, again with major benefits to consumers. At the end of 1995, the Interstate Commerce Commission, the oldest independent federal regulatory agency, dating to 1887, was abolished and its remaining functions transferred to the Surface Transportation Board in the Department of Transportation. Financial institutions were partially deregulated in 1980 and 1982, and telecommunications underwent revolutionary changes when a federal court broke up the Bell Telephone System in 1984. (For more information on this deregulatory episode, see Weidenbaum

1986, 178–202.) After the mid-1980s, the deregulatory movement lost its momentum, and not much significant deregulation occurred during the next two decades.

The limited and quickly terminated deregulatory episode was an aberration. Much more notable was the relentless, ongoing flood of regulations—many of which purport to protect health, enhance safety, or prevent discrimination—that have poured forth every year on the strength of the multitude of existing statutes authorizing agencies to impose such rules at all levels of government. As late as the 1950s, the *Federal Register,* which publishes the official announcements of each year's new final and proposed rules, contained only 107,000 pages for the entire decade; then the ten-year total jumped to more than 450,000 pages in the 1970s; it continued to rise each decade thereafter; and in the early years of the twenty-first century it is running at a rate of more than 731,000 pages per decade (Crews 2003, 11). Federal regulatory agencies alone now issue more than four thousand new rules each year (Crews 2003, 12), and state and local regulators add countless others. An old rule is hardly ever removed from the books, so the aggregate mass of regulations in effect grows ever more immense, as even a casual inspection of the *Code of Federal Regulations* attests.

In countless ways, postwar governments have also actively engaged in doling out subsidies, some of them direct (for example, cash and in-kind services), others indirect (for example, tariffs on imported, competing products). Agricultural interests began to reap such subsidies early in the twentieth century and acquired them whole hog during the latter half of the century. Defense contractors also gained huge subsidies, often disguised as reimbursed costs in their supply contracts for military goods and services. Once the federal government got into the business of extending college loans, millions of college students every year became the beneficiaries of credit extended at below-market rates of interest. Government loan guarantees likewise effectively subsidized a multitude of business and household borrowers. The entire real-estate sector became pervaded by various forms of subsidized lending. Joseph P. Stiglitz observed in 1989, "In the US today, approximately a quarter of all lending (to the private sector) is either through a government agency or with government guarantees.... The magnitudes of the implicit subsidies and costs—both the total value, and who receives how much—are hidden" (63). Inspection of the government's organization chart reveals many federal agencies that supply subsidized credit (for example, the Maritime Administration, the Small Business Administration, the Export-Import Bank, the Farm Credit System, the Rural Utilities Service). Besides doling out subsidized credit and loan guarantees to privileged recipients, the postwar U.S. government has stood ready to bail out firms deemed "too big to fail," among them defense contractors (e.g., Lockheed in 1974), industrial firms (e.g., Chrysler in 1979), banks (e.g., Continental Illinois Bank in 1984), and other financial institutions (e.g., Long-Term Capital Management in 1998), regardless of whether bad luck or bad management brought them to the brink of bankruptcy. Because loan guarantees do not automatically entail a government outlay, their extension ordinarily does not leave any trace in conventional measures of the size and growth of government.

## FISCAL DIMENSIONS OF THE GROWTH OF GOVERNMENT

Although a great deal of government growth has taken forms that do not leave heavy footprints in government budgets—the bulk of the cost of regulations, for example, takes the form of higher private costs, higher prices, and sacrificed individual liberties—much of it has required increases in taxation, borrowing, and expenditure. Table 7.2 provides data on certain dimensions of the fiscal growth of government in the post–World War II era from 1948 to 2005.

By the measures presented in the table, government grew enormously during these fifty-eight years. Before considering just how much it grew, however, we might well consider one or two adjustments. First, we might wish to adjust the data for changes in the purchasing power of the dollar. Because of the government's gross mismanagement of the money supply, the excessive creation of money during this period caused a reduction of more than 85 percent in the dollar's purchasing power (alternatively, we can say that the overall price level rose more than 6.88 times, according to the official chained price index for GDP). Thus, merely to maintain the same level of real expenditure, governments would have needed to spend 6.88 times more in 2005 than in 1948. Second, we might also wish to adjust for changes in the population, which increased by 102 percent during this period. Multiplying the dollar-depreciation factor (6.88) and the population-growth factor (2.02), we find that government in 2005 would have needed to increase its spending by approximately 13.9-fold in order to maintain the 1948 level of real expenditure per capita. Let us use this growth factor of 13.9 as our standard for assessing how much government spending actually grew. The United States in 1948 was an economically advanced and relatively civilized country with actively engaged governments at all levels, so the standard is a reasonable one. Although social scientists often also adjust government spending for the growth of the national product, this adjustment is highly problematic (see Higgs 1991), and I do not make it here (the figures in table 7.1, column 4, show military spending adjusted for inflation and for growth of GDP).

Looking first at the growth of the total expenditures of all governments—federal, state, and local—between 1948 and 2005, we see that the growth was 88-fold, or more than 6 times the amount necessary to maintain the 1948 level of real expenditure per capita. The spending component associated with the nation's expansive global military activities (shown under the rubric "defense and international" in the table), grew nearly 39 times, or by almost thrice enough to maintain the standard. The greatest growth of all, however, occurred in the welfare-state elements of the budget; these transfer payments are shown in the table under the rubric "federal payments to individuals" but also include expenditures, not shown separately, that compose a substantial part of the state and local spending shown in the table's farthest-right column). Federal Social Security and Medicare expenditures expanded by a mind-boggling 1,704 times, and "other" federal transfer payments expanded by 75 times. Although the federal government's growth was in many respects the most remarkable, state and local governments certainly plunged into the tax-and-spend fray with full force as well. Spending at state and local levels (from their own revenue sources) increased more than 97-fold, or by more than seven times beyond the amount needed to maintain the 1948 standard of real spending per capita. This growth would be even greater if the amounts financed by federal revenue sharing were included, too.

Perhaps the most notable aspect of the postwar growth of government was its relentlessness. In these fifty-eight years, only twice (in 1954 and 1955) did total government spending decline, and then only because of a $10 billion cutback in defense spending after the fighting ended in Korea (see table 7.2). From time to time, defense spending fell slightly for a while, but not once did Social Security and Medicare spending fall, and not once did state and local spending (from their own sources) fall. Thus, besides relying on the certainty of death and taxes, postwar Americans also could expect that every year the welfare state would spend more dollars. The so-called entitlement system, whereby governments fix an eligibility formula and then make transfer payments to everyone who demonstrates eligibility in accordance with that formula, has effectively placed the growth of the welfare state on autopilot for a guaranteed steep ascent.

## CONCLUSION

"The natural progress of things," said Thomas Jefferson, "is for liberty to yield and government to gain ground." Yet, until the early twentieth century, the growth of government, especially the federal government, remained slow by comparison with its growth afterward. The difference between the two eras reflects in various degrees the political consequences of cumulative long-term structural changes (urbanization, industrialization, improvements in transportation and communication, and so forth), the enduring effects of great national emergencies (especially the world wars and the Great Depression), and the political consequences of collectivist-leaning ideological changes that were themselves fostered by the structural changes and the national crises (for more extended discussion, see Higgs 1987 and 2005a). These fundamental changes promoted the formation of political interest groups in growing abundance, each seeking in some way to use the power of government to promote its members' ends at the expense of the general community. The combination of ideological change and political maneuvering also brought about the abandonment of constitutional doctrines that had long restrained the growth of government. The upshot was that by the beginning of the postwar era nothing fundamental remained to restrain the rapid growth of government except workaday politcal wrangling, and the politicians proved resourceful in working around their differences in order to provide something for everybody (everybody, that is, who possessed political resources and was organized for effective political action). Thus, government has taken the course that Jefferson perceived long ago as its natural tendency. To be sure, the growth of government cannot continue forever, if only because an ever-more-devouring predator ultimatly must destroy its prey and therefore its means of sustenance. At present, however, there is no end in sight.

For some, the foregoing account of the postwar growth of government and the correlative shrinkage of private-property rights and economic liberties may seem unbalanced. Where else, they might ask, can we find so much security of private-property rights and such expansive economic liberties as we have in the United States? Sure enough, in systematic studies of economic freedom the United States in recent times always stands near the top in the ranking of the world's nation-states (see, for example, Gwartney and Lawson 2005). Even today, people throughout much of the world look to this country as a safe haven for their investments and bank deposits and as a relatively free labor market in which workers can find ample opportunities for well-compensated employment. Nevertheless, there is no contradiction between these undeniable facts and my account of the vast growth of government in the United States since World War II. We must recognize that government has grown enormously in *all* the economically advanced countries during this era (Higgs 2005a). Therefore, despite the enormous growth of government here, this country's economy remains, overall, *relatively* free of government burdens and restraints. Nonetheless, a great deal has been lost over time. As a British admirer of the United States has remarked recently, "If the Americans today remain the freest people in the world, that is only because they started with so much more to lose" (Gabb 2003).

## NOTES

1. This section draws heavily on Higgs 1994b.
2. This section draws heavily on Higgs 1987, 246–56, and Higgs 1996.

## REFERENCES

Ambrose, Stephen E. 1985. *Rise to Globalism: American Foreign Policy since 1938,* 4th ed. New York: Penguin.

Bernstein, David E. 2003. *You Can't Say That! The Growing Threat to Civil Liberties from Antidiscrimination Laws.* Washington, D.C.: Cato Institute.

Bradley, Robert L. 1995. *Oil, Gas, and Government: The U.S. Experience.* Lanham, Md.: Rowman and Littlefield and the Cato Institute.

Browning, Edgar K., and Jacquelene M. Browning. 1983. *Public Finance and the Price System,* 2nd ed. New York: Macmillan.

Butos, William N., and Thomas J. McQuade. 2006. Government and Science: A Dangerous Liaison? *The Independent Review* 11, no. 2 (fall): 177–208.

Chapman, Stephen. 1980. The Gas Lines of '79. *The Public Interest* (summer): 40–49.

Corwin, Edward S. 1947. *Total War and the Constitution.* New York: Knopf.

Crews, Clyde Wayne, Jr. 2003. *Ten Thousand Commandments: An Annual Snapshot of the Federal Regulatory State. 2003 Edition.* Washington, D.C.: Cato Institute.

De Jouvenel, Bertrand. [1945] 1993. *On Power: The Natural History of Its Growth.* Indianapolis, Ind.: Liberty Fund.

Eisenhower, Dwight D. [1961] 1973. Eisenhower's Farewell Address, January 17, 1961. In *Documents of American History,* vol. 2, *Since 1898,* 9th ed., edited by Henry Steele Commager, 652–54. Englewood Cliffs, N.J.: Prentice-Hall.

"Employment Act of 1946, February 20." 1946. in *Documents of American History,* vol. 2, *Since 1898,* 9th ed., edited by Henry Steele Commager, 514–16. Englewood Cliffs, N.J.: Prentice-Hall.

Fishback, Price V., and Shawn Everett Kantor. 2000. *A Prelude to the Welfare State: The Origins of Workers' Compensation.* Chicago: University of Chicago Press.

Friedberg, Aaron L. 2000. *In the Shadow of the Garrison State: America's Anti-statism and Its Cold War Grand Strategy.* Princeton, N.J.: Princeton University Press.

Gabb, Sean. 2003. Why Criticising American Foreign Policy is Not Anti-Americanism. *Free Life Commentary,* no. 102 (April 28). Available at: http://www.seangabb.co.uk/fl-comm/.

Gieringer, Dale H. 1985. The Safety and Efficacy of New Drug Approval. *Cato Journal* 5 (spring–summer): 177–201.

Glasner, David. 1985. *Politics, Prices, and Petroleum.* Cambridge, Mass.: Ballinger.

Glazer, Nathan. 1975. *Affirmative Discrimination.* New York: Basic Books.

Gwartney, James D., and Robert Lawson. 2005. *Economic Freedom of the World, 2005: Annual Report.* Washington, D.C.: Cato Institute.

Higgs, Robert. 1979a. Blaming the Victim: The Government's Theory of Inflation. *The Freeman* 29 (July): 397–404.

———. 1979b. Inflation and the Destruction of the Free Market. *Intercollegiate Review* 14 (spring): 67–76.

———. 1980. Carter's Wage-Price Guidelines: A Review of the First Year, *Policy Review* 11 (winter): 97–113.

———. 1981. Wage-Price Guidelines: Retreat and Defeat. *The Freeman* 31 (November): 643–52.

———. 1987. *Crisis and Leviathan: Critical Episodes in the Growth of American Government.* New York: Oxford University Press.

———. 1989. Beware the Pork-Hawk: In Pursuit of Reelection, Congress Sells Out the Nation's Defense. *Reason* 21 (June): 28–34.

———. 1991. Eighteen Problematic Propositions in the Analysis of the Growth of Government. *Review of Austrian Economics* 5: 3–40.

———. 1993. Private Profit, Public Risk: Institutional Antecedents of the Modern Military Procurement System in the Rearmament Program of 1940–1941. In *The Sinews of War: Essays on the Economic History of World War II,* edited by Geofrey T. Mills and Hugh Rockoff, 166–98. Ames: Iowa State University Press.

———. 1994a. Banning a Risky Product Cannot Improve Any Consumer's Welfare (Properly Understood), with Applications to FDA Testing Requirements. *Review of Austrian Economics* 7: 3–20.

———. 1994b. The Cold War Economy: Opportunity Costs, Ideology, and the Politics of Crisis. *Explorations in Economic History* 31 (July): 283–312.

———. ed. 1995. *Hazardous to Our Health? FDA Regulation of Health Care Products.* Oakland, Calif.: The Independent Institute.

———. 1996. The Welfare State: Promising Protection in an Age of Anxiety. *The Freeman* 46 (May): 260–66.

———. 2001. The Cold War Is Over, but U.S. Preparation for It Continues. *The Independent Review* 6, no. 2 (fall): 287–305.

———. 2004. The U.S. Food and Drug Administration: A Billy Club Is Not a Substitute for Eyeglasses. In *Against Leviathan: Government Power and a Free Society,* 59–73. Oakland, Calif.: The Independent Institute.

———. 2005a. The Ongoing Growth of Government in the Economically Advanced Countries. *Advances in Austrian Economics* 8: 279–300.

———. 2005b. *Resurgence of the Warfare State: The Crisis since 9/11.* Oakland, Calif.: The Independent Institute.

———. 2006a. *Depression, War, and Cold War: Studies in Political Economy.* New York: Oxford University Press for The Indpendent Institute.

———. 2006b. War Weariness. Independent Institute commentary. November 26. Available at: http://www.independent.org/newsroom/article.asp?id=1856.

Higgs, Robert, and Anthony Kilduff. 1993. Public Opinion: A Powerful Predictor of U.S. Defense Spending. *Defence Economics* 4: 227–38.

Holzman, F. D. 1992. The CIA's Military Spending Estimates: Deceit and Its Costs. *Challenge* 35: 28–39.

Kolodziej, E. A. 1966. *The Uncommon Defense and Congress, 1945–1963.* Columbus: Ohio State University Press.

Leebaert, Derek. 2002. *The Fifty-Year Wound: The True Price of America's Cold War Victory.* Boston: Little, Brown.

Matusow, Allen J. 1984. *The Unraveling of America: A History of Liberalism in the 1960s.* New York: Harper and Row.

McClosky, Herbert, and John Zaller. 1984. *The American Ethos: Public Attitudes toward Capitalism and Democracy.* Cambridge, Mass.: Harvard University Press.

Mueller, John E. 1973. *War, Presidents, and Public Opinion.* New York: Wiley.

Neu, C. E. 1987. The Rise of the National Security Bureaucracy. In *The New American State: Bureaucracies and Politics since World War II,* edited by Louis Galambos, 85–108. Baltimore: Johns Hopkins University Press.

Page, Benjamin I., and Robert Y. Shapiro. 1992. *The Rational Public: Fifty Years of Trends in Americans' Policy Preferences.* Chicago: University of Chicago Press.

Patterson, James T. 1996. *Grand Expectations: The United States, 1945–1974.* New York: Oxford University Press.

Rockman, B. A. 1987. Mobilizing Political Support for U.S. National Security. *Armed Forces and Society* 14: 17–41.

Sapolsky, H. M. 1987. Equipping the Armed Forces. *Armed Forces and Society* 14: 113–28.

Sherry, Michael S. 1995. *In the Shadow of War: The United States Since the 1930s.* New Haven, Conn.: Yale University Press.

Simon, William E. 1979. *A Time for Truth.* New York: Berkley Books.

Smith, R. B. 1971. Disaffection, Delegitimation, and Consequences. In *Public Opinion and the Military Establishment,* edited by C. C. Moskos Jr., 221–51. Beverly Hills, Calif.: Sage.

Sowell, Thomas. 1984. *Civil Rights: Rhetoric or Reality?* New York: William Morrow.

Stein, Herbert. 1984. *Presidential Economics: The Making of Economic Policy from Roosevelt to Reagan and Beyond.* New York: Simon and Schuster.

———. 1996. Wage and Price Controls: 25 Years Later. *Wall Street Journal,* August 15.

Stiglitz, Joseph E. 1989. On the Economic Role of the State. In *The Economic Role of the State,* edited by Arnold Heertje, 9–85. Oxford: Basil Blackwell.

Twight, Charlotte A. 2002. *Dependent on D.C.: The Rise of Federal Control over the Lives of Ordinary Americans.* New York: Palgrave.

U.S. Department of Defense, Office of the Under Secretary of Defense (Comptroller). 2006. *National Defense Budget Estimates FY2007.* Washington, D.C.: U.S. Department of Defense, March.

U.S. Office of Management and Budget. 2006. *Budget of the United States Government, Fiscal Year 2007, Historical Tables.* Washington, D.C.: U.S. Office of Management and Budget.

Weidenbaum, Murray L. 1986. *Business, Government, and the Public.* 3rd ed. Englewood Cliffs, N.J.: Prentice–Hall.

Weinberger, Caspar W. 1987. *Annual Report of the Secretary of Defense to the Congress, Fiscal Year 1988.* Washington, D.C.: U.S. Government Printing Office.

Weiner, Tim. 1990. *Blank Check: The Pentagon's Black Budget.* New York: Warner Books.

Williams, Benjamin H. 1954. *Emergency Management of the National Economy.* Vol. 21, *Reconversion and Partial Mobilization.* Washington, D.C.: Industrial College of the Armed Forces.

# The Ongoing Growth of Government in the Economically Advanced Countries

I maintain that in the economically advanced countries, government continues to grow, as it has grown for more than a century, although the growth now takes a somewhat different mix of forms than it did in earlier times. Some leading analysts, in contrast, have concluded that the growth of government has slowed or even stopped in the past twenty-five years. In this chapter, I first show how those analysts have erred because of their excessive reliance on conventional measures of the size and growth of government. I then discuss the logic of the growth of government in the economically advanced countries. Finally, I contrast my own interpretation with the interpretation developed by Ludwig von Mises (and elaborated by Sanford Ikeda), which concludes that a mixed economy is inherently unstable and must transform itself into either laissez faire or complete socialism. In my own view, neither of these two extreme forms of politicoeconomic organization is now realizable, although the reasons for their unrealizability differ. As a feasible politicoeconomic order, pure socialism is dead; so is laissez faire. In the real world of the near and intermediate terms—at least for the next several decades—the likely prospect is for moderate movements back and forth along the middle segment of the spectrum occupied by different degrees of mixed economy, some more severely hampered by government than others.

## MISLEADING MEASURES OF THE GROWTH OF GOVERNMENT

Many of us who believe that governments continue to grow relentlessly, at least in the economically advanced countries, have been criticized by analysts who claim that in fact the growth of government has petered out or slowed substantially. Those who advance such claims perceive us to be needlessly alarmed, and they fault us for a failure to acknowledge the decisive turn of events associated with the so-called Reagan and Thatcher revolutions of the 1980s. Not to worry, they exhort us; the statists are on the run, and a brave new world of market-oriented liberalism shimmers on the horizon (Boaz 2003).

I maintain that the seemingly level-headed realists are the ones who have failed to perceive correctly the ongoing growth of government.[1] A major reason for their failure is their reliance on certain conventional measures of the size and growth of government. Some of these measures have a built-in tendency to exhibit deceleration even when a more compelling representation indicates continued steady growth. In other cases, the conventional measures simply miss the growth of government that has been diverted into channels beyond the scope of their measurement. To some extent, governments have been growing in important but unmeasured or poorly measured ways all along, and they continue to grow in these ways, perhaps more menacingly than ever before. Off-budget spending, for example, is a well-known resort of political scoundrels, but it is only one example among many of how governments employ hard-to-measure means to achieve their usual ends, especially when tax resistance or formal spending limits frustrate their chronic desire to tax and spend at a greater rate.

## Government's Share of Gross Domestic Product

The most common measure of the size of government is the amount of government spending relative to gross domestic product (GDP). In Vito Tanzi and Ludger Schuknecht's recent monograph on the growth of government, for example, the authors present much of their data in the form of government-spending variables relative to GDP. A major theme of the book is: "Government spending [measured in this way] increased rapidly until about 1980. Since the early 1980s, it has been growing more slowly and in some instances has even declined" (3).

To see what is wrong with this view, we must recognize first that a sure-fire way to make nearly any economic magnitude appear small is to divide it by GDP, because the latter, which purports to be the total value at market prices of all final goods and services produced within a country in a year, is always an enormous dollar (or euro or peso or other currency unit) amount. Government spending of $2,855,200,000,000, as in the United States in fiscal year 2001, seems to be an astronomical amount, but simply divide it by the value of concurrent GDP and, *voilà*, it is a mere 28 percent—surely nothing to be alarmed about, especially in comparison with corresponding figures for many European countries that exceed 50 percent.[2]

(It is worthwhile to note that GDP, a measure that includes a large component for capital consumption allowances—13.3 percent of the total for the United States in 2002—makes an inherently ill-suited aggregate for use as a benchmark in assessing the size of government. Certainly, net national product [NNP] or national income [NI] would be a more defensible aggregate. The difference is not trivial. Thus, again for the United States in 2002, for example, the current receipts of all governments amounted to $2,875 billions, or 27.5 percent of GDP, 31.8 percent of NNP, 34.4 percent of NI.)[3]

The next thing to notice is that because government spending for currently produced final goods and services is itself a component of GDP, the ratio of the former to the latter is immediately compromised. Any addition to such government spending increases the denominator as well as the numerator of the ratio. Suppose that in year one the government spends $100 dollars for currently produced final goods and services, and the GDP in that year is $500. Now suppose that in year two the government spends twice as much—that is, it increases the amount of its purchases by 100 percent—but nothing else changes. In year two, the government's share of GDP will be 33.33 percent (or $200/$600), as compared to 20 percent in year one. An analyst who focuses on the government's spending *share* then concludes that government has grown not by 100 percent, as it plainly has, by construction, but only by 66.66 percent (that is, [(33.33/20) – 1] • 100). The greater the government's initial share is, the greater the bias is in moving from its absolute spending to the share concept to measure its growth. If government had begun with spending of $100 out of a GDP of $200, then doubled its amount of purchases, other things being unchanged, it would have increased its spending share from 50 to 66.66 percent—a mere 33.33 percent rate of growth.

The governments of many economically advanced countries have maintained a fairly steady "exhaustive" share of GDP during the final two decades of the twentieth century (Tanzi and Schuknecht 2000, 25), but this steadiness merely attests that a government's purchases of currently produced final goods and services grew as fast as the sum of nongovernmental purchases of final goods and services during that same period of substantial economic expansion, not that the government became quiescent or stuck in the mud. In the United States, for example, the total government share of GDP was 22.1 percent in 1975 and 17.6 percent in 1999. Lest one think that the government ran out of steam during that quarter-century, however, one ought to notice that the government increased its purchases of currently produced final goods and services from $361.1 billion in 1975 to $1,634.4 billion in 1999, which is to say, it increased the annual rate of such spending by $1,273.3 billion during that period (U.S. Council of Economic Advisers 2001, 274–75). To be sure, inflation accounts for some of that increase, but even in constant (1996) dollars, the increase was from $942.5 billion to $1,536.1 billion, or 63 percent (277)—hardly a retrenchment. Population growth cannot justify the increased spending: the U.S. population grew by just 26 percent during the period (315).

Of course, in recent decades the really gigantic increases in government spending have taken the form of transfers (including subsidies), which are not components of GDP and therefore do not give rise to the exact same numerator-denominator bias that arises when government increases its purchases of currently produced final goods and services ("exhaustive" spending). Transfer spending also, however, is commonly placed for purposes of analysis in relation to GDP, which then serves as a sort of "normalizer" or standard of comparison, and whenever this ratio is used, some of the same problems identified earlier arise again. Even if one grants that such benchmarking is appropriate, one still might ask why the government's transfer spending should be placed in a ratio to GDP rather than, say, in a ratio to population or some other base. And if the ratio to GDP remains constant, one might ask why such constancy should prevail. That is, why should government's transfer spending increase whenever the economy's output of final goods and services increases? Indeed, such constancy would seem to signal a kind of relative growth of government in its own right, inasmuch as people in a higher-income society presumably can get by more readily without government assistance, and hence the ratio of transfers to GDP might be expected as a rule to fall in a growing economy, rather than rise or even remain constant.

However this matter is viewed, in reality the ratio has risen enormously in all the economically advanced countries during the past several decades, and it now stands at more than 20 percent on average for a group of seventeen important industrial countries studied by Tanzi and Schuknecht, up from less than 10 percent as recently as 1960 (2000, 31).[4] Increasingly, transfer spending is becoming recognized as the Godzilla that threatens to consume New York, Tokyo, Berlin, and nearly every other city on the planet. A few countries, such as Chile, have taken effective measures to deal with this looming threat to government fiscal viability, but so far most politicians in most countries have kept their heads planted firmly in the sand, ignoring everything beyond the next election, while their government's transfer spending grows ever more bloated and the severity of the adjustments that will have to be made in the future grows ever greater.

## Government's Share of Employment

Government employment as a percentage of total employment also has served as an index of a government's size. This measure, too, however, has a built-in bias toward suggesting that the rate at which government is growing is decelerating over time even when government increases its share of employment by, say, one percentage point every year. Thus, for example, when government's employment share increases from 2 percent to 4 percent, the government grows by 100 percent, but when the share increases from 20 percent to 22 percent, gobbling up the same incremental proportion of total employment, the government grows by just 10 percent.

In the group of seventeen advanced countries analyzed recently by Tanzi and Schuknecht, the government's average employment share increased from 5.2 percent in 1937 to 12.3 percent in 1960 to 18.4 percent in 1994 (2000, 26). The rate of increase of this ratio declined during the final two decades of the twentieth century in most countries, but one ought not to make too much of that deceleration, for reasons already explained.

In the United States, increases in the amount of "contracting out" of government functions have led to a replacement of formal government employees by a growing "shadow army" of many millions of seemingly private employees—grantees, contractors, and consultants—who are doing what they are doing only because the government arranges it and pays for it to be done (Blumenthal 1979; Hanrahan 1983; Light 1999a, 1999b). According to Paul Light's estimate's, the U.S. federal workforce as of 1996 was not the fewer than 2 million persons officially reported, but nearly 17 million persons, "and the count does not even include the full-time equivalent employment of the people who work on a part-time or temporary basis for Uncle Sam—for example, the 884,000 members of the military reserves"—though it does include some 4.7 million already counted as employees of state and local governments (1999a, 1).

In a recent update of his estimates, Light concludes that "the government's largely-hidden workforce created through contracts and grants has reached its highest level since before the end of the Cold War.... [F]ederal contracts and grants generated just over 8 million jobs in 2002, up from just under 7 million in 1999, and 7.5 million in 1990.... [G]overnment is now growing, almost entirely in off-budget jobs that are invisible to the American public in federal budget and headcount documents" (2003, 1–2). For 2002, Light estimates that true total federal government employment, including the estimated 4,650,000 state and local employees engaged in federally mandated tasks, amounted to 16,765,000 persons. To this total, we must add the remaining 13,700,000 state and local employees (calculated from data in U.S. Bureau of the Census, 2006,

307), which gives us a grand total of 30,465,000 persons, or 22.3 percent of total employment in the United States (calculated from total employment data at 387)—almost one out of every four employees in 2002 was getting paid directly or indirectly by the governments at various levels.

Moreover, governments increasingly have established regulations that in effect require bona fide private parties to work for the government. Tanzi and Schuknecht take note of such "quasi-fiscal policies," which they describe as regulations that "become alternatives to taxing and spending" (2000, 203). In this recognition, they follow in a long line of analysts stretching back at least to Richard A. Posner in his capacity as the author of the oft-cited 1971 article "Taxation by Regulation."

The relevant class of regulations, though, is much wider than it is usually recognized to be in the standard literature of economics and public choice. To be sure, all sorts of economic, environmental, health and safety, and social regulations continue to spew out of Washington and Brussels, among many other places (Grow 2003). In addition, the U.S. government especially requires ever more uncompensated information collection and reporting by its subjects in order to slake the Surveillance State's insatiable craving for the minute details of everyone's conduct (Bennett and Johnson 1979; Twight 1999). These Big Brotherish demands are justified by the despicable slogan that only those with something to hide will object, but in truth this vile rain falls on the righteous and the wicked alike and, in any event, one would have to be pretty dimwitted to expect the latter to report truthfully.

According to Clyde Wayne Crew's recent summary of U.S. federal regulation:

- The 2001 *Federal Register* contained 64,431 pages

  . . .

- In 2001, 4,132 final rules were issued by agencies.

  . . .

- Of the 4,509 regulations now in the works, 149 are "economically significant" rules that will have at least $100 million in economic impact. Those rules will impose at least $14.9 billion yearly in future off-budget costs.

  . . .

- The costs of meeting the demands of off-budget social regulations were as high as $229 billion according to the Office of Management and Budget. A more broadly constructed competing estimate that includes economic regulatory costs and paperwork costs pegs regulatory expenditures at $854 billion in 2001, or 46 percent of all [fiscal year 2001] outlays. (2002, 1–2)

The foregoing, shocking as it is, describes the regulatory burden being imposed at only the federal level of government. Simultaneously, the state and local governments as well as various international bodies continue to pour out endless streams of their own regulations, all of which entail resource costs and sacrifices of citizens' liberties.

Because the public has less awareness of the burdens imposed by these regulations, many of which remain obscure and indirect in their operation and effects, governments encounter less resistance to their ongoing imposition of regulatory burdens than they encounter in their quest to collect greater revenue from explicit taxes laid on incomes, sales transactions, and property values. So far, there seems to be no political limit to the number of regulations that governments can and will impose. Hence, we are fast approaching a condition in which everything that is not forbidden is required, even as Americans, acting for all the world like faux-patriotic zombies, continue to reassure themselves incessantly that "it's a free country."

For present purposes, the point is that people occupied with regulatory compliance are not truly privately employed. Instead, they are in effect stealth government servants, working not for their own ends, but doing the bidding of their political masters. In the present Western world, then, nearly all of us are actually government employees, but rather than getting a government paycheck for our efforts, most of us are required to pay the government for the privilege of our own serfdom and to bear the risk of prosecution and imprisonment should our unpaid work on the government's behalf prove unsatisfactory to our merciless de facto "employer."

## THE LOGIC OF THE GROWTH OF GOVERNMENT IN THE ECONOMICALLY ADVANCED COUNTRIES

The growth of government has had many sources. In a sense, nothing less than a comprehensive social, political, legal, and economic history can tell the story fully. Within this vast empirical complexity, however, we can perceive patterns and identify crucial types of changes that have promoted the rise of a Leviathan state in many countries since the mid–nineteenth century, a time when government was still (except during wartime) small by comparison with its subsequent dimensions. By appreciating the major patterns, we can begin to understand better not only why governments have grown historically, but also why they continue to grow currently and most likely will continue to do so for a long time to come in the economically advanced countries.

For understanding the dynamic process of the growth of government, I find it useful to separate causal factors into two categories. One category includes what I designate here as structural-ideological-political (SIP) changes; the other category includes crisis-ideological-political (CIP) changes. To some extent, these two classes of factors correspond to what John J. Wallis (1985) has called "trend" and "trigger" events. Later, I will insist that these two classes of factors are not independent, but interact with each other in important ways.

## SIP Changes

In the nineteenth century, earlier in some countries than in others, a number of interrelated changes began to accelerate. All had something to do with the processes that have come to be known collectively as modernization; they included industrialization, urbanization, the relative decline of agricultural output and employment, and a variety of significant improvements in transportation and communication. As these events proceeded, masses of people experienced tremendous changes in their way of life. In response, they turned to their governments to seek assistance in order to gain from, or at least to minimize the losses attendant upon, the social and economic transformations in which they found themselves swept up.

The structural changes associated with modernization altered the perceived costs and benefits of collective action for all sorts of latent special-interest groups. For example, the gathering of large workforces in urban factories, mills, and commercial facilities created greater potential for the successful organization of labor unions and working-class political parties. New means of transportation and communication reduced the costs of organizing agrarian protest movements and populist political parties. Urbanization created new demands for government-provided infrastructure, such as paved streets, lighting, sewerage, and pure water supplies. All such events tended to alter the configuration of political power, encouraging, enlarging, or strengthening certain special-interest groups, while discouraging, diminishing, or weakening others. At nearly every step, opposing factions clashed, sometimes violently.

Simultaneously, the structural transformations altered the perceived costs and benefits of government responses to various demands. For example, it became cheaper for governments to collect income taxes when more people received their income in the form of pecuniary payments traceable in business accounts, as opposed to unrecorded farm income in-kind. The modern welfare state is often seen as originating in Imperial Germany in the 1880s, when the Iron Chancellor Otto von Bismarck established compulsory accident, sickness, and old-age insurance for workers. Bismarck was no altruist. He intended his social programs to divert workers from revolutionary socialism and to purchase their loyalty to the Kaiser's regime and, to a large extent, he seems to have achieved his objectives. The lesson was not lost on governments elsewhere. By 1914, similar programs had been enacted in most other western European countries, and even the United States—a laggard in this regard—was moving in the same direction, albeit only at the state or local levels of government and in federal programs restricted to war veterans and their dependents (Higgs 1996).

This development calls to mind another important aspect of SIP events—namely, ideological change. From the mid–nineteenth century onward, collectivist ideologies of various stripes, especially certain forms of socialism, gained greater intellectual and popular followings, whereas traditional conservatism and classical liberalism increasingly fell out of favor and, with a lag, suffered losses in their political influence. By the early twentieth century, the intellectual cutting edge in all of the economically advanced countries had become more or less socialistic (or, in the United States, in greater part, "Progressive"), and the masses also had become more favorably inclined toward support for various socialist or Progressive schemes, from regulation of railway rates to municipal operation of utilities to outright takeovers of industry on a national scale (Hayek 1949; Higgs 1987, 113–16).

Political developments mirrored the changes in the economy and the dominant ideology. Throughout the nineteenth century, democracy tended to gain ground. The franchise was widened, and more popular parties, including socialist parties and labor parties closely allied with the unions, gained greater representation in legislative assemblies at all levels of government—more so, however, in Europe than in the United States. Everywhere the trend toward universal manhood suffrage and even women's voting became seemingly irresistible. People insisted on casting a ballot in periodic contests to select their political leaders. Even Adolf Hitler came to power via the ballot box.

Whether structural, ideological, or political, the foregoing changes proceeded gradually. With the passage of time, various changes reached a threshold at which the balance of forces tipped in favor of a new outcome with regard to government action. Modernizing economic transformation, collectivist ideological drift, and democratic political reconfiguration tended to bring about a changing balance of forces that not always but as a rule favored increases in the size, scope, and power of government. Such trends now have continued for more than a century and a half in the economically advanced countries.

## CIP Changes

Superimposed on the gradually unfolding SIP transformations has been a series of discrete crises, of which the most significant were wars and economic depressions, especially the two world wars and the Great Depression. These crises also tended to promote the growth of government, although in certain cases, such as Germany and Japan after World War II, the consequences of the crisis took a different form because of the wartime regimes' defeat and these countries' occupation by victorious powers intent on reshaping the vanquished societies' basic politicoeconomic institutions.

War is the preeminent government undertaking, and great wars, such as those of 1914–18 and 1939–45, have elicited the fullest expression of government power over economy and society. In World War I, all major belligerents adopted some form of "war socialism" in order to mobilize resources and place them under government control for the prosecution of the war (Mises [1919] 1983, 133–76; Higgs 1987, 123–58). Many measures figured prominently in the warring governments' economic management, including price, wage, and rent controls; inflationary increases in the money stock; physical allocations of raw materials and commodities; conscription of labor; industrial takeovers; rationing of consumer goods and transportation services; financial and exchange controls; vast increases in government spending and employment; and both increases in tax rates and the imposition of new kinds of taxation (Porter 1994, 161–67).

After World War I, Mises called attention to "the stupidities of the economic policy of the Central Powers during the war," noting that "measures and countermeasures crossed each other until the whole structure of economic activity was in ruins" ([1919] 1983, 146), and similar problems plagued the war socialism of other countries as well. And the war left institutional and ideological legacies everywhere that promoted subsequent resort to similar measures, not only in wartime but in peacetime crises as well. World War II, an even bigger exercise in mass human slaughter and massive property destruction, prompted similar measures and had similar results (Porter 1994, 167–69; Klausen 1998). As Bruce Porter has written, "The mass state, the regulatory state, the welfare state—in short, the collectivist state that reigns in Europe today—is an offspring of the total warfare of the industrial age" (1994, 192). In the United States, World War II left society permanently shackled to what Americans aptly call "Big Government" (Higgs 1987, 196–236).

In addition, especially in the United States, the economic crisis of the Great Depression elicited similar government responses and left similar legacies of swollen state power and permanently lost liberties (Wallis 1985; Higgs 1987, 159–95, 1996, 261–63). Three decades later, the crisis events that crowded into the troubled years from 1964 to 1974—turmoil that for Americans sprang initially from U.S. involvement in the Vietnam War and from urgently contested race relations—had similar, if somewhat less sweeping, consequences (Shultz and Dam 1977; Matusow 1984; Higgs 1987, 246–54, 1996, 264–65).

## SIP-CIP Interactions

Analysts have not been blind to the operation of both SIP and CIP events in bringing about government growth in the economically advanced countries, but as a rule they have considered the two classes of factors as if they were independent. They have often, if only implicitly, viewed the SIP factors as systematic and the CIP factors as stochastic; some analysts have gone so far as to exclude wartime periods from their empirical analysis of long-term changes in the size of government (for citations of examples, see Higgs 1987, 288 n. 3). To proceed in this manner is a mistake because SIP and CIP events are interrelated in important ways.

On the one hand, SIP events precondition how societies will respond to the outbreak of crisis. During the process of gradual structural, ideological, and political change, the various special-interest groups and ambitious political actors maneuver to position themselves so that when the opportunity arises, they will be better placed to realize their objectives. For a time, they may be stymied by opposition, but they understand that in a crisis the ordinary checks and balances of social and political life will be attenuated, and new possibilities will arise. Therefore, they prepare themselves for that day, and on occasion they may even take actions to precipitate the very crisis they long for—more than one "burning of the Reichstag" has occurred in the past century.

This routine ideological and political activity creates a configuration of forces that to some extent predetermines how crises will be dealt with and therefore what consequences they will have for the operation of the society in the period of postcrisis (altered) normality. Mises described an important instance of this phenomenon when he discussed the causes and consequences of wartime socialism during World War I:

> War socialism was only the continuation at an accelerated tempo of the state-socialist policy that had already been introduced long before the war. From the beginning the intention prevailed in all socialist groups of dropping none of the measures adopted during the war after the war

but rather of advancing on the way toward the completion of socialism. If one heard differently in public, and if government offices [*sic*], above all, always spoke only of exceptional provisions for the duration of the war, this had only the purpose of dissipating possible doubts about the rapid tempo of socialization and about individual measures and of stifling opposition to them. The slogan had already been found, however, under which further socializing measures should sail; it was called *transitional economy.*

The militarism of General Staff officers fell apart; other powers took the transitional economy in hand. ([1919] 1983, 176)

Similar events took place in the United States, where socialist "liberals" and Progressives viewed the war as their long-awaited opportunity to put in place permanently many of the expanded government powers they favored, which they and their political friends hoped to wield during and after the war (Rothbard 1989).

If SIP events precondition how crises will be handled and what consequences they will have, it is no less true that CIP events determine the character and operation of the political economy during postcrisis periods of normality and therefore condition the unfolding SIP events, sometimes for decades after the crisis at hand. Countless examples of such interdependence might be given (see Higgs 1987, 150–56, 189–93, and 225–34 for discussions of the "legacies, institutional and ideological," of World War I, the Great Depression, and World War II in the United States). I continue to adhere to the general understanding of such CIP-SIP interdependency that I described a number of years ago as follows:

The expansion of the scope of governmental power was path-dependent; where the political economy was likely to go depended on where it had been. Those who brought about the growth of government were motivated and constrained at each moment by their beliefs about the potentialities and dangers, the benefits and costs of alternative policies under current consideration. Their beliefs derived in turn from past events as they understood them. A genuine "return to normalcy" was unlikely after a crisis had provoked an expansion of the scope of governmental powers.

The irreversibility obtained not only because of the "hard residues" of crisis-spawned institutions (for example, administrative agencies and legal precedents), few of which necessarily show up in conventional measures of the size of government. More important, the underlying behavioral structure could not revert to its prior condition because the events of the crisis created new understandings of and new attitudes toward governmental action; that is, each crisis altered the ideological climate. Though the postcrisis economy and society might, at least for a while, appear to have returned to their precrisis conditions, the appearance disguised the reality. In the minds and hearts of the people who had passed through the crisis and experienced the expanded governmental powers (that is, at the ultimate source of behavioral response to future exigencies), the underlying structure had indeed changed. (Higgs 1987, 58–59)

Thus, what appear to be "trends" are what they are at least in part because of the "triggers" associated with great national emergencies. A complete understanding of the dynamic process of the growth of government requires not only that analysts take both trends and triggers into account, but also that they give careful consideration to the interactions between them.

## MISES AND IKEDA ON THE INSTABILITY OF THE MIXED ECONOMY

In several articles published during the 1920s and included in a collection titled *Critique of Interventionism* ([1929] 1996), Ludwig von Mises argued that the mixed economy (he called it "the hampered market order"), which by definition is subject to chronic and pervasive government intervention, is an unstable form of political economy. During the following years, he returned from time to time to the same theme, most notably perhaps in his magnum opus *Human Action* (1966), in which part 6 is called "The Hampered Market Economy" and includes ten chapters, the last of which deals with "the crisis of interventionism."

Mises maintained that with respect to the politicoeconomic order, no "middle way" is possible: "There is no other choice: government either abstains from limited interference with the market forces, or it assumes total control over production and distribution. Either capitalism or socialism; there is no middle of the road" ([1929] 1996, 9, see also 18, 27, 28, 54).

Mises's argument for the "impossibility" of the mixed economy rests on three interrelated claims: (1) the government's interventions in the free market cannot achieve the aims that the interventionists seek; (2) because of the adverse effects of the interventions, more interventions will be required, which will produce even more adverse effects; and therefore (3) the government will ultimately be driven to abandon the market system completely and to adopt full-fledged socialism with its total government control of the means of production—unless, on the contrary, the government has the wit to recognize that socialism is unworkable and so instead gives up all its interventions and reverts to a full-fledged free-market order ([1929] 1996, 54 and passim). In *Human Action*, Mises added a fourth factor: "Interventionism aims at confiscating the 'surplus' of one part of the population and at giving it to the other part. Once this surplus is exhausted by total confiscation, a further continuation of this policy is impossible" (1966, 858).

In a probing and thorough reconsideration and elaboration of Mises's analysis of interventionism, Sanford Ikeda calls attention to "the paradox of interventionism"—namely, that despite the mixed economy's alleged instability, "among existing politico-economic systems, the interventionist mixed economy, all of its contradictions notwithstanding, is by far the most popular, widespread, and persistent of them all" (1997, 46). Indeed, Mises himself explicitly recognized this seeming paradox, remarking that "interventionist norms survived for hundreds of years, and since the decline of liberalism, the world is ruled again by interventionism. All this is said to be sufficient proof that the system is realizable and successful, and not at all illogical" ([1929] 1996, 21).

In response to his own recognition of the paradox, Mises declared: "The fact that measures have been taken, and continue to be taken, does not prove that they are suitable. It only proves that their sponsors did not recognize their unsuitability" ([1929] 1996, 21). Mises proceeded to blame the "the empiricists" for failing to apply economic theory properly and hence for failing to understand what the actual consequences of various interventions had and had not been. Whatever the analytical shortcomings of the Historical School and other empiricists or of the sponsors of interventionist measures, however, Mises's response does not resolve the paradox. The point is not whether analysts or sponsors of interventionism did not see the failure of the middle way, but whether that failure constitutes a fatal flaw that necessarily renders the system unstable and thus guarantees its replacement by either all-out socialism or a free-market order.

Ikeda provides a much more satisfactory resolution of the paradox. In his view, "the key to resolving this paradox is to realize that to claim the mixed economy is unstable is not the same thing as asserting that it is *transitory*. . . .

By introducing contradictions into the system, interventions generate a process that causes the mixed economy continually to adjust and to evolve into novel and diverse forms over time" (1997, 215). Still, it need not become nonviable quickly: "the roads between the minimal and maximal states can thus be very long and winding, and state expansion very gradual" (215). Indeed, it turns out that because socialism is unworkable in the long run (for reasons that Mises and Hayek explained persuasively) and because, in Ikeda's view, laissez faire is also unstable (owing to "governmental error" and "shocks in ideological preferences" [216]), *all* politicoeconomic orders are unstable and the mixed economy is the *least* unstable among them: "paradoxically, therefore, it appears that the product of interventionism, the mixed economy, though unstable, is likely to be more enduring than the pure forms of either collectivism or capitalism, offering as it does a much wider range of (ultimately futile) adaptive forms than either of its rival systems" (216). Hence, the first of Ikeda's eight pattern predictions: "At any given time, nearly all economic systems will be mixed economies" (216).

Much more might be said about the endogenous logic of interventionism as explicated by Mises and elaborated by Ikeda, but because Ikeda has plowed this ground so thoroughly, I make no attempt to do so here. Before leaving the topic, however, I offer a few additional observations. In doing so, my intention is to appraise not so much the structure of the arguments already advanced as their applicability to the present-day reality of the economically advanced countries.

First, in much of their writing on interventionism and even on socialism, Mises, Hayek, and Ikeda assume good will on the part of the interventionists; that is, they assume that the interventionists seek to promote the broad public interest, not merely to achieve their personal ends or those of special-interest groups. Thus, the recurrent assertion is made that the interventionist measures cannot "achieve what their advocates expect of them" (Mises [1929] 1996, 5, see also 20, 28, 36), and there is an expressed need to explain "the failure of [intelligent, well-intentioned, and public-spirited] public authorities to learn from their mistakes" (Ikeda 1997, 49, see also 104, 110–12, 121, 137; but compare 145–51 on "relaxing the assumption of benevolent public interest"). Although one may defend this assumption as a methodological device not intended to be descriptively accurate, I see only a minor purpose at best being served by proceeding with analysis on this basis. As Hayek compellingly argued, the worst get on top in political life, and the "ruthless and unscrupulous" thrive in positions of government power (1944, 151; see also Bailey 1988). Although Hayek was writing with socialism in mind, the same tendency prevails in the mixed economy, though perhaps in slightly lesser degree (Higgs 1997). In addition, public affairs are rampant with rent seeking by one and all. Ikeda properly notes that although "it is possible initially to abstract to a large extent from political self-interest and exogenous ideological change in order to isolate analytically a unique Austrian method of political economy … completely removing these two factors is … neither possible nor desirable in a realistic theory of political economy" (1997, 53)—that is, in a political economy genuinely applicable in the interpretation of current public affairs.

The idea that well-intentioned authorities make mistakes is closely connected to the concept of "failed policies" that has come to play such a frequent part in popular criticism of government intervention in the market order. As I have argued elsewhere (Higgs 1995), however, notwithstanding the fair-mindedness of Austrian political economists with regard to the interventionists they analyze, very few failed policies last long. The all-too-numerous seemingly failed policies really fail to achieve only their *ostensible* objectives; but they succeed in achieving their *actual* objectives. In brief, the world of government affairs is the world of humbuggery; things are almost never what they are represented to be. All sides consider that they stand to gain by disguising their self-serving programs with a public-spirited rationale, and invariably they do so. Only rarely, however, is political talk anything but spin and counterspin, and we will sooner find chastity in a brothel than truth or honest pursuit of the public interest in a political setting (Higgs 2004, xv–xix). As analysts, we do well never to lose sight of this pervasive smoke-and-mirrors aspect of politics. Our task in this respect is to understand the operation, effects, and limits of the humbuggery.

In much of their work on politicoeconomic systems, both Mises and Hayek wrote as though the nature of the system itself were the object of choice. Thus, for example, in the preface of *Critique of Interventionism,* Mises wrote: "Nearly all writers on economic policy and nearly all statesmen and party leaders are seeking *an ideal system* which, in their belief, is neither capitalistic nor socialistic" ([1929] 1996, xi, emphasis added). Rarely, however, is the object of political choice the system itself; as a rule, this stark choice presents itself only in consequence of the violent revolutionary overthrow of a regime or its total defeat in war (for example, in Russia in 1917, in Germany and Japan after World War II, or in eastern Europe after the collapse of communism and the Soviet Empire). In general, political choices pertain only to programs that make piecemeal, ad hoc changes in the context of an existing politicoeconomic framework, whatever its overall character may be. Of course, owing to many partial changes, the overall character of a system may be transformed eventually, as it was in the United States between 1885 and 1945. Even then, however, the resulting system is an artifact—a product of human action, but not of human design.

This aspect of the workings of politics bears on the Austrian idea that the mixed economy may reach a point at which, the public choosers having piled intervention on intervention and the society having come to suffer all of the resulting ill effects, "the recognition at some level of a systemic failure becomes *inevitable*" (Ikeda 1997, 123, emphasis in original). Although such a recognition may occur—perhaps New Zealand in 1984 provides a case in point (see Sautet 2006, 575)—it is highly unlikely. Rather than recognizing that the system has reached a point at which, "interventionism having lost its legitimacy, there is no longer a middle ground" (Ikeda 1997, 137), the political decision makers are much more likely to respond in the classic manner of Franklin Delano Roosevelt, who proposed amid the Great Depression to try something and, if it didn't work, to try something else, rather than abandon the whole system of interventionism. So long as an interventionist system retains any viability at all, its kingpins will cling to it, as the history of nearly all times and places bears witness. So long as the public will tolerate the countless burdens and insults of interventionism—a toleration that hinges almost entirely on the dominant ideology rather than on the system's objective conduct and performance—then the response to even severe systemic difficulties is likely to be more muddling through, perhaps a moderation of the worst abuses, but not an overthrow of the system or a drastic retrenchment within it. In short, as Robert Bradley (2003) has observed, in the mixed economy even a crisis may lead only to "halfway measures of a new form" (Ikeda's pattern prediction number 2 [1997, 217] also accords with this conclusion).

Finally, we must recognize the severe limitations of the Misesian model of the dynamics of the mixed economy (even as expanded by Ikeda) that arise from its inability to incorporate the effects of war on the course of the politico-economic order. As Ikeda acknowledges, "perhaps the most important omission, especially from the standpoint of empirical observation, is the effect of *war and domestic conflict* on the interventionist process. This means that the rapid growth of government in the United States during the twentieth century owing to war and similar national crises lies outside [the] scope" of the model (1997, 226, emphasis in original). Directly and indirectly, however, war and preparation for war have been by far the most significant wellsprings of government growth during the past century. And they are again in the United States at the present time, owing to the so-called war on terrorism and the boost it has given to U.S. military intervention abroad, the police state at home, and unbridled government spending across the board as all parties have joined in an enormous logroll in Congress. A model of the dynamics of the mixed economy that excludes this aspect of the historical process, however useful it might be for illuminating the endogenous forces at work, must be judged severely deficient for purposes of aiding the interpretation of actual events (which Austrian school analysts recognize as always being "complex" events immune to formulaic explanation).

## DOUBLE-ENDED CONSTRAINT: THE ACTUAL DYNAMICS OF THE MODERN GROWTH OF GOVERNMENT

In light of the foregoing discussion, I can be brief in presenting my own scheme for understanding the past and likely future course of the growth of government in the economically advanced countries. I maintain that in the short and intermediate terms—at least for the next few decades—reversion to laissez faire or anything close to such a system is impossible, but a resort to full-fledged, centrally planned socialism is scarcely more likely. As Jeffrey Rogers Hummel has remarked, "Rather than being inherently unstable, interventionism is the gravity well toward which both market and socialist societies sink" (2001, 530). Mixed economy, social democracy, democratic socialism, participatory fascism—whatever one's preferred name for it—this system clearly has demonstrated its superior survival power under present conditions against all feasible alternatives. The politicoeconomic order of each of the economically advanced countries will remain within the broad middle of the spectrum because this order is effectively constrained at both ends from transforming itself into one of the alternative, extreme systems.

Mises, Hayek, and Ikeda, among others, have correctly diagnosed the ills of interventionism and explicated its characteristic mode of operation and change. Such a system does generate tremendous burdens and opportunity costs, and its absurdities do compound themselves over time. However, the chief political decision makers have come to recognize that so long as private enterprises are allowed to retain a modicum of room to maneuver, then continued high levels of productivity and even some economic growth can be expected. As Mises noted, the corruptibility of public officials helps to mitigate some of the most idiotic elements of interventionism, allowing a certain amount of important business to get done despite taxes and regulations that, if fully enforced, would preclude all progress. More important, however, "the adaptability of the capitalist economy has negated many obstacles placed in the way of entrepreneurial activity. We constantly observe that entrepreneurs are succeeding in supplying the markets with more and better products and services despite all difficulties put in their way by law and administration" ([1929] 1996, 12–13, 14). This remark, so reminiscent of Adam Smith's observation that there is a lot of ruin in a nation, deserves much weight. So long as entrepreneurs are not crushed utterly, they will prove astonishingly creative in finding ways to satisfy market demands, whether the market be legal or "black," and "interventionism is seen as a tribute that must be paid to democracy in order to preserve [the remnants of] the capitalistic system" (Mises [1929] 1996, 13).

In no event will public choosers opt for full-fledged socialism. The economic disasters wreaked by central planning in the Soviet Union, China, and other countries during the twentieth century have been taken to heart everywhere. No substantial support exists anywhere for the maintenance of such a politicoeconomic system, and where its remnants remain, as they do in Russia, China, Vietnam, and Cuba, they are gradually being phased out. The verdict is in—socialism does not work—and the world has accepted it. People want a system that can "deliver the goods" for a modern standard of living. Therefore, the extreme collectivist end of the spectrum is no longer regarded as a viable option.

Nor is the political dictatorship that accompanied economic central planning any longer a promising option. As noted earlier, all over the world, for better or worse, people want to cast meaningful ballots to select their political leaders. Democracy, ugly duckling that it is, bids fair eventually to become and remain the only acceptable political system everywhere.

Laissez faire is unrealizable, too, but not because it cannot "deliver the goods." Indeed, it can deliver them in undreamed of abundance if it is allowed to operate. Nevertheless, no population anywhere will allow it to operate. In today's world, no substantial group of people is prepared to accept the personal responsibilities and to shoulder the personal risks inherent in genuine capitalism—which is, after all, as Joseph Schumpeter emphasized, a system of creative *destruction.* Certainly throughout the economically advanced world, people have come to demand that governments relieve them of nearly every personal responsibility, from caring for their own health to preparing for retirement to teaching their children about sex. In more ways than anyone can count, people now expect the government to take care of them, in the classic phrase, from the cradle to the grave. Thus, in the European Union, whose peoples exemplify this syndrome at its worst, "the European social-welfare system is thriving despite a decade long call for change," even as "a report from the European Commission shows Europe faces a looming crisis unless it enacts changes" (Grow 2003). Personal responsibility has become too painful for the citizens of the economically advanced countries even to contemplate. Locked in an ideology of dependency on state provision and of belief in the capacity and rectitude of such provision, they have no interest in living in a free society. (They forget or do not understand that a government cannot provide even a semblance of the demanded personal security unless it regulates and controls the people in countless ways and taxes them heavily to pay for its many "services.") Thus, the dominant ideology of modern populations has rendered them uninterested in and incapable of living in a full-fledged market system, and by their participation in modern democratic political processes they can make sure that no such system ever comes close to realization.

Thus constrained on both ends, the politicoeconomic systems of all the economically advanced countries stand condemned to fluctuate within the great middle of the spectrum. Should matters become too unbearably botched by high taxes or by intervention compounding intervention, then small retrenchments are possible, but in no event will such retrenchments move the system close to laissez faire, and, in every case, once the retrenchments have served their purpose for a while, new pressures will be brought to bear on the system, compounding once again the absurdities of the existing mixed economy. More than a decade ago, Bruce Porter wrote that "a shrinkage of the American state appears about as remote as a drying up of the oceans" (1994, 294). Nothing has happened since then to change that prospect, and with good reason we may express the same expectation for all of the other economically advanced countries.

## NOTES

1. For my earlier defenses of this thesis, some of which deal with matters not discussed here, see Higgs 1983; 1987, esp. 20–34; 1991a, esp. 5–8; and 1991b, esp. 66–68.
2. U.S. ratio computed from figures reported in U.S. Office of Management and Budget 2002, 292–93; ratios for various European countries from Tanzi and Schuknecht 2000, 6–7.
3. Calculated from data in U.S. Bureau of Economic Analysis n.d., tables 1.9 and 3.1.
4. The group includes Australia, Austria, Belgium, Canada, France, Germany, Ireland, Italy, Japan, the Netherlands, New Zealand, Norway, Spain, Sweden, Switzerland, the United Kingdom, and the United States.

## REFERENCES

Bailey, F. G. 1988. *Humbuggery and Manipulation: The Art of Leadership.* Ithaca: Cornell University Press.

Bennett, James T., and Manuel H. Johnson. 1979. Paperwork and Bureaucracy. *Economic Inquiry* 17 (July): 435–51.

Blumenthal, Barbara. 1979. Uncle Sam's Army of Invisible Employees. *National Journal* (May 5): 730–33.

Boaz, David. 2003. Is Freedom Winning? *Cato Policy Report* (January–February): 2.

Bradley, Robert L. 2003. A Typology of Interventionist Dynamics. Unpublished typescript.

Crews, Clyde Wayne, Jr. 2002. *Ten Thousand Commandments: An Annual Snapshot of the Federal Regulatory State. 2002 Edition.* Washington, D.C.: Cato Institute.

Grow, Brian. 2003. Despite Criticism, It's Business as Usual in Europe: EU Nations Are Doing Little to Change Policies Hurting Growth, Recent Reports Say. *Wall Street Journal,* January 7.

Hanrahan, John D. 1983. *Government by Contract.* New York: Norton.

Hayek, F. A. 1944. *The Road to Serfdom.* Chicago: University of Chicago Press.

———. 1949. The Intellectuals and Socialism. *University of Chicago Law Review* 16 (spring): 417–33.

Higgs, Robert. 1983. Where Figures Fail: Measuring the Growth of Big Government. *The Freeman* 33 (March): 151–56.

———. 1987. *Crisis and Leviathan: Critical Episodes in the Growth of American Government.* New York: Oxford University Press.

———. 1991a. Eighteen Problematic Propositions in the Analysis of the Growth of Government. *Review of Austrian Economics* 5: 3–40.

———. 1991b. Leviathan at Bay? *Liberty* 5 (November): 64–70.

———. 1995. The Myth of "Failed" Policies. *The Free Market* 13 (June): 1, 7–8.

———. 1996. The Welfare State: Promising Protection in an Age of Anxiety. *The Freeman* 46 (May): 260–66.

———. 1997. Public Choice and Political Leadership. *The Independent Review* 1, no. 3 (winter 1997): 465–67.

———. 2004. *Against Leviathan: Government Power and a Free Society.* Oakland, Calif.: The Independent Institute.

Hummel, Jeffrey Rogers. 2001. The Will to Be Free: The Role of Ideology in National Defense. *The Independent Review* 5, no. 4 (spring 2001): 523–37.

Ikeda, Sanford. 1997. *Dynamics of the Mixed Economy: Toward a Theory of Interventionism.* New York: Routledge.

Klausen, Jytte. 1998. *War and Welfare: Europe and the United States, 1945 to the Present.* New York: Palgrave/Macmillan.

Light, Paul Charles. 1999a. The True Size of Government. *Government Executive Magazine* (January 1). Available at: http://www.govexec.com/features/0199/0199s1htm.

———. 1999b. *The True Size of Government.* Washington, D.C.: Brookings Institution Press.

———. 2003. Fact Sheet on the New True Size of Government. September 5. Available at: http://www.brook.edu/gs/cps/light20030905.pdf.

Matusow, Allen J. 1984. *The Unraveling of America: A History of Liberalism in the 1960s.* New York: Harper and Row.

Mises, Ludwig von. 1966. *Human Action: A Treatise on Economics,* 3rd rev. ed. Chicago: Contemporary Books.

————. [1919] 1983. *Nation, State, and Economy: Contributions to the Politics and History of Our Time.* Translated by Leland B. Yeager. New York: New York Press.

————. [1929] 1996. *Critique of Interventionism,* 2d rev. ed. Irvington-on-Hudson, N.Y.: Foundation for Economic Education.

Porter, Bruce D. 1994. *War and the Rise of the State: The Military Foundations of Modern Politics.* New York: Free Press.

Posner, Richard A. 1971. Taxation by Regulation. *Bell Journal of Economics and Management Science* 2 (spring): 22–50.

Rothbard, Murray N. 1989. World War I as Fulfillment: Power and the Intellectuals. *Journal of Libertarian Studies* 9 (winter): 81–125.

Sautet, Frederic. 2006. Why Have Kiwis Not Become Tigers? Reforms, Entrepreneurship, and Economic Performance in New Zealand. *The Independent Review* 10, no. 4 (spring): 573–97.

Shultz, George P., and Kenneth W. Dam. 1977. *Economic Policy Beyond the Headlines.* New York: Norton.

Tanzi, Vito, and Ludger Schuknecht. 2000. *Public Spending in the 20th Century: A Global Perspective.* New York: Cambridge University Press.

Twight, Charlotte. 1999. Watching You: Systematic Federal Surveillance of Ordinary Americans. *The Independent Review* 4, no. 2 (fall): 165–200.

U.S. Bureau of the Census. 2006. *Statistical Abstract of the United States: 2006.* Washington, D.C.: U.S. Government Printing Office.

U.S. Bureau of Economic Analysis. n.d. *National Income and Product Accounts Tables.* Washington, D.C.: U.S. Bureau of Economic Analysis. Available at: http://www.bea.doc.gov/bea/dn/nipaweb/TableViewFixed.asp.

U.S. Council of Economic Advisers. 2001. *Annual Report of the Council of Economic Advisers.* Washington, D.C.: U.S. Government Printing Office.

U.S. Office of Management and Budget. 2002. *Budget of the United States Government, Fiscal Year 2003: Historical Tables.* Washington, D.C.: U.S. Office of Management and Budget.

Wallis, John Joseph. 1985. Why 1933? The Origins and Timing of National Government Growth, 1933–1940. In *Emergence of the Modern Political Economy,* edited by Robert Higgs, 1–51. Greenwich, Conn.: JAI Press.

Acknowledgments: I am grateful to Sanford Ikeda for careful and helpful comments on a previous draft. An earlier version of this chapter was published in the periodical *Advances in Austrian Economics* 8 (2005). By the terms of my Transfer of Copyright Agreement with Elsevier Ltd., the publisher acknowledges my right to use that previously published material in this volume.

# Index

# About the Author

ROBERT HIGGS is Senior Fellow in Political Economy for The Independent Institute and Editor of the Institute's quarterly journal *The Independent Review: A Journal of Political Economy*. He received his Ph.D. in economics from the Johns Hopkins University, and he has taught at the University of Washington, Lafayette College, Seattle University, and the University of Economics in Prague. He has been a visiting scholar at Oxford University and Stanford University.

Dr. Higgs is the author seven previous books: *The Transformation of the American Economy 1865-1914: An Essay in Interpretation* (1971), *Competition and Coercion: Blacks in the American Economy, 1865-1914* (1977), *Crisis and Leviathan: Critical Episodes in the Growth of American Government* (1987), *Against Leviathan: Government Power and a Free Society* (2004), *Resurgence of the Warfare State: The Crisis since 9/11* (2005), *The Political Economy of Fear* (2006, in Czech), and *Depression, War, and Cold War: Studies in Political Economy* (2006). His edited books include *Emergence of the Modern Political Economy* (1985), *Arms, Politics, and the Economy: Historical and Contemporary Perspectives* (1990), *Hazardous to Our Health? FDA Regulation of Health Care Products* (1995), *Re-Thinking Green: Alternatives to Environmental Bureaucracy* (2004), *The Challenge of Liberty: Classical Liberalism Today* (2006), and *Opposing the Crusader State: Alternatives to Global Interventionism* (2007). A contributor to numerous scholarly volumes, he is also the author of more than 100 articles and reviews in academic journals of economics, demography, history, and public policy.

His popular articles have appeared in the *Wall Street Journal, Los Angeles Times, Providence Journal, Chicago Tribune, San Francisco Examiner, San Francisco Chronicle, Seattle Times, Seattle Post-Intelligencer, St. Louis Post-Dispatch, San Diego Union-Tribune, Journal of Commerce, Financial Times,*

*Society, Reason, Liberty, The Freeman,* AlterNet, LewRockwell.com, Online Journal, AntiWar.com, Media Monitors Network, and many other newspapers, magazines, and Web sites, and he has appeared on NPR, NBC, ABC, C-SPAN, CNBC, PBS, Radio America Network, Radio Free Europe, Voice of America, Newstalk TV, the Organization of American Historians' public radio program, and scores of local radio and television stations. He has also been interviewed for articles in the *New York Times, Washington Post, Al-Ahram Weekly, Terra Libera, Investor's Business Daily,* UPI, *Congressional Quarterly, Orlando Sentinel, Seattle Times, Chicago Tribune, National Journal, Reason, Washington Times, WorldNetDaily, Folha de São Paulo, Newsmax, Financial Times, Creators Syndicate, Insight, Christian Science Monitor, Atlanta Journal-Constitution,* and many other news media.

Dr. Higgs has spoken at more than 100 colleges and universities in North America, Latin America, and Europe and to such professional organizations as the Economic History Association, Western Economic Association, Population Association of America, Southern Economic Association, International Economic History Congress, Public Choice Society, International Studies Association, Cliometric Society, Allied Social Sciences Association, American Political Science Association, American Historical Association, and many others.

# INDEPENDENT STUDIES IN POLITICAL ECONOMY

*For further information and a catalog of publications, please contact:*

**THE INDEPENDENT INSTITUTE**

100 Swan Way, Oakland, California 94621-1428, U.S.A.

510-632-1366 · Fax 510-568-6040 · info@independent.org · www.independent.org